D0350987

Mama's Boy, Preacher's Son

Mama's Boy, Preacher's Son

A Memoir

KEVIN JENNINGS

Beacon Press
Boston

Beacon Press
25 Beacon Street
Boston, Massachusetts 02108-2892
www.beacon.org

Beacon Press books
are published under the auspices of
the Unitarian Universalist Association of Congregations.

Printed in the United States of America

09 08 07 06 8 7 6 5 4 3 2 1

This book is printed on acid-free paper that meets the uncoated paper ANSI/NISO specifications for permanence as revised in 1992.

Text design by Patricia Duque Campos
Composition by Wilsted & Taylor Publishing Services

Library of Congress Cataloging-in-Publication Data

Jennings, Kevin
Mama's boy, preacher's son : a memoir / Kevin Jennings.
p. cm.
ISBN 0-8070-7146-3 (hardcover : alk. paper)
1. Jennings, Kevin. 2. Gay men—United States—Biography.
3. Gay teachers—United States—Biography. 4. Gay students—United States.
5. Gay, Lesbian, and Straight Education Network—History. I. Title.

HQ75.8.J46A3 2006
306.76'62092—dc22 2006001275

For Claudette,
who has always been family

One person's truth, if told well, does not leave anyone out.

PAUL MONETTE

Contents

Prologue

The first thing I remember is the oxygen tent.

It's 1966. We're living in North Carolina, where my dad has chased a job in construction. I'm three and a half (halves are important when you're three) and in a hospital in Roanoke Rapids because I have whooping cough, a disease that nobody gets—nobody, that is, who isn't poor, so poor that you don't get vaccinated, so poor that you don't have health insurance, so poor that you don't go to the hospital until your fever breaks 102 degrees and your mom thinks she'd better take you now because, if it goes any higher, you might be brain damaged for life. We're that poor.

The oxygen tent is made of plastic and is large enough that my entire three-and-a-half-year-old body fits comfortably within it. I can sit up without hitting the top, stretch out my legs without hitting the wall at my feet, and spread my arms out without touching the sides. I love tents: my cousins and I make them when playing indoors in my family's trailer, draping blankets and sheets to create hiding places, using flashlights to illuminate them from within, delighting in the idea that we are invisible to the outside world.

But this isn't a fun tent like those. Inside this tent, I dwell in the land of the sick. My body is wracked with coughing fits that end with the characteristic "whoop" from deep inside my lungs that gives the disease pertussis its common name. The fits are so powerful they make me vomit. On the other side, through the wrinkled plastic that distorts and blurs my view, is the real world. The room outside the tent seems enormous, like a cavern, making me feel even more tiny than I already feel. Occasionally hands reach in from the real world, those of nurses dressed in white and wearing cupcake hats, who give me yet another injection. I receive so many injections that I begin to cry and scream when I see a nurse enter because my arms and legs are so swollen they are starting to give them to me in my stomach. I will learn later that the nurses told my family that they waited too long to bring me here, that there's a good chance I won't get out, but even though I don't know this at three and a half I can sense the deep concern on the other side of the tent and their fear only magnifies my own. I am small and imprisoned in an oxygen tent, cut off from everyone and everything, with troubled adults on the other side of the plastic curtain peering in, trying unsuccessfully to mask their worry. I am terrified.

There's only one constant, reassuring presence in this world, a small woman who is there whenever I wake up. She doesn't seem small to me, of course, because I am only three and a half, but she barely breaks five feet and a hundred pounds. She feeds me, she smiles at me through the opaque plastic, and she comforts me when I have my coughing fits, and when my cousin (who is in an oxygen tent on the other side of the room) has his fits—which, as I watch him thrash and vomit and gasp, terrify me even more than my own—she makes sure I know I am never alone. She is, of course, my mom, Alice Verna Johnson Jennings.

I'm not supposed to be here at all. As Mom would tell me repeatedly throughout my childhood, I was not a wanted child. She had her first kid, my sister Carol, seventeen years before I was born, in 1946, the war having ended barely a year before. Her fourth child, my brother Paul, was born in 1956, nearly seven years before I was. At thirty-eight, she wasn't planning on a fifth in 1963, during Camelot, with a bright and shiny John F. Kennedy in the White House and the Vietnam War just getting underway. She was done. But I came anyway and, preacher's wife that she was, Mom would say, "The Lord works in mysterious ways," believing that I must have been sent for a reason. I was supposed to be reassured that my birth was part of God's plan, but when the troubles and misery of the years to come struck and I witnessed my mother's struggle to take care of this unplanned, unwanted child—of me—knowing this story only made me feel like a burden who should never have been born.

"The Lord giveth and the Lord taketh away," was the family mantra I heard in my childhood whenever death occurred. Everything was the Lord's will, and we were to give thanks or at least understand it was what He wanted, no matter how disastrous the event might be for us. But Mom must have thought "the Lord be damned" in that hospital in Roanoke Rapids in 1966, because she wouldn't let me die.

She prays and she feeds me and she doesn't sleep and—backed by her iron will—I don't quit (she won't let me quit). I fight my way out of that hospital, I get better, and I go home to my family's two-bedroom trailer in Weldon, North Carolina. I live through the upcoming winter and my first snowfall and I make my first snowman. Then it's Easter and I get a live little yellow chicken and a live baby duck dyed blue like most Southern children get on the day our Lord rose from the dead. I love them, they're my babies until the next-door neighbor's dog eats them and I cry and my brothers tell me not to be such a baby. But the whooping cough incident marks me: when your first memory is of fighting to live, you feel fragile, you develop a fear of being struck down unexpectedly, and you have a deep sense of being different from the normal, healthy kids. My mother is left paranoid after the whooping cough attack; she fusses over me, fiercely protective of this fragile child who had been so unexpectedly brought into her life and just as unexpectedly nearly taken away. I become "Mama's boy," which is, of course, the worst thing any self-respecting Southern male child can be. I can't remember a time when that wasn't my name.

So I guess there was never a time when I felt like I was a normal boy.

CHAPTER 1

Deathbeds Are Waiting

I figured out early on that my dad cared about two things: God and sports.

When it came to sports, I never had a chance. My sister, Carol, had it even worse, being a girl in the pre–Title IX era, meaning she didn't even register on Dad's radar screen and never got any attention at all. She married at nineteen, when I was two, mainly to get out of a house where she was always the moon to her brothers' suns. She grew into an adult who craved attention, provoking it with outrageous behavior when necessary, determined to get herself noticed some way, any way. Once free of our parents' home, she stopped going to church and dyed her hair blonde and wore halter tops and short shorts, all behaviors that scandalized Mom and Dad. I had to give her one thing: she found a way to get their attention.

My brothers had it easier. The one family commitment I can remember Dad always keeping was attending any sporting event in which my brothers competed. Alan, the oldest, was the handsome, responsible kid who ran relay on a high school track team with two guys who later won Olympic gold medals. Alan was always my favorite. While my relationships with Mike and Paul were characterized by long spans of inattention interrupted by bursts of terror and mockery, Alan always paid me attention. He gave me the only nickname I ever liked—"Champ"—and he actually tried to *teach* me to swim rather than throwing me in the deep end of the pool to see if I would literally sink or swim, as Mike and Paul did. He was my hero.

Mike, the middle boy (I was too young to really count), suffered from the same problems as many middle kids; he was always overlooked a bit, always overshadowed a bit. He ran track too, but he was never quite as good as Alan. He played football too, but he was never as good as Paul, which must have especially galled him as he was the older of the two. Skinny and nervous, he would bite his fingernails to the quick, so I remember them as only nubs. He was often angry, and he scared me.

Paul, the youngest of my brothers, was the golden child. Handsome, athletic, he was good at the most sacred of sports—football—and talk of him "going pro" floated around the house for as long as I can remember. Everything seemed to come effortlessly to Paul—sports, friends, girls, biceps, washboard abs—all of which I spent my own early years noticing I lacked. Absorbed in himself and his own world, Paul barely noticed my existence. But Paul's golden status curdled as he became a bullshit artist as an adolescent and an adult, one who never took responsibility for his actions, always telling tales that were beyond belief to avoid the consequences of his behavior. He totaled Mike's car while driving it illegally at fourteen, claiming that he lost control because he was trying to get a grasshopper off the windshield. Thanks to his good looks and charm, he pulled off these tall tales time and time again, and never learned the lessons of hard work and responsibility that Mom sought so desperately to impart.

Like a white-trash version of the Kennedys, our family recreation revolved around intensely competitive games of touch football, church softball games, and basketball at the Y. I was always expected to get on the field and play alongside my dad and brothers. This was a bit of a challenge, as my brothers and their friends outweighed me by as much as fifty to a hundred pounds. Most of the time, I just ran around, waving my arms frantically, calling "Me! Me! Throw it to me!"—as if someone was actually going to throw me the ball (hope springs eternal). On the occasions when I did get the ball—events as frequent as appearances of Halley's comet—my six-, seven-, eight-year-old hands would invariably fail to grasp the adult-size basketball or football, and after exclaiming their disgust—"Come on, Kevin! Catch the damned ball!"—they'd go back to ignoring me and I'd go back to running around like a chicken with its head cut off. When playing on the opposing team, if I got the football, my brothers saw golden opportunities to create fumbles and would nail me as hard as possible to jar the ball loose. I would fly five, ten, fifteen feet before landing and coughing up the ball, watching helplessly as someone picked it up and ran it back for a touchdown. The basketball court was even worse: if I had the ball, my brothers and their friends would either quickly steal it or, if I managed to hoist a shot, they would slam the ball back in my face with a force that would do Shaquille O'Neal proud. I got my revenge some two decades later, at a family reunion in the late eighties, when I, a healthy twenty-something, ran circles around my overweight, middle-aged brothers on the basketball court, stealing the ball at will, until my sister-in-law Claudette (always my biggest champion within the family) yelled out from the stands, "Payback's a bitch, now, ain't it!" She remembered.

Strangely enough, I did not develop an aversion to sports. My dad and brothers set the standard for masculinity, part of which was participating in sports, and I yearned to live up to it. At age six, Dad tried to sneak me into Pop Warner football two years before I was old enough to play. I was big for my age and Dad—ever the con artist—thought he could convince the coach to make an exception for me. One warm Florida evening, just after he had gotten off work, Dad brought me along to the playing field where he was picking up Paul from practice. The sun was just starting to go down and I stood by the car while Dad took the coach by the arm and walked him out onto the playing field. I had never been so nervous in my life: somehow, I thought, if I got onto the football team, I could make Dad proud and he would love me just as much as he loved Paul and Mike and Alan. I pictured myself in my shoulder pads, helmet, and jersey, Dad on the sideline cheering me on, giving me the same kind of attention my brothers got. I was sure Dad would succeed: he was my dad, and a minister, how could the coach say no? But when he got back to the car, he had a look of disappointment on his face. Once we were all in the car he told us that the coach said I was just too young to play and would have to wait. Since Dad couldn't have been the one who had failed, I was filled with shame: there had to be something wrong with me, I must not have measured up in some way and that was why the coach rejected me. I just wasn't enough of a man.

Having failed at sports, I tried the other way to get Dad's attention: church. Dad's journey to his ministry as a fundamentalist preacher was a bit unusual. Born in 1924, Dad hailed from Taunton, Massachusetts, one of the mill towns that dot that state and fueled the industrial revolution of the nineteenth century. His parents had a classic mill-town marriage. His father, Marlitt Fisk Jennings, was a flinty old "swamp Yankee" (in other words, someone whose family had somehow failed to make any money despite English ancestors who had come over in the 1600s) who emoted a little less than the Plymouth Rock he took me to see when I was six. His mother, Merilda Ora (Carmel) Jennings, was a French Canadian whose family was among those who had immigrated to work in the mills in the late 1800s, speaking not a word of English, replacing the Irish as the lowest of the low in New England's white ethnic pecking order.

A restless, rebellious kid, Dad jumped at the chance to join the merchant marine during World War II, having been rejected from the "fighting" armed forces because of his medical exam, and he ended up in Miami. There he met my mom, whose family had migrated from the Appalachian hill country of Tennessee, their ancestral home, to take advantage of the jobs the war had created. Mom was already engaged to another man, who was fighting in the Pacific, but the five-foot-eight, athletic, dark-haired, olive-skinned, handsome Yankee swept the little dark-haired lady off her feet with his jitterbugging (she always loved to dance) and his "foreign" ways. (His resemblance to his Quebecois ancestors was passed down to me, complete with the big nose.) She wrote the fighting man a Dear John letter, and Chet and Alice were married in 1945.

Theirs was indeed a mixed marriage. When Mom brought Dad home to meet her parents, his thick Yankee accent and their molasses Appalachian ones were so dissimilar that Mom finally had to translate for them, as each was baffled by what the other was saying. Descended from Confederate veterans, the Johnson family looked askance at the Northerner. When my mother's older brother Fred returned from fighting in Europe, he met my dad, was polite, waited until Dad left the room, and then snarled, "I can't believe you married a fucking Yankee," before stalking out.

As countless bumper stickers promise, "Jesus Saves," and he would save my dad and his marriage. When Mom and Dad were visiting her family in Knoxville in the early fifties, Mom's brother Fred—the one who had cursed her for marrying a Yankee—introduced Dad to Jesus, and Dad accepted him as his personal Savior and decided to start his life over with a clean slate, as Jesus had cleansed his soul. Dad told Mom of his plans, of how he wanted to move south and become a preacher and save men's souls so they could find Jesus the way he had. As a preacher's wife, Mom would have to accept Jesus too, of course, and (despite having no religion growing up) Mom eagerly did so, happy to be saved—and saved from the North, a land that she hated, where the water in the toilet of her lakeside cottage froze in the winter. She must have been skeptical about the leopard changing his spots, but she went back to Massachusetts, packed up her three kids and their belongings (easy to do as they didn't own much of anything), and headed south.

Dad went to a seminary in New Orleans, with Mom working as a telephone operator to put him through school, connecting calls all night and then tending babies all day while Dad was in class. Dad got his first church in Pleasant Home, Alabama, in the mid-fifties. With the church and the parsonage a mile from the nearest electricity, it wasn't the best post. Mom cooked on a woodstove and literally swept rattlesnakes out of the house. She bore a fourth child, Paul, in nearby Andalusia, Alabama, in 1956. These were all hardships, but they were making a new start, and things would assuredly get better from here. Southern Baptist ministers are somewhat akin to free agents in professional sports; they are hired and fired by congregations at will, with the more entrepreneurial ones starting their own congregations. A minister's personal charisma was the foundation of his success, and his ability to deliver a knockout sermon was the only guarantee of any kind of job security. Dad believed he had the gift, "the Calling," and Dad and Mom thought Pleasant Home was but the start of his journey to bigger and better things.

But Dad was soon booted from Pleasant Home, the first of a series of congregations that would fire him before and after my birth. As a kid, from my view in the front pew, I thought Dad was great and couldn't figure out why he could never seem to get or hold on to a congregation. I didn't understand yet that his Yankee accent was alienating to his Southern audiences or know that he had an unfortunate habit of sleeping with the deacon's wives, making it hard to hold on to a pulpit once he got it. Listening to Mom (who doctored the truth for her own purposes and wouldn't come clean about Dad until I was in my midthirties), I learned that Dad was too strong in the Gospel for the Pharisees and hypocrites who occupied the pews behind ours. Like Jesus, he was a prophet being scorned in his own land for telling the truth too clearly and too often.

By the time I was born they were back in Florida, where Mom and Dad had first met in 1945. Florida was Dad's Promised Land. He too hated the cold, snow, and ice of New England, and had vowed as a child that he would live in a warm climate one day. The late fifties were a good time to land in southern Florida, as the region was just beginning to take off economically and was made habitable by air-conditioning (Florida would aptly choose John Gorrie, considered the father of refrigeration and air-conditioning, as its representative in the National Statuary Collection in the U.S. Capitol building). Celebrated Northerners like Jackie Gleason were moving down to the Sunshine State. Jobs were plentiful, and Dad could always find something to do between congregations.

The Southern Baptist Church was the central institution of our lives. First there were the services: Sunday morning, Sunday evening, and Wednesday night prayer meeting. Then there were the choir rehearsals one or two nights a week; Dad loved to sing, and Mom had a mean alto that made her a frequent soloist at Sunday services. And then there were the softball leagues, which Dad and my brothers always played in. Throw in the "pageants" we rehearsed for Christmas and Easter, the potlucks (where my dad would never eat, as he had a paranoia about flies; he would heap his plate with food, flattering the church ladies on their congealed salads and potato salads and macaroni salads and then quietly dump it all behind the nearest bush while no one was looking), and your week was pretty much filled up. Religion, arts, athletics: the church provided it all. If we had just moved, we'd simply find the nearest Southern Baptist church and plug into a ready-made community.

On the nights when we weren't playing church softball or at Wednesday night prayer meeting or rehearsing with the choir, my family would attend revivals or "crusades." These gatherings, held in open fields or tents or churches or indoor arenas, depending on the reputation of the preacher, would go on for hours, often extending over multiple nights. Crusades were thrilling events: the big ones, like Billy Graham's, would attract thousands of people, feature choirs with hundreds of voices, and had all the excitement of a rock concert. The smaller, local ones, in churches or tents or fields, provided a chance to see friends and to check out new talent, unknown preachers who were making a name for themselves on the traveling revival circuit. The crowd would always provide entertainment as well: when especially moved by a preacher, some participants would fall to their knees and call out "Hallelujah, thank you Jesus!" or run down the aisles sobbing to find a counselor to whom they would witness that they had accepted Christ. As entertainment, it beat the hell out of church softball.

The main attraction of each crusade (there was always one preacher who was the headliner, like Billy Graham) needed warm-up acts in the form of local preachers. Dad saw this as his chance to grab the golden ring. If he could get up at a crusade and wow the crowd, he'd surely win a congregation and we could finally settle down. Crusades became for Dad what auditions are for aspiring actors, and we often found ourselves on hot summer nights swatting mosquitoes in some tent while Dad tried to summon the Spirit to give the sermon that would bring security to our lives.

One such crusade took place in a small town called Goulds, south of Miami. It was a hot, humid Florida night, when I couldn't have been more than six. Humidity and heat notwithstanding, we always dressed up when headed to the house of the Lord. I had on my requisite short-sleeved white dress shirt and clip-on tie (Dad wore the same, but he wore long sleeves and a real tie), and Mom had on her pink suit, my favorite of her outfits. The church hosting the crusade was a modest one, newly constructed, white stucco like everything else being thrown up in south Florida during the boom of the sixties, but lacking air-conditioning, so that the windows were wide open and bugs swarmed in. Over the din of whirring fans and flapping church programs parishioners used to try to cool themselves, Dad made his pitch for their immortal souls. He painted his picture of the terrors of hell, lakes of fire where you would burn for eternity, which surely awaited you if you did not accept Jesus as your personal Savior. He warned that death could come at any time, even on the drive home tonight, and that you had to be prepared to meet your Maker, you had to be right with God, or else the jaws of hell yawned wide for you. I was terrified and thrilled by his oratory: Dad was going to save people tonight, save them from eternal damnation. I was so proud to be his son.

At the end of his sermon, Dad made the Call. The Call was a fervent plea by the preacher for you to accept Jesus as your personal Savior and thereby be washed clean of your sins and be saved from burning in a lake of fire for eternity. After making the Call, Dad always asked the choir to sing "Softly and Tenderly" as he waited for sinners to come down the aisle to repent and accept Jesus. I can hear it to this day...

Softly and tenderly Jesus is calling,
calling for you and for me;
see, on the portals he's waiting and watching,
watching for you and for me.
Refrain:
Come home, come home;
ye who are weary come home;
earnestly, tenderly, Jesus is calling,
calling, O sinner, come home!
Time is now fleeting, the moments are passing,
passing from you and from me;
shadows are gathering, deathbeds are coming,
coming for you and for me.

I would wait anxiously, breathlessly, to see if any of the sinners would come home, would accept Jesus, or if they would leave him at the portal, waiting and watching. Would they continue to risk eternal damnation should they lose control of the steering wheel, skid off the road, and perish on the drive home?

After the sinners had accepted Jesus and the crusade wound down, I walked hand in hand with my dad that night across the darkened church grounds toward the parking lot. I had never loved him the way I loved him that night—as he stood at the pulpit, making the Call, holding the hands of the sinners who stumbled sobbing down the aisle into his grasp to find Jesus, to find salvation. I desperately wanted to be special to him, to bring to his face the joy I saw when the sinners responded to the Call, so I decided it was time to be saved myself.

I looked up hopefully into his face and said, "Dad, I want to accept Jesus as my personal Savior."

Instead of joy on his face, I found a frown. "Kevin, you're too young to be saved."

This wasn't the response I was hoping for. "Why?" I asked.

"Accepting Jesus as your Savior means giving your life over to him. It's a big decision that you need to be able to make knowing what that means, and you're too young to know what it means yet."

I strenuously objected. "That's not true, Dad! I do know what it means!"

"No, Kevin, you don't. You can't yet. We're not like Catholics, who baptize babies at birth before they know anything. That doesn't count. You have to *choose* to be baptized, and you're just not old enough to make that choice yet. You'll just have to wait."

I would have to wait. I was crestfallen. Once again, I didn't measure up. Would I ever?

But there was a deeper, darker, scarier implication than disappointing my dad to the problem of not being saved. The next day I waited until Dad had left for work and approached Mom in the kitchen to ask her some questions.

"Mom, is it true what Dad preaches, that people who don't accept Jesus will go to hell?"

"Of course it's true," she answered. "You have to accept Jesus as your personal Savior to be saved. The Bible says, 'For God so loved the world that He gave his only begotten Son, that whosoever believeth in Him shall not perish but have everlasting life.... But he that believeth not is condemned.'"

This was troubling news. "But what about people who've never heard the Gospel, Mom, who live in Africa or someplace where there are no preachers? Will they go to hell?"

"Well, yes, that's sad, but they will still go to hell."

"But that's not fair! They've never heard the Gospel! It's not their fault!"

"The Bible says, 'No man may cometh unto the Father except by me,' Kevin, and those folks don't get an exception just because they didn't know any better."

I took a deep breath and then I asked the question that was really on my mind.

"What about little kids, babies even, who weren't old enough to accept Jesus before they died—will they go to hell?"

Here Mom paused, caught between her maternal instinct to tell her obviously distraught son that it would all be okay and the rigid truth of the Gospel as we practiced it. She was torn, but she couldn't deny the Gospel, so she replied, "Well, I guess they go to hell, too."

I was stunned: I was going to go to hell, and Dad was going to let it happen! The sermons, the crusades, the hymns always emphasized that death was lurking, that

Time is now fleeting, the moments are passing,
passing from you and from me;
shadows are gathering, deathbeds are coming,
coming for you and for me.

Deathbeds were coming for me. I just knew it. And I was going to hell.

So, by age six, I had figured out that the world was unfair, that death and damnation loomed at every turn, and that God was more intent on punishment than mercy. I had a profound sense that disaster was always about to strike, and that we were powerless to stop it from destroying our lives. The world was a bad place, where bad things happened, like they did to the sinners in darkest Africa, like they did to babies who never got to accept Jesus. It was only a matter of time until our turn came.

And then I turned eight.

CHAPTER 2

Happy Birthday to Me

By my eighth birthday we were back in North Carolina, this time in a trailer park in Lewisville, a small town next to Winston-Salem. The preaching thing was going nowhere in Florida, and when Uncle Fred called and offered my dad a construction job, he decided to take it and try his luck in a new town. We'd been there about nine months when I turned eight and, so far, no pulpit. When Dad asked what I wanted to do for my eighth birthday, on May 8, 1971, I asked him to take me and my brothers Mike and Paul to the Y. We set off late on that Saturday morning.

Why I picked this way to celebrate my birthday I'll never know, as to choose to play sports with my brothers was to be a glutton for punishment. We started off by playing a pick-up basketball game. Mike was twenty, Paul fourteen and a half (halves still matter when you're eight), and the other players were all their size or bigger. It was a typical game, with the four-foot, eight-year-old sapling ignored by the six-foot monsters *("Me! Me! Throw it to me!")*. My brothers' competitive natures boiled over, as they were wont to do, and one of them got into a fight with another player, so Dad decided we should go swimming instead.

This was much more to my liking, as I wouldn't have to compete for the ball. The pool at the Y seemed like a palace to me. My brothers told me it was "Olympic size," which to me meant "really big." Kids like me were restricted to one small area of the pool, at the shallow end, because it was for serious athletes only. It had floating buoys that marked lanes for races, a springboard *and* a stationary platform for diving, and even bleachers for fans, so it was easy to imagine my dad as an Olympic athlete when he mounted the diving board for his first dive. At forty-seven, Dad was still a stud, with remnants of a washboard stomach, impressive biceps, and a body-fat ratio I would kill to have today. I was even prouder of him standing on the diving board than I was when he stood at a pulpit. He was a *man*, and I prayed I'd grow up to be just like him.

Dad approached the end of the board, turned, stretched his arms out, and prepared to dive. This was too good to be true: Dad was going to do a back flip, showing off that he still had it, middle aged or not. He bounced on the board a couple of times, leapt, did the flip, and broke the surface cleanly with hardly a splash. In my pride and joy, I applauded wildly when he surfaced, and ran to him as he swam to the side of the pool, got out, and lay down. I was eager to get him to do it again, but when I reached him, he was oddly not himself. He seemed upset, like he was in pain, hardly ready to do another dive. Dad told me to go get my brother Mike.

Nervous, I skedaddled quickly over to Mike, tugging him out of the pool and over to Dad. By the time we got back, Dad was having trouble breathing. Mike bent over to talk with Dad and I began to panic, saying "Get up, Dad! Get up! What's wrong?" Mike may not have fully realized what was going on, but he knew it was bad, and he turned and barked at Paul to get me out of there. A small crowd was beginning to gather as Paul hustled me out toward a nearby locker room. I started screaming and struggled against Paul to break free and go back to Dad's side, to no avail.

Sobbing and scared, I spent probably only a few minutes in the locker room, but it seemed like an eternity. Eventually Mike reappeared. I rushed toward him, expecting to hear everything was okay, asking, "Where's Dad?" But Mike seemed upset now too, telling us curtly to get dressed fast, that we needed to go, Dad was going to the hospital. From the locker room, we had to go back through the pool area to get out of the Y. As we passed through, I could see Dad being taken away on a stretcher by the emergency medical crew, covered up to his neck by a white sheet, across the bleachers where minutes before I had pictured the cheering fans being wowed by his back flip.

It was the last time I saw him alive.

Mike went with Dad in the ambulance and Paul and I went in my cousin Nathan's car to the trailer where we lived to grab some dry clothes. Nathan worked for his dad, Uncle Fred, in construction, and had used his earnings to buy a snazzy convertible. We raced, top down, behind the ambulance carrying Dad on I-40, the wind and high speed adding to my terror. I was crying and hysterical, and their efforts to convince me that Dad would be okay fell on deaf ears *(shadows are gathering, deathbeds are coming, coming for you and for me...).* When the ambulance peeled off to go to the hospital, we continued down I-40 and headed out to Lewisville.

Mom had been preparing a family celebration for when we got back from the Y, preparations that were interrupted by the phone call telling her that Dad was on the way to the hospital. The phone call was so upsetting that she dropped half of my birthday cake into the sink, where I found it when I got home, an image so bizarre that it is still burned into my brain over three decades later; it was not like my mom to leave a mess. After grabbing some dry clothes, we went on to Uncle Fred's, where I was sent out to the screened-in porch to play with my cousins. Everyone told me it would be okay, that Dad would be home soon. I tried to concentrate on playing, but annoyed the adults every few minutes by asking when Dad would be back. The afternoon wore on, and I began to have a sinking feeling that maybe Dad wouldn't be coming back. But shortly before sunset, I looked up and saw a small caravan of cars, including ours, come down the road and pull into Uncle Fred's driveway. Dad *was* coming home! I ran out with delight and latched on to Mom as soon as she got out. Dad was nowhere to be seen, though, so I asked when he would be coming home. She looked down at me with the saddest smile I've seen to this day, but said nothing. Perplexed, I chased Aunt Nannie back inside, where she was running through the house looking for Uncle Fred, screaming, "He's gone, he's gone, he's gone!" Dad had had a minor heart attack at the Y and then a second, more devastating one after arriving at the hospital and had died almost instantaneously. It was then I realized that Dad wouldn't be coming home ever again, and that the cake in the sink would never get iced. I would never look at my birthday the same way again. Happy Birthday to me.

Mom didn't talk much that night or the next day, as relatives began to gather from Florida and Massachusetts and Tennessee for the funeral. I didn't understand that she was having a nervous breakdown, and I was simply left wondering why she seemed so odd and so distant. On Sunday night I came down with yet another case of the strep throat/bronchitis/whatever that plagued my childhood, and my temperature spiked to 103 degrees, meaning it was time to go to the hospital now because if it went any higher I might be brain damaged for life. Perhaps it was the idea that her youngest child might now succumb to an unexpected illness, as I had almost done at age three and a half, or perhaps it was reentering the emergency room where less than twenty-four hours earlier she had been told that her healthy, active, forty-seven-year-old husband was dead—but whatever it was, my mom became hysterical when we reached Forsyth Memorial Hospital. The doctors took her first, and I now know they sedated her, but back then I wondered who the zombie was who returned because she didn't seem much like my mom. In less than a day, both my dad and my mom had disappeared.

The next few days were confusion as everything was turned upside down and no one was available to explain what had happened. The main message I got, reinforced by brothers and uncles and cousins, was that I should "be strong for your mother," which meant not to cry or show any feelings at all that might upset her. The periodic arrival of out-of-town relatives added to my confusion. I wasn't supposed to be happy, but seeing these visitors from far away *did* make me happy, leading to stern warnings that I shouldn't seem so happy, shouldn't laugh or smile at a time like this. This left me no options: don't seem happy, don't seem sad; so I decided to just try to be as invisible as I could.

On Monday night we had the first viewing of Dad's body in Vogler's Funeral Home. The place was creepy: with heavy drapes, thick carpets, and hushed tones, it fulfilled every stereotype of a funeral home. Dad was laid out in an ornate casket because Mom had insisted on buying the most expensive one available, determined that, if Dad had little in the way of material goods during life, he was going to have only the best in death. It sat on a riser at the front of a large room, surrounded by enormous mounds of floral bouquets, with rows and rows of seats arrayed in front of the coffin for viewers to sit in, a perfect aisle dividing them down the middle. Approaching the casket for the first time, I didn't get it. How could this thing, this inert, unmoving thing with its eyes closed, lying in a box, be my dad, who had just been showing off with a back flip at the Y? Maybe he was sleeping (he *looked* like he was sleeping) and would wake up soon. In the meantime, I didn't want to go anywhere near *it*, this thing that looked like my dad but clearly wasn't, at least not until he woke up. I hid at the back of the viewing room for the rest of the evening. If I didn't look at him, all this wasn't real.

Toward the end of the night, my sister, Carol, came to me and explained that it was time to go home, and asked if I wanted to say goodnight to Dad. I said yes, and Mom and Carol walked me up the aisle to the coffin. When I got to the coffin I decided I would do what I normally did when I said goodnight to Dad, which was kiss him. I secretly thought that, Sleeping Beauty–like, he might then awaken and apologize for scaring everyone so much. But I was too short to reach him and had to ask Mom and Carol to lift me up so I could kiss him. They each grabbed an arm to hoist me over the lip of the coffin, and when I planted my lips on Dad's forehead, the fact that he was dead became real. He wasn't warm. He was cold, ice cold. I felt horror, complete and total horror, at his iciness. I wanted to scream but, knowing that I was supposed to be "strong for my mother," I swallowed my horror and walked silently to the car to go home. But there was no doubt anymore: he wasn't waking up. He was gone.

Within another day or so the extended Johnson-Jennings family had gathered as the funeral was imminent. My brother Alan was home from the Marines, having gotten a hardship furlough, and arrived in his dress uniform. Alan sat with me and gave me some hard candies, and I began to think that maybe things would go back to normal someday. With Dad gone and Mom still acting weird, the sight of Alan in his dress uniform, so stable and upright and adult (at age eight, someone who is twenty-three is an adult), made it seem like the world was not entirely upside down. He helped me get dressed for the funeral, to which I wore the new jacket, dress shirt and dress pants, shoes, and clip-on tie I had gotten for Easter, just a couple of weeks before. Before we left he reminded me to be strong for Mom, tousling my hair and telling me to "keep my chin up." I promised him I'd try.

The service at Robinhood Road Baptist Church, the tiny church we had joined just a few months before, was packed with aunts and uncles and cousins and friends, an overwhelming array of people, many of whom I couldn't ever remember seeing before and would never see again, all of whom stopped me, patted my head, and said with a shake of their heads how sad it was that such a young boy had lost his father (in case I hadn't yet figured that out myself). All the flowers had been transferred from Vogler's to the church and encircled Dad's casket, which lay open before the pulpit, seeming to float in a sea of mums and carnations. Mom and I and Carol and her husband Tim and Alan and Mike and Paul all sat in the front row, the place of honor for the immediate family of the deceased. A soloist from the choir Mom and Dad sang with did "How Great Thou Art," Dad's favorite hymn, and one Mom would never again be able to hear without fleeing the church to cry outside. Mom fainted repeatedly. Alan put the spent smelling-salt capsules that were used to revive her in his military dress uniform hat, a collection that soon seemed to near the brim. At last it was over, and we were ushered into the Vogler limousine for the trip to the cemetery, where there would be a smaller, family-only graveside service.

Three days after my eighth birthday, I stood between Mom and my brothers as Dad was laid to rest in Forsyth County Memorial Cemetery. It being a mid-May afternoon in North Carolina, it was a beautiful day. Spring had sprung at Forsyth Memorial Park and everything was in bloom, as if nature herself was denying the death that had torn apart my eight-year-old world. When we got to the cemetery, Mom fainted again as she tried to get out of the car and, terrified, I began to cry. My brother Mike looked down at me and barked, "Don't cry. Be a man. Don't be a faggot." I stopped crying.

By age eight, I had learned everything I needed to know about being a man from my dad and my brothers. Being a real man meant taking advantage of anyone smaller or weaker than you. Being a real man meant never showing emotions or "weakness," even if you were eight and at your dad's funeral. And any male who deviated from those standards had a name. That name was *faggot.*

That would be me.

CHAPTER 3

The Road to Salvation, Part One

Praise God, from Whom all blessings flow;
Praise Him, all creatures here below;
Praise Him above, ye heavenly host;
Praise Father, Son, and Holy Ghost.

Although Dad was now gone, I still had a Father above.

The teachings of the Southern Baptist Church shaped my understanding of the world as a child. And those teachings came with a definite point of view. The Southern Baptists broke away from mainstream Baptists in 1845 because those who belonged to Southern congregations held slaves and saw it as their God-given right to do so. Today it is the largest organization of Protestants in the United States, with over sixteen million members, second only to the Catholic Church among U.S. Christian denominations. In the mid-nineties the Southern Baptist Convention issued a formal apology for defending slaveholding. The mid-*1990s*. That's about as current and progressive as the Southern Baptist Church's thinking on social justice gets. Suffice it to say, they aren't on the cutting edge.

I found it baffling when I moved North to go to college and was asked, "What are you?," with my interrogators expecting me to say Irish or Italian or some such European nationality. That's not how it works back home. First, you're white or you're black.

Then you're (in order of social prestige) Episcopalian, Lutheran, Presbyterian, Methodist, Baptist, or Pentecostal. We knew there were things called Catholics and Jews, but we didn't know any and they didn't count: the latter were definitely going to hell, and the former might be, too. I remember when we'd visit my Northern aunts, who planted strange little statues of what I later learned was the Blessed Virgin Mary in their back yards. This made my mom cluck disapprovingly, mutter about the sin of idolatry, and wonder aloud (out of earshot, of course, because she was Southern and you are never impolite to someone's face in the South) if Catholics were really Christians at all, with their strange ways, worshipping the Pope and all, and whether God would let them into heaven or if they would burn in a lake of fire for eternity with the Jews and other heathens. The jury was out. But I, thank God, was white, and I was a Baptist. I was fine. That's all I needed to know.

Catholic guilt and Jewish guilt have been explored at length, but few educated urban professionals have fundamentalist Protestant backgrounds, so Southern Baptist guilt is little understood. Urban sophisticates would laugh in 1976 when presidential candidate Jimmy Carter, in an interview with *Playboy* magazine during which he was asked if he'd committed adultery, said he had "lusted in his heart after other women." They laughed because they didn't get it. We did. For Southern Baptists, *thinking* you want to commit a sin is just as bad as actually committing it. They're the same. And God writes them all down, time, day, and date, and reads them all back to you on Judgment Day before the final verdict on your immortal soul is rendered. It doesn't matter if you actually *do* anything; you get to feel guilty and you get to go to hell even if you never act on your evil desires.

George Orwell must have felt creative when he wrote about "thoughtcrime" in *1984*, but Southern Baptists were *way* ahead of him on that one. For us, every thought could be a sin, a thoughtcrime against God. The major difference between us and the denizens of Orwell's nightmarish fantasy was who the police were. As Southern Baptists, we are our own policemen. The voice of the Church was inside my head early in life, telling me which thoughts were sins. It was *my* responsibility to police my thoughts, to stop the sinful ones from happening. But given my natural inquisitiveness, controlling my thoughts was impossible. I was set up to fail because evil thoughts—evil being anything that questioned the Southern Baptist orthodoxy—would creep in anyway, despite my best efforts, confirming that I was a bad, despicable person (only a bad person would have these thoughts, right?) who could only be saved through God's grace.

My tendency to ask questions as a child started getting me into trouble early. Once, when I was six or seven and my mom was at the kitchen table during one of her smoking and coffee-drinking marathons, I decided it was time to ask her to clarify some particularly confusing matters in the Gospel. I knew we were supposed to take the Bible literally, but some parts just didn't make sense. I began with Adam and Eve.

"Mom, Adam and Eve were the first two people, right?"

"Right."

"All of us descended from them, right?"

"Right."

"I don't understand something, Mom. If we all descended from Adam and Eve, that means their kids had to marry each other and have kids, which is wrong, isn't it?"

Mom was momentarily thrown back, and paused between drags on her cigarette. I could see the wheels turning. "Well, yes, that would be wrong, but there were some other people around for them to marry, too."

"There were?" I responded, incredulous. "What were their names? Why aren't they mentioned in the Bible?"

By now Mom was really stumped, and gave her standard reply: "These questions just show how strong the devil is, Kevin, how he can plant doubts in your mind. These questions are so confusing because he is so wicked. You have got to be careful not to be fooled by his clever ways. You have to have faith."

The circular logic of the Church foiled me at every turn. Mom struggled to do her best to come up with logical explanations but, when completely stumped, she'd always play the trump card.

"Mom, if drinking is wrong, why did Jesus turn water into wine at the wedding, and drink wine at the Last Supper? That just doesn't make sense."

Answer: The devil makes you think that way.

"Mom, how did people in olden times live to be several hundred years old when they didn't even have doctors, and people die so young today? That just doesn't make sense."

Answer: The devil makes you think that way.

This answer was never very satisfactory and doubts began to creep in, competing with a feeling of guilt for having asked the questions in the first place, as my tendency toward questioning and doubt was one more piece of evidence of my weakness and depravity. Maybe I was possessed by the devil, I thought, because I had so many troubling questions. Not to worry, though: In my Father's house there are many mansions, as we are told in John 14:2, and salvation is open to all. With one important exception: my Father didn't seem to have a House for Homos. I'm not sure when and where I got this message, but I can't remember a time when I didn't know it.

"When did you know you were gay?"

I get asked this question every time I speak in a school. My stock answer is, "I always knew," but that's not the full truth. There are times when I think back and ask myself, "When *did* I really know?" and the honest answer is: I'm not really sure.

Did I *know* when I was transfixed by my dad's friend's five-o'clock shadow when I was five? Did I *know* when I was inexplicably drawn to the bodybuilding ads in my brothers' magazines when I was seven? Did I *know* when I developed an obsession with Jan-Michael Vincent after watching *Buster and Billie* when I was ten? Did I *know* when I cut out and taped to my bedroom wall pictures from *Sports Illustrated* of Pittsburgh Steelers linebacker Jack Lambert, weightlifting shirtless, when I was twelve? Did I *know* when I swiped my sister's *Playgirl* from her grocery bag when I was fourteen?

Just as Bill Clinton told Kenneth Starr that it all hinges on what your definition of "is" is, I guess it all hinges on what your definition of "know" is. If "knowing" means "I know these feelings mean I am a homosexual," then the answers to these questions would be no, no, no, no, and no. Looking back, the signs are so obvious that it is almost laughable, and I wonder, "How could I *not* have known?" *Because I wasn't allowed to know.* Being gay was unthinkable. After all, my parents weren't, my sister wasn't, my brothers weren't, no one I knew was. I didn't make the connection between my feelings and what I was. I couldn't. It was the ultimate thought-crime.

And the Church would make it much harder for me to acknowledge the truth. With Dad now gone, the Church became more important than ever; it became a way to try to remain connected to him. I threw myself into the void Dad left. On Sundays, seated in one of the front pews at Robinhood Road Baptist Church, I would sing in an affected bass next to Mom during hymns in hopes of taking his place in their duets, earning befuddled looks from everyone. I became the Sunday school nerd who actually *read* the lessons and the verses before class, a sure sign to the other boys that I was weird. I was chosen as the "youth minister" every year on the Sunday when a young'un was picked to preach the Gospel. "You're just like your daddy," the church ladies would coo when the minister and I would shake their hands as they left the service. "Alice, he's following in his father's footsteps." I would preen in response to their praise, hoping against hope that they were right, suspecting deep down that I wasn't my daddy at all, praying that Jesus would indeed save me, but suspecting that I was simply too bad a person to merit His mercy.

I just couldn't let myself know I was gay. It was too horrible.

Things were bad enough already in the aftermath of Dad's death. At first things looked up. Mom got a small life insurance settlement and used it to buy a double-wide trailer. I was unbelievably excited to live in a double-wide. By age eight I could already count at least seven different homes, and it may have been more. Moving as often as we did, I was always the new kid, and being the new kid sucks. I had no way of understanding the pecking order of my new classmates, no allies to turn to, no "you taught my older brother" rapport with teachers. Being the most isolated student, the new kid is always the easiest to target. The fact that we were usually poorer than my classmates, that I was the new kid who lived in a trailer park, made it even easier to single me out. And, on the rare occasions when I'd make friends and start to feel as if I belonged, we'd up and move again. But it was all going to be different now that we had a double-wide.

The dwellings of my childhood were a mix of things—apartments, rented houses—but the dominant form of housing during my preteen years was a trailer. When I talk about growing up in a trailer to my educated, professional friends today, I may as well be describing growing up in something like an igloo or a tepee, but far trashier and less exotic. I often have to explain that trailers aren't RVs, nor are they the things you tow behind a car. A trailer is a manufactured home, no less than eight feet wide and twenty-eight feet long, but typically fourteen feet wide by fifty or more feet long. A trailer gets parked on a lot, generally at least fifty feet wide and a hundred feet long, where it is connected to services like electricity and sewage, and it tends to stay there for its natural life. Hence the term "trailer park," as it is where trailers are parked (although I am sure some developer coined the phrase because he thought it sounded more bucolic and inviting than "parking lot").

"Mobile home" is something of a misnomer: it's mobile until it gets parked in the trailer park, then it's stationary.

The trailers of my childhood had very predictable layouts. They had two doors, as fire regulations mandated two exits, located in the midsection of the trailer. The midsection usually had an open living room/eat-in kitchen area that occupied the bulk of the trailer. At either end would be bedrooms and bathrooms: usually a "master bedroom suite" at one end and one or sometimes two smaller bedrooms at the other. They came furnished but generally did not have washers and driers. Better trailer parks provide a laundry facility where you can wash your clothes; otherwise, you find a laundromat.

When things were going poorly, we rented trailers. When things were going well, we'd shop for new ones to buy. New trailer shopping was one of the great thrills of my childhood. Trailers are sold on lots like those that sell Christmas trees, so you can compare a wide variety in a very short period of time. I loved dashing in and out of dozens of trailers, comparing and contrasting their various features. It was like being in a giant toy store where you get to live in the toy once you bought it.

The one downside to new trailer shopping was new-trailer smell. This is kind of like new-car smell. Except it sucks. Very new trailers will give off an intensely chemical smell that burns your eyes and singes your nose hairs to the point that you cannot get through the salesman's tour. It's sort of like the smell you get a whiff of when you drive by a paper manufacturing plant, except you have to then live inside the plant. You always avoid very new trailers for this reason. Let a few weeks pass, until the new-trailer smell wore off, and then it would be livable.

Rented trailers came with special features of their own. Like rats. One of the first trailers we rented in North Carolina had them, and I would often hear them scampering around when they came out at night. Since I was younger, I got the bottom bunk and my older brother Paul the top one, putting me closer to the rats, a fact Paul would gleefully remind me of every night when he turned the lights off. I would lay awake, rigid with fear, a fear that proved justified when one night a rat ran across my bed (to get to the other side, I suppose). I ran into my parents' bedroom and refused to sleep anywhere but between them for the remaining months we lived in that trailer.

(Years later this experience would be important glue in the bond between me and my best friend in college, Luis. A fellow scholarship kid, Luis had grown up in the South Bronx, where his housing project was also infested with rats. But he and his brothers took a different approach than I did, viewing the rats' presence as a chance to play a fun game they called "beat the rats to death." They would turn off all the lights, wait until the rats assumed they were asleep and then came out, and would then flick the lights on, racing around with baseball bats, clubbing the rodents senseless. There, in a nutshell, is the difference between gay men and straight men, I suppose.)

So I was incredibly excited to move into a double-wide, which isn't a regular trailer but much more like a house, the kind of place "rich people" lived in. For those unfamiliar with manufactured homes, a double-wide is a big step up from a trailer. The term "double-wide" comes from the fact that this home consists of two trailers that are open on one side. They are transported to a lot (its own lot, not a space in a trailer park), placed on a foundation, and joined together. It is a permanent structure. Mom bought a lot across from Uncle Fred, which was great because I then had cousins to play with. She had enough to make a down payment, to put in an in-the-ground pool in the backyard, and to take out a mortgage. We *owned* it. I felt like we'd won the lottery.

Lewisville was unincorporated when I was a child, so there were no municipal services to speak of. Our street was unpaved, you only got a streetlight if you paid for one, and if you wanted your garbage picked up you had to pay someone to do so. Mom thought that this was a big waste of money, so she decided we'd dispose of it ourselves, and we began to burn our trash periodically in the backyard. I loved burning trash, especially when we'd do it at night during the summer. The sparks from the trash would float off into the night sky, fireflies would gather, and we would be enveloped in a magical twinkling of light. Trash burning was up there with new trailer shopping as one of the special treats of my childhood.

For me, the best part of the double-wide was our in-ground pool. All the kids in Lewisville were nice to me because we had one of the few in-ground pools in town and I controlled access to it on the steamy Southern summer days that stretch from June through August. But having an in-ground pool presented challenges as well. One was water moccasins. Water moccasins are deadly amphibious snakes that, when they can't find sources of natural running water, will settle for a pool. Mom warned us to check carefully to see if there were any snakes in the pool before diving in, which I always did. Cleaning out the pool filter was a terrifying chore, as you could never be sure if a water moccasin had been sucked in along with the frogs you would always find.

Other, less terrifying things also found their way into our pool. Our backyard, where the pool was, was abutted on the north by a fenced-in horse pasture, to the east by a cornfield, and to the south by an undeveloped lot. Further south from that lot was a family that kept some cows, which had a tendency to get loose and wander the neighborhood. One morning Mom and I were in the kitchen, and when she got up to go refill her coffee cup she looked out the kitchen window and exclaimed, "Well, I'll be damned!" One of the neighbor's cows had fallen in our pool and, unable to get out, had drowned. Its corpse was now floating in the deep end. Mom phoned up the neighbors and indignantly demanded they come fish out the cow. They demanded just as indignantly that she reimburse them for the cost of the cow, as they blamed its death on her. As they proceeded to duke it out verbally, I got annoyed:

the longer that thing floated in the pool, the more delayed my summer fun would be. I don't recall who paid for what but, by the next day, the cow was gone and my friends and I were back to our favorite game, which consisted of throwing golf balls in the deep end and seeing who could retrieve the most from the bottom before having to surface for air.

While being in a rural setting brought disadvantages, like water moccasins and dead cows in your pool, it had its advantages, too. My favorite dessert growing up was Mom's blackberry cobbler. Blackberry bushes tend to grow in edge areas, like the boundaries between woods and cornfields, which we fortuitously had right behind our house. On the days when Paul and I were brave enough, we'd venture out into the cornfield to find blackberry bushes, pick as many berries as we could, and then bring them home so Mom could make a fresh cobbler. Blackberry picking had its risks, though. First, there was always the ever-present danger of snakes but, if you stomped your feet and made enough noise, they'd know you were coming and slither away. Second was the problem of bees and wasps and hornets, which tended to like blackberries as much as we did. Sometimes you'd reach into a bush and inadvertently disturb a wasp's nest. I remember Paul doing so on one occasion and bolting through the cornfield screaming, a swarm hot on his tail. Mom spent much of the night pulling stingers out of Paul's face, which was covered with welts just like the plastic bumps that were used to depict topographical features on the new globe I had gotten for Christmas. But the lure of a fresh blackberry cobbler (preferably as dessert following our favorite meal, Mom's chicken and dumplings) was simply too strong to resist, and we were back out in the cornfield picking blackberries again a few days later, winged threats or no.

We had a yard and a pool and a permanent home, but Mom's financial planning skills weren't the best, and we soon found ourselves in trouble. When the life insurance money ran out, Mom faced the reality of mortgage payments and bills and found that

Dad's Social Security check was woefully inadequate. She needed to get a job, fast. But she had little education and had been out of the workforce for more than two decades, thanks to my father's dictum that "a woman's place is in the home." Essentially, she was unemployable in an economy experiencing a decade-long downturn during the seventies. Her options were few.

Mom tried getting various manual labor jobs—serving in my school cafeteria, for instance—but nothing came through. I could see the tension and pressure she faced and her growing sense of desperation. We began to do things Mom vowed we'd never do. For one, she hated charity, but our dwindling resources forced us to apply for food stamps. Trips to the grocery store became laden with anxiety. Food stamps covered only some items, that is, those that were edible, so we had to separate our basket into those they covered—bananas, milk, cereal—and those they did not—laundry detergent, cleaning supplies—paying cash for the latter. If we made a mistake, the cashier would loudly say, "Ma'am, you can't buy this with food stamps." Mom's humiliation would be compounded by being portrayed as a foiled cheat, so she took special care to be scrupulous in the division of goods. At the checkout this complex process—"Hot dogs, Mom?" "Yes." "Toothpaste, Mom?" "No."—slowed everything down so that the line behind us ground to a halt, annoying the other customers. Mom would wait until the last minute to furtively pull out the food stamps, trying to minimize the possibility that someone would see her using them. As the clerk rang us up, Mom would stand tightlipped, head held high, trying to hide her shame and anger at being forced to accept a handout from the government.

I experienced my own version of this every day in the school lunch line after I went on the free lunch program. Getting my lunch became a daily ordeal. Things were normal at the beginning of the line, when I got the same entrée as everyone else. It got more complicated the further down the line I went. With free lunch, you got only one carton of milk, while the kids who were paying for lunch always took two. Dessert was not included—don't want to spoil the freeloaders—so I longingly looked at the brownies or cookies or pie on offer every day, pretending to choose not to have them, but knowing that I couldn't afford to put them on my tray. The nearer I got to the cashier, the more my stomach churned. Those of us on free lunch had to announce this fact to her every day, a ritual seemingly designed to embarrass us as, in our small town, the cashier knew us all and knew who was on free lunch and who wasn't. The primary reason for this requirement seemed to be to force poor children to make a daily admission that they were freeloading in hopes that the attendant humiliation would get us to drop out of the program. My face would flush red as I said "free lunch" to the cashier. I tried to find a way to lean close to her and say it loudly enough for her to hear but quietly enough so that no one else did. It never worked: the other kids knew, and one of the boys would from time to time inevitably announce, "Hey, guys! Did you know Kevin gets free lunch?"

But no matter how miserable it was, I was always reminded that it could never be as bad as my mom's childhood. The roots of her own miserable childhood lay in the misery of her mother's life.

My memories of Grandma are fragmentary as she died in 1973, when I was nine. But the stories of Grandma's life and my mother's childhood were epic in my childhood, Homeric practically, and were recited as a liturgy of misery to me whenever I "felt sorry" for myself, that is, when I noticed that my life sucked pretty bad, too. Mom would tell these stories to me at the kitchen table, always her favorite place to sit no matter where we lived, chain smoking three packs of Herbert Tareyton cigarettes a day and drinking cup after cup of coffee, lightened by a bit of evaporated milk from the can she kept in the fridge. Grandma was born in the Appalachian hills of Tennessee in 1900. Her mom had died when she was very small (tuberculosis was the family legend) and her shiftless, no-good, no-account father abandoned the little girl, who was then shuttled between orphanages, cousins, and a pair of delightfully named aunts, Myrtle and Gyrtle, throughout her childhood. The fact that her relatives pawned her off on one another as fast as possible is not evidence that they were uncaring. Grandma grew up in an impoverished land in an era when the government provided no assistance whatsoever to poor people; every mouthful of grits, gravy, or fatback that she ate literally came right off their plates or those of their own children, creating an incentive to get her married and out of the house as soon as they possibly could.

Her relatives were undoubtedly relieved when William Johnson, a man considerably older than Margaret, asked for her hand in marriage. So my grandmother was married off, a teenaged bride, and started having kids. First William Jr., then Frances, then Fred, then my mom, Alice Verna, in 1925, the fourth of the nine children she bore by her early thirties. William Johnson proved to be just as shiftless, no-good, and no-account as Margaret's father had been, drinking all day, slapping her around, unable to hold a job, and yanking his kids out of school as soon as they were able to work in the fields so they could bring home some money for the often-bare family coffers. Whenever I would complain as a kid, Mom would respond with stories of sleeping in abandoned churches when there was nowhere else to go, or of picking cotton at age six or seven to earn some money, making clear that my experience was the lap of luxury when compared to hers.

My mom hated her father, telling me as a child that she and her sister Frances seriously debated spitting on his corpse at his funeral. He died in the mid-fifties, before I was born, and Mom's desire to erase his existence was so strong that I would never even see a picture of him. I have no idea how tall he was, what he weighed, what he looked like: he would become a faceless monster to me, the villain who ruined Grandma's life. Partly Mom hated her father because of how he treated my grandmother and because he didn't even bother to try to provide for his family. But mostly, she hated him because of how he treated her. One night when Mom was eight, nine, ten—she couldn't be exactly sure, it was so many years ago—my grandfather showed up at her bedside and "went at her," as she put it to me. A feisty girl even then, Mom fought him off and ran out of the house. Later she would come home and find out from her older sister, Frances, that her dad had already had at her, and would probably move on to one of Mom's three younger sisters, having failed with her. The next day, little Alice snuck her mother's butcher knife out of the drawer, hid it, and waited for her dad to come home. When he got there, she showed it to him and told him that, if he ever touched her or one of her sisters again, she'd kill him in his sleep. Grandpa laughed, until he saw the look in her eyes and realized she was dead serious and mean enough to do it. Apparently he never went at any of the girls again.

Mom's childhood stories were all of chores and deprivation. Growing up in shacks with no electricity or running water until her teens, Mom performed tasks that were totally foreign to my experience: washing the insides of the globes of the kerosene lanterns that lit her home (which she was assigned because her hands were the only ones small enough to reach inside them), minding her five younger siblings (a duty she would get out of by pinching the babies so hard they screamed, prompting her mom to take over, allowing little Alice to go out and play), and pressing clothes with an iron that had to be heated on their wood-burning stove (a task she especially detested in the sweltering Tennessee summers when the combination of the woodstove's heat and the Southern humidity would raise the temperature so high she would sometimes faint). If I wanted new clothes, Mom would remind me she had but two dresses as a child, sewn by her mother from the patterned fabric of flour sacks, a pattern all the other kids knew because they bought the same flour, marking her as the poorest of the poor. If I complained about school lunches, Mom would remind me that her school lunch, when she was lucky enough to have one, was a piece of bologna on a biscuit, a meager one even by Appalachian standards, of which she was so embarrassed she would hide behind a tree while eating it. If I said I was hungry, Mom would remind me of how she would wake up crying from hunger as a child, and that her mom would cry too, because often she had no extra food to feed her.

Mom's stories might have been meant to teach me "how good I had it" (one of her favorite phrases), but the result was to silence and terrify me. I quickly learned what the biggest sin in my mom's book was. It wasn't adultery, or not honoring thy father or thy mother, or coveting thy neighbor's ass: it was "feeling sorry for yourself." In Mom's world, talking about difficulties or problems (or feelings at all) was feeling sorry for yourself, and that was just not to be done. Noticing you didn't have something and asking for it was being greedy, and being disappointed if you didn't get it was feeling sorry for yourself. Mom's life had taught her that you probably weren't going to get what you wanted, therefore you shouldn't hope for it too much. Noticing your deprivation and your feelings about it served no purpose. It was just feeling sorry for yourself.

Seeing the increasingly dire straits we were in as the life insurance money dwindled, I was determined not to feel sorry for myself, and I wracked my brains for ideas about how to help out. I read an article about saving money in *Reader's Digest* and approached Mom with some ideas during one of her kitchen table cigarette-smoking/coffee-drinking jags.

"Mom, I read that you can save money by using a hand towel instead of paper towels to dry the dishes, so I am going to start doing that from now on."

"Okay, honey, that's nice," she replied.

"I also read that it is cheaper to eats eggs for breakfast than cereal, and I wanted you to know I'd like to switch to eggs then."

Now Mom put down her cigarette and turned to give me her full attention. "Kevin, where are you getting all these ideas?"

"I read an article in *Reader's Digest* about ways to save money. I know we need to save money, so I thought we could try some of these ideas out."

Mom gave me a bemused smile. "Honey, those are good ideas, but they will only save pennies. We need some dollars."

Foiled in my attempt to help, I tasted a bit of the desperation that Mom ingested daily, a desperation borne of having no idea where to turn, a desperation that grew so intense that it led her to do the unthinkable, something beyond taking food stamps and free lunches. It was a warm summer day when Mom told me to get in the car, that we were going to Thruway Shopping Center. That in itself was odd: Thruway was in Winston-Salem, and we didn't venture into the city that often. I rode quietly in our blue Galaxy 500 for the half hour it took to get from our double-wide in Lewisville to the shopping center, where Mom parked not in front of the A&P or W. T. Grant's or Ben Franklin's—the places we would usually shop—but in front of a store I'd never been in before, where all the things in the windows looked used and were covered with a fine layer of dust.

"Let's go," Mom barked, and out we got. "Now, I don't want you to say anything while we're in this store, you understand?" I nodded yes, and into the store we went. There was only one man working in the dimly lit, forlorn store, and he came over to us immediately. "Can I help you?" he asked.

"Yes," Mom replied, and took a deep breath. "I'm not here to buy, but to sell."

Huh? Sell? I thought Mom was confused. You *bought* things in stores, you didn't *sell* them.

"What do you have?"

Mom removed a cloth from her purse and unwrapped it. "These two rings."

My eyes widened. These were her engagement and wedding rings, things she had gotten from Dad. How could she sell them? I looked up at her in surprise, but didn't dare speak.

Mom wouldn't look at me. She was trying to keep her head up, to maintain her dignity, but I could see the shame on her face.

The man quoted a price. Mom was clearly disappointed, and looked down at the rings. "That's not very much. Is that the best you can do?"

"Yes, ma'am."

She sighed, resigned. It was just one more disappointment in a lifetime filled with them. "Okay, I'll take it. But can I ever get them back?"

"Yes, ma'am. You'll be on a monthly payment plan and, as long as you keep up the payments, they won't be sold."

"Okay, then."

Mom took the man's money and we headed back to our car. When we got there, she turned and looked at me. "Kevin, you are never to tell anyone about this trip today. Do you understand?"

I couldn't look back at her, so filled with shame was I at her decision to trade away these emblems of my father. "Yes, ma'am."

She reached out and grasped my chin, wrenching my face toward hers, leaning in close to me. "Anyone. Ever. *Do you understand?*"

Trembling now, I blurted out, "Yes, ma'am."

With that, Mom turned around and put her key in the ignition. But she didn't turn the car on. She lowered her head and started to cry, silently—but only for a minute. A minute was how long you got to feel sorry for yourself. Then she regained her composure, turned the key, and drove us home.

(I would never tell anyone about this trip, not until I gave the eulogy at my mother's funeral thirty years later. One of my cousins would read the eulogy and—predictably—write back that I was "trying to make people feel sorry for you.")

Shortly after that, Mom finally landed a job—at McDonald's. We had a steady, if meager, income stream, between Dad's Social Security, Mom's earnings, and the contributions my brother Mike made from his paycheck, and things stabilized for a while. Mom was thrilled, and the first thing she did was take us off food stamps and free lunch, even though in the early years of her working at Mickey D's we were still eligible for them. Charity was something you resorted to if you had absolutely no other choice, and she finally had that choice. I was thrilled because dinner often became a quarter pounder with cheese and a large fries, as Mom came home too tired to cook and it was just easier to bring something from "the store," sparking in me an addiction I've never fully shaken. I came to see the "golden arches" as a symbol of home cooking, and to this day, when I bite into a Big Mac, it's as if I am tasting my mom's handiwork.

Mom was a star at McDonald's. She worked like a fiend, never took a sick day (being an hourly worker, she couldn't: it came right off her paycheck), and had a natural gift for math that made her the fastest employee on the register. Customers would come to the counter and say, "I'd like three Big Macs, two large fries, two shakes, and a hot apple pie," and Mom would tell them their total before the machine had finished ringing it up, amazing both them and her coworkers. I asked her if she ever got the total wrong. She said yes, once, when a bus came through the drive-through and ordered food for the forty-some people on it. I asked her how much she missed by, and she replied, "three cents: I calculated the sales tax, which is 4.5 percent, wrong in my head." I would always remember this story, and remember the injustice that a woman with a gift for math like hers would spend her days solving the value for three Big Macs, two large fries...

The bottom fell out when I was in fifth grade. Mike met a local girl, fell in love, and got married. Carol and Alan were off starting their own families, being in their early twenties, and Paul was still too young to work, so Mike had been filling a critical role in the family finances. We were barely staying afloat, and the loss of his contribution to the household income when he married tipped the boat. Mom began to realize that she couldn't make the mortgage payments anymore and that we would have to sell the double-wide and buy a trailer instead.

I was devastated. This was a huge step backward, going from a double-wide to a trailer. We had lived in one place for more than three years, the longest stretch ever, and I felt like I belonged. Now my world was being upended: there would be no more yard, no more in-ground swimming pool, no more cousins across the street. My brother Paul also moved out about this time, dropping out of high school, unwilling to live by Mom's (or anyone else's) rules any longer. It was just Mom and me now, against the world.

By sixth grade we were ensconced in a new trailer in a trailer park a few miles away, but this disruption was only one small part of my misery, which was due more to the fact that I was starting to go through puberty. While "cleaning myself" in the bathtub one day, I discovered masturbation. I was horrified by it, and even more horrified by the physical reactions my body was beginning to have to cute boys. I began praying that God would somehow help me avoid this evil act; "lead us not into temptation, but deliver us from evil" took on a new and more urgent meaning. I started keeping a small journal in which I would track how many days I could make it without engaging in the sin of Onan. I think the high was three. I distinctly remember that streak being broken after watching Andy Gibb on some TV show, gazing enraptured as he performed his mega-hit "I Just Want to Be Your Everything" in full, feathered-hair seventies glory. I was simply overcome and had to rush to the bathroom to "relieve" myself. Afterward, I was stunned that the power of the Brothers Gibb seemed to overwhelm that of the Almighty. But then I remembered: as pop singers, they were in league with the devil, and I was a weak and willing pawn in his game.

I hadn't actually acted on any of my feelings or engaged in the prepubescent antics that so many others have related to me, had never played a game of "doctor," but no matter: I was having so many impure thoughts that I couldn't figure out how God was going to record them all in his Book for retelling on Judgment Day. As a child I pictured myself before the throne for a *very* long time. The transgressions of one gym class seemed to be enough to keep God busy for hours. "At 9:30 and twenty-two seconds, you had lustful thoughts about Todd. At 9:30 and twenty-seven seconds, you had lustful thoughts about Mike. At 9:30 and thirty-four seconds, you had lustful thoughts about Tripp," and so on. My thoughtcrimes, my sins, were innumerable, and my inner policeman seemed helpless to do anything about it. My prayers for these thoughts to stop went unanswered: God had abandoned me, undoubtedly because I was too evil for redemption.

To add to my horror, my dad and our Father had merged together. Right after Dad's funeral, Mom told me that when people die, they go to heaven, where they look down upon you and know your every thought and every action. Whether she said this because she thought it would comfort me to think Dad was always with me or because she thought this would help keep me on the (literally) straight and narrow, Mom had delivered very, very bad news to a preteen struggling with his sexual orientation. I pictured Dad sitting at the right hand of the Father, knowing my every thought (including those about Todd, Mike, Tripp, and Andy Gibb), shaking his head mournfully. The thought that he also saw me masturbating, and knew what I was thinking when I did so, filled me with a shame and horror that is simply indescribable, a shame and horror that would truly make Portnoy complain. Every ejaculation shamed my father in front of his Father, and left me feeling like I was the dirtiest, most loathsome creature on the earth, some kind of human worm with no rock to hide beneath. No matter how carefully I concealed my thoughts and deeds from my mom, my brothers, my classmates, there was no escaping the ever-watchful eyes of my fathers. There was *no way* I was going anywhere but hell, that was for sure.

I had additional, and equally unspeakable, reasons to fear Dad's wrath reaching out from beyond the grave to smite me. Perhaps it is because the power of guilt in our faith is so strong but, for whatever reason, my family felt a need to fix the blame on someone whenever anything went wrong. Since God was merciful, punishments were visited upon us because of our own actions, and thus the perpetrator of those actions must be found out so future recurrences of disaster can be avoided. The thing that had most "gone wrong" in our family was the untimely death of my father, and someone had to be to blame. Given his health and relative youth, we searched and searched for explanations for his demise, and eventually settled on the idea that somehow the cold water of the swimming pool into which he dove after playing basketball at the Y had brought on his heart attack. Perhaps, had he never gone to the Y, he would have lived, we concluded. And why did he go to the Y in the first place? Because I had asked him to. So I was to blame.

This wasn't a conclusion I came to on my own. No, my older brothers told me explicitly that it was my fault that Dad was dead. Because she had difficulty letting go of Dad, Mom literally refused to let go of his clothes and belongings, and kept them in a closet in our double-wide. I never wanted to go anywhere near this closet, a fact my brothers knew and took advantage of. On more than one occasion, when I did something that displeased them, they shoved me into the closet where Mom kept Dad's old clothes, snarling, "Now Dad's going to come back and get you," and held the closet door tightly closed so I couldn't get out. A sense of absolute terror would overcome me in the gloom of the closet. I expected Dad to step out from some deep recess at any moment and demand to know why I had killed him. When I brushed up against his suits, I would scream, as I was sure their arms were about to reach out and grab me, strangling me as punishment for patricide. Panicked, desperate to escape the sudden death I thought was about to be visited upon me, I would struggle against my brother's hold on the door and cry when I could not overpower him, my tears proving what a "sissy" I was. I never told Mom about these episodes; my brothers told me they'd kill me if I did.

It wasn't only my past actions that put me in peril; my present and future ones could as well. If I upset my mom—easy to do, as Dad's death and my childhood illnesses made her more and more jumpy, and an inexplicable absence of more than two minutes would often throw her into a paroxysm of hysteria—my brothers pulled me aside and whispered, "What are you trying to do, kill your mother like you killed your father?" Only the most horrible of children would be capable of such an act.

The fact that I was capable of it made sense to me. I was clearly evil anyway, filled with doubts and questions the devil had placed in my mind, possessed by cravings that I knew were wrong and that I could not best. Convincing me that I was guilty of patricide was an easy. Plus, they were my older brothers, and were real men who knew what was right and good. I was the opposite, and deserved what I got.

My internal policeman would remind me every day:

You are bad.

You are bad.

You are bad.

So bad you killed your father and want to kill your mother.

I had broken the Fifth Commandment ("Honor thy father and thy mother, that thy days may be long upon the land which the Lord thy God giveth thee"), committed one of the sins that was unforgivable. There was no chance for me. I would go to hell. It didn't matter, though, because I felt like I was already there.

CHAPTER 4

The Road to Salvation, Part Two

I loved learning. School, on the other hand, was a problem.

My first-grade class portrait says it all. It's picture day in 1969 at Edgewood Elementary School in Ft. Lauderdale, Florida, and Mom has dressed me appropriately. I'm wearing my nicest sweater, my hair has been slicked down to within an inch of its life, and I am good to go. For the class picture, we're all seated at the long wooden tables we have instead of the individual desks the "big kids" in third and fourth grade have. As the big moment approaches, a silence falls over the room. We listen intently as our teacher instructs us—in a tone nearly as serious as that used by bailiffs asking witnesses to pledge to tell "the truth, the whole truth, and nothing but the truth"—that we are to fold our hands together and face the camera. Solemnly, we all strike the pose as directed.

"Kevin!" the boy next to me whispers frantically.

"What?"

"You're doing it the wrong way!"

"No, I'm not! Leave me alone!"

An elbow in the ribs. "Yes, you are! Stop being so queer!"

"Shut up! I'm doing it the right way!"

The flash goes off.

Days later, when we get the pictures, I realize he was right. Everyone is turned at an angle, facing the camera, hands folded together in front of them on the table: I am the only one facing forward, away from the camera, my elbows on the table, my arms upright, my hands clasped in a praying posture. I look at the picture and am filled with shame. The other boy was right and I was being queer. I even *look* queer in the photo. The picture proves that I am a weirdo, that I do things the wrong way. What I don't know yet is this: this feeling will persist for the next twelve years.

Somewhere early in life, amidst the many negative things I was learning, I did get one extremely positive message: You are smart. Just as I can't remember exactly when and how I learned that being gay was "wrong," I can't recall a time when I wasn't being told that I was smart. Somehow I mastered the basics of reading and arithmetic before getting any formal schooling, a talent that my dad loved to show off. I would be called to the kitchen table when my parents were playing Uncle Eddie and Aunt Judy in one of their weekly pinochle games, Patsy Cline or Johnny Mathis or Nat King Cole playing in the background, and—like a trained monkey—would be handed a pocketful of change by my father and asked to add it up. While they smoked and drank coffee, I would count the coins, and then tell Dad the total. I was always right, having apparently inherited Mom's gift for basic math. The adults would laugh and applaud and I would preen, having finally found something I was good at. I learned early on that my brains were my best trait, the one that could get me positive attention from Dad and Mom, and I became intensely focused on learning.

I picked up my love of learning not in a classroom, but from my mom. She taught me to love history through her passion for the Civil War and the trips we took to its battlefields each vacation. Paul had no interest in these excursions, so they were always a time for Mom and me to indulge our shared fascination with the past. The Civil War was a bit of an obsession for Mom, who had heard stories of her great-grandfather fighting in it from her dad; consequently, we didn't just take trips to battlefields—we made pilgrimages. We never had much money, so at times we had to sleep in the car, but the thrill of the sites made our privations seem minor, especially in light of the suffering of our Confederate ancestors.

We completed our own Confederate Stations of the Cross in our blue Galaxy 500. At Chancellorsville, the site of our greatest victory, Mom and I stood in hushed awe in the room where Stonewall Jackson had died, our greatest tragedy, the clock on the bedside table forever stopped at the moment when he died. At Gettysburg, Mom and I gazed out over the battlefield and imagined what might have been, had Pickett's Charge crested Cemetery Ridge and turned the tide of the war, me thinking, like Faulkner, "For every Southern boy... there is the instant when it's still not yet two o'clock on that July afternoon in 1863... and it's all in the balance, it hasn't happened yet, it hasn't even begun yet.... *Maybe this time* with all this much to lose and all this much to gain: Pennsylvania, Maryland, the world, the golden dome of Washington..." At Washington and Lee College, we stood before Robert E. Lee's sarcophagus with the same reverence that pilgrims to Jerusalem stand before Golgotha. For us, it was as Faulkner said, "The past isn't past. It isn't even over," and the events of the 1860s seemed as alive to me as those of the 1970s, maybe more so. My life was drab and depressing; through history I found a way to escape into a more exciting time with my mom, just the two of us, away from a world that was proving not so kind to either of us.

Mom's intellectual curiosity was not limited to the 1860s. She made me want to see the world by buying me an entire set of the *World Book Encyclopedia* with money she did not have to spend. I read these volumes cover to cover, imprinting mental images of the Potala in Tibet and Angkor Wat in Cambodia and Machu Picchu in Peru so clearly that it would become a lifetime obsession to see these places. Together we watched nature films, learning about the wonder of the natural world. This habit continued throughout her life: my partner, Jeff, once remarked, "You know, there's always some animal eating another animal on the screen whenever your mom watches TV. It's kind of gross." With Dad and her older kids gone and her own intellect hardly challenged by McDonald's, Mom needed someone to talk to about her many interests. I grew up fast so she could have a conversation partner.

Above all, she taught me to love books and reading. Mom was a voracious reader, a trait she passed down to me. The highlight of our week would be our Saturday trips to the downtown public library in Winston-Salem—the "big one" and just about the only site that would get Mom regularly to venture out of the safety of Lewisville into "the city." It was always just me and her, as the only thing that bored Paul more than Civil War battlefields was a library. I *loved* the downtown library. It was beyond a church—it was a cathedral, filled with holy objects, books, so many that I despaired that I would ever be able to read them all. The librarians were friendly and thought it was great, not weird, that I liked to read so much. I would check out as many books as I could carry, usually a stack so large I couldn't see over them, and would devour them all during the course of the week, returning the next Saturday, eager for more. Library trips were the best. They even beat new trailer shopping.

At first I would go to the children's section and Mom to the adult section. By fourth grade or so, I had read all the books that interested me in the children's section and decided that the rest were too childish for this budding intellectual snob to bother with. I told Mom that I wanted to go where she went, the adult section. This created a crisis for Mom: in the adult section, there was a replica of the Venus de Milo. Mom felt it was inappropriate to have a nude statue in a public place, period, and especially inappropriate for a young boy to see it. (If she only knew...) I begged and pleaded and finally she relented, but only if I first promised not to look at the statue of the "naked lady." Ignoring the naked lady, I raced in and returned with a forehead-high stack. I was in heaven.

Because books were for learning, I couldn't be bothered with novels. Novels were *made up*, they weren't *true*, so they had nothing to teach me. My favorites were titles like *Decisive Battles of the Civil War* or *Lee's Lieutenants*—a turgid, multivolume tome by Douglass Southall Freeman—books no one else within two decades of my age would even think to pick up. Occasionally I would allow myself an indulgence, usually a book about football, but that was a rarity. Books were serious business, so you read about serious things, like war.

The great tragedy of my mother's life is that she never got much of a formal education. Mom loved school as a little girl, oh, she just loved it. She loved to read and could do the multiplication tables faster than any of her classmates. She mastered subjects so quickly that they started skipping her ahead in elementary school because her classmates couldn't keep up with her. Plus, when she was at school, she didn't have to watch after little ones or wash kerosene lantern globes or do any of the hated chores her mom made her do—she could just *learn.* My grandfather, however, thought that children should first and foremost earn money. He had definitive views on how much education his daughters needed: if they knew how to read, 'rite, and "figure," as he put it, they'd had enough education, and it was time for them to get on with the real purpose of their lives—helping out around the house and earning money to support the family. During Mom's sixth grade year, my grandfather determined that she'd had enough education and made her drop out of school to go to work at whatever jobs she could find to earn money to support her eight siblings during the bleakest years of the Depression. Having been skipped ahead so much, Mom was only nine when she left school.

Mom hated her father for this, even more than she hated him for "having at" her sisters. Over the years her disappointment would morph into a fierce determination that her kids would get what had been denied to her. She would educate herself through her incessant reading, through her daily crossword puzzles, through the documentaries she watched on TV, developing a vocabulary and a breadth of knowledge about history and politics and the natural world that would secretly intimidate the hell out of my partner, Jeff, his M.B.A. notwithstanding. But throughout her life her minimal schooling was a source of secret shame. She drove without a license for twenty years because she was terrified to take the written test, thinking her lack of formal education would somehow trip her up. She lived in fear that her slight inflation of her résumé on job applications—she always said she had been to junior high—would someday be discovered and she'd be exposed as a fraud. In her later years, she would sheepishly ask me to proofread her personal letters so I could find and correct any grammatical errors that might reveal her as unlettered. Among the many secrets I was to keep, this one was paramount: she never, ever wanted anyone to know how little formal education she'd had. It might make people think we were white trash.

Having gotten no support herself as a child, my mom was fiercely supportive of her youngest's intellectual proclivities, as I would learn in second grade. I loved maps. I could spend hours pouring over them, imagining what places looked like, memorizing capital cities, major landmarks, and natural features, like the points of highest elevation, that distinguished state from state, nation from nation. (Alaska has the highest "highest point" in the United States, Mt. McKinley, at 20,320 feet; Florida the lowest, Britton Hill, at 320 feet.) This knowledge came in handy when, during the first weeks of second grade, my teacher at Vienna Elementary School in Pfafftown, North Carolina, told our class that you could not drive across the United States without crossing the Mississippi River. Being a map buff, I knew this was not true. I was the new kid, having just moved to North Carolina but, having absorbed the notion that I was the smartest person in any room, I wasn't afraid to tell the teacher she was wrong. I raised my hand.

"That's not true."

"Excuse me, young man?" she replied, startled to be challenged by a seven-year-old.

"I said, that's not true. You *can* drive across the United States without crossing the Mississippi River."

"No, you cannot," she said, incredulous that I was standing my ground and challenging her status as the all-knowing teacher.

"Yes, you can. The Mississippi River begins in Minnesota and, if you drive up to the tip of Minnesota, you can avoid crossing it."

Miffed, she replied, "Well, that may be so, but there are no roads in that region, so you still can't drive across the United States without crossing the Mississippi River." With this, she folded her arms in triumph, and smiled.

"That's not true. There are roads. I have seen them on maps."

The smile faded. She'd had it. "Are you calling me a liar, young man? I want you to admit to the class you are wrong, right now."

I was now in uncharted territory. My classmates stared at me, bug-eyed. Our teachers still routinely spanked us with yardsticks, and I was clearly heading for a whuppin'. What was I to do? I had been taught in Sunday school to always tell the truth, and I knew what I was saying was true, but she was the teacher. The lady or the tiger? Punishment from her or from God? That made it easier. I swallowed hard and tried a Solomonic solution.

"I didn't call you a liar, Miss Smith. I just said you could drive across the United States without crossing the Mississippi River. It's the truth."

She blew her top. "Young man, I want you to go stand in that corner, and you'll remain standing in that corner until your mother comes and gets you from school today."

Given that the trailer park we lived in was only about a mile from the school and Mom was still a homemaker (Dad was still alive at the beginning of second grade), Mom must have been there in only a few minutes, but it felt like I stood in that corner for an eternity. Before handing me over, Miss Smith spoke with Mom, telling her I had been disrespectful and called her a liar in front of the class. Mom was steaming, but she kept her composure until we got to the car. (Never show feelings to outsiders.) Then she wheeled on me.

"Young man, I do not know what has gotten into you. I cannot believe you called a teacher a liar, in front of an entire class. You are in for a spanking you will never forget when you get home."

"But Mom . . ."

"Don't 'but Mom' me. Be quiet. We'll talk about this when we get home."

As we rode in silence, my dread grew: not one of *Mom's* spankings! Dad's spankings were painful, always featuring his black leather belt, but they were predictable and rational. Dad spanked us with a cold fury, telling you the number of whacks you were going to get before he started, using a carefully calibrated system where that number was tied to the severity of the crime. Mom, on the other hand, was a wild, creative genius, the Stravinsky of Spanking, inventing new and unforeseen methods, going on as long as the spirit moved her, which could be a few seconds or could be ten minutes. She loved to experiment: why restrict oneself to belts when there were things like slotted spatulas and wooden spoons around? When Mom said she was going to spank me, my fear was greater by multiples than when Dad said he was going to, as I never knew exactly how it was going to turn out.

To make matters worse, since moving to North Carolina, Mom had a new technique that took advantage of the change in vegetation from Florida. I would be sent outside to "pick a switch" from a bush with which she would whip my bare legs when I brought it to her. This created a veritable "Sophie's choice." The first problem was finding the right switch. The goal was to find a switch that could last long enough to let Mom get some of her fury out but would break quickly thereafter, minimizing the damage to my legs. This was not easy and was fraught with risk. Pick one too sturdy, and she might go on for hours. Pick one too flimsy, one that broke too quickly, and Mom would go out and choose what she thought was an appropriate switch, which was usually similar in size and weight to a maple tree sapling. In addition to switch size and sturdiness, I also had to gauge how much time I should take looking for the switch. Come back too quickly, and Mom's rage would be so white hot she'd wale on me. Take too long, and she'd be enraged that I was trying to avoid my whipping and would wale on me even more than if I came back too fast. Switch selection was a complex calculus, with multiple variables; I was never good at complex equations, so I was doomed.

Finally we got to the trailer. Mom walked in, flung her purse across the room, and said, "Kevin, you go pick yourself a switch, and be quick about it."

"But Mom . . ."

"Don't 'but Mom' me, young man. Now!"

"But Mom, I didn't call the teacher a liar. I didn't!"

Mom paused. She knew her youngest well enough to know that I wouldn't lie to her. She granted a stay of execution. "Okay, then. What happened?"

Out the story came, words rushing out of me like water over a falls. I even got our atlas and showed Mom on the map that I was right. "Mom, you always say to tell the truth, that the truth will set you free. I told Miss Smith that I wasn't calling her a liar, but that what I was saying was true. Isn't that the right thing to do?"

Mom took a drag off her cigarette and thought for a moment, pondering the moral dilemma I had presented her with. "Okay. I am going back to that school to talk to Miss Smith and we'll get to the bottom of this." She picked up her purse and headed toward the door. "Oh, and give me that atlas." Before leaving, she turned to me one last time. "Kevin, you had better be telling me the truth because if you aren't, so help me God, I will whip the living daylights out of you when I get home." And with that, she was off.

I couldn't believe it: I had talked Mom out of a spanking. There *was* a first time for everything! But I also was filled with fear. What if Miss Smith convinced her I was lying? Adults *did* tend to stick together, after all. If she did, the Mother of All Whippings was coming my way, because I would have both lied to her *and* embarrassed her in front of outsiders. Time stood still while she was gone.

When Mom got to the school, she asked Miss Smith to repeat what had happened. Miss Smith once again said I was disrespectful and had called her a liar in front of the whole class. Mom then repeated my version of the story, and asked Miss Smith if my account was accurate, if the whole controversy was over whether or not you could drive across the United States without crossing the Mississippi River. Miss Smith said that it was, and that I would have to apologize to her for being so disrespectful in front of the whole class before she'd let me return. Mom's fury now turned on Miss Smith. She took out my atlas and carefully showed Miss Smith where the Mississippi River ended and how one could indeed drive across the tip of Minnesota without crossing it, just like I had showed her. Exposed as a fraud, Miss Smith held her ground.

"Mrs. Jennings, that may all be true, but your son was still disrespectful and will still have to apologize."

"He will do no such thing," Mom replied. "My son was right, and he simply told the truth. You were wrong. He knew more than you and you were embarrassed by that. Maybe you ought to get your facts straight first, lady, before you teach your lessons. Seems like you owe my boy an apology, not the other way around. He'll be back in class tomorrow, and he will apologize over my dead body. Have a good day." Miss Smith was nearly apoplectic with rage, but I never did apologize, and I never did get whipped for being disrespectful to her.

(This happy ending aside, Mom and Dad's spankings, and my brothers' bullying, would leave their scars in the form of a clear lesson: when people get angry, they hit you. I developed a lifelong, nearly paralyzing fear of angry people, so much so that I would do anything to avoid getting others angry—anything, no matter how damaging it was to me.)

An unintended side effect of all this positive reinforcement around my "smarts" was that I became an insufferable know-it-all "teacher's pet" as a child—except when I was challenging their intelligence, that is. I liked school—at first. But it didn't take me long to begin to notice I was "not like other boys." Recess seemed to be the most interesting part of the day for them; I hated it, as my brothers never gave me the ball as a boy so I "threw like a girl" and was lousy at kickball/softball/anykindaball. Girls thought it was cool to learn, and so did I; boys sneered at those who raised their hands in class, calling them "nerds" and "queers." I took to sitting with the girls and playing with them at recess, which further cemented my reputation as a sissy and a queer. It didn't help any that I wouldn't let other boys cheat off my tests (God and Dad were watching—how could I?), which further enraged them, as my refusal denied them the one thing I was good for.

Once mandatory busing to foster racial integration was introduced and I had an hour-long bus ride to school in fifth grade, it was open season on the sissy. I tried sitting near the front of the bus, figuring the driver and the student "safety patrol" might protect me. This didn't stop the taunts of "sissy" and "faggot," nor did it lessen the launching of paper airplanes, spitballs, and paper footballs at my head, acts that never drew a reprimand from the driver or safety patrol. I tried ignoring it, but this seemed to only encourage them to taunt me louder or throw an increasing number of objects at me. On the occasions when I would turn and tell them to stop, a whoop of victory at having broken my composure would go up and the taunts would escalate. "What are you gonna do, faggot? Why don't you come back here and make me?" Here I would lose my nerve *(when people get angry, they hit you)*, and would turn back around, inviting a new and intensified level of invective since I was a sissy who wouldn't stand up for himself. Two hours a day, every day, this routine repeated itself.

By sixth grade Mom and I had moved out of the double-wide and were living in a trailer park, where my bookish proclivities made me seem even odder and more out of place. One boy in the trailer park, John, took special delight in humiliating me at the bus stop every day. His favorite thing to do was to wait until we got off the bus in the afternoon and, with all the kids on the bus still watching and all the other kids from the trailer park gathered around, order me to sit down on the pavement and not move until he was out of sight. Faced with the seemingly impossible odds against successfully fighting off John and his posse, I would sit down. This brought howls of laughter from the other kids, laughter that echoed as the bus pulled away. Once the bus pulled away, John and his buddies would saunter off, but this didn't mean my ordeal was over. Sometimes they would hide so that, when I turned the corner, John would scream at me for having gotten up without his permission and would order me to sit a second time, as I was once again within his sight. On some days they would do this repeatedly, so that the half-mile walk to our trailer could take me an hour or more. When they finally got bored, they would walk away, walking backward, shouting the whole way, "Don't you get up, you little faggot! Don't *dare* you get up! We'll kick your ass!" until they were so convulsed with laughter they couldn't shout any more. I would burn with shame. I was a sissy, and John proved it every day.

By sixth grade, I dreaded going to school. On Sunday nights I would get what I called my "Sunday funny feeling," which was a euphemism for the fear-induced nausea I felt at the prospect of going back to school on Monday morning. Mom and I would watch the *Wonderful World of Disney* every Sunday night and, as the theme music began and Tinker Bell flew over the Magic Kingdom's Cinderella Castle at the opening of each show, my stomach would begin to turn, on cue, as the weekend was officially drawing to a close and the start of the school week loomed. I would try to think of reasons I could avoid going to school the next morning, feigning illness when I could, placing hot cloths on my forehead in the bathroom and then racing back to the living room to ask Mom if I felt like I had a fever, having also drunk some hot water in hopes that my temperature would be elevated when Mom put the thermometer in my mouth. Mom, having had to play physician to five kids, would see through my imaginary ailments and order me to go to school. Unable to get out of school for artificial reasons, I rejoiced at any hint of snow. Luckily for me, North Carolina school officials went into a panic the minute a snowflake drifted down from the sky and often called off school immediately. (We once got a week out of school when six inches fell.) Anything, anything that got me out of school was a good thing. I would make complex charts of how many days remained in the school year, how many until the next big school vacation, eagerly crossing them off as each day passed and freedom grew closer.

I also began to gain weight in middle school, offering my peers another target for their derision. Some people can't eat when they're upset; I can't *not* eat. It became a vicious cycle: the more I hated school, the unhappier I was, the more I ate—which made me fatter, which made other kids tease me more, which made me even more unhappy, so I ate even more, which made me fatter. The fact that we had moved out of the double-wide meant that it was even easier to pack on the pounds: I had no pool to splash around in for hours and no cousins to play with; my brothers were now gone, taking their humiliating but calorie-burning sports with them; and I was terrified to venture outside—I might run into John and his buddies. "Sedentary" is the word for my then lifestyle. Mom could tell I was unhappy and the easiest thing she could buy me to console me was food, so she'd buy whatever I wanted—Doritos, Three Musketeers bars, a cornucopia of junk soon filled our cabinets. When Mom started working nights when I was in sixth grade, I was on my own for dinner, and I found that a bag of Doritos made a good chaser to a can of Chef Boyardee. A half pound of sugar really helped liven up a glass of iced tea or a bowl of Rice Krispies as well. I ballooned and one of my brothers dubbed me "Baloney Boy" because I was so fat. This became the nickname that stuck, used much more regularly by them than "Champ" ever was.

Then junior high came. The part of Piggy in the daily production of *Lord of the Flies* at Southwest Junior High School in Clemmons, North Carolina, in 1975 was played by one unhappy boy named Kevin Jennings. Everything I hated about fifth and sixth grades just got worse when I started junior high with seventh grade. Studying was even more uncool now and sports moved from semifriendly games of kickball at recess to cutthroat games like "smear the queer" in gym class. For the uninitiated, smear the queer is a game where one boy gets the football and all the others try to hit him hard enough to make him fumble, after which another boy picks up the ball and the cycle begins all over. What "physical education" this imparted was unclear to me, unless it was intended as an object lesson in Darwinian survival. Having had a little too much of this particular reindeer game with my brothers in grade school, I would do anything to avoid getting the ball. On the rare occasions when the ball inexplicably ended up in my hands, my classmates seemed to turn on me with a special relish, screaming "queer" especially loudly as they belted me. Thanks to gym class, this queer now got both verbal *and* physical smearing regularly.

The locker room was my undoing. With my and the other boys' hormones raging, I couldn't help but notice that I wasn't becoming interested in girls like they were, but was being drawn more and more to the increasingly muscular boys around me. The locker room brought all of this into especially high relief. I had to undress, revealing source of shame number one: I was fat, something other boys delighted in taking note of, with one remarking to me, "Do you ever wonder what it would be like to see your feet while you're standing up?" Then the other boys undressed, leading to source of shame number two: I was highly, highly aware of which boys were *not* fat, much to my dismay. For me, the junior high locker room was a veritable Garden of Eden, where Satan tempted me with his wares—the forbidden fruit. It wasn't fun, it wasn't hot—it was torture.

Then came gym class itself. Calling it a "class"—which, according to the dictionary, is "a group of students who are taught together"—would be to give it a dignity it did not deserve. It may have been a group of students, but if we were ever "taught" (a verb meaning "to impart knowledge or skill to"), I must have missed that session. Mr. Cultrou was our "teacher," a term I use loosely, as the definition—"one whose business or occupation is to instruct others"—rarely reflected what Mr. Cultrou did. Mr. Cultrou was in his midtwenties, an ex-jock still in good shape who was filled with a repressed rage that expressed itself in screaming fits at any boy whose performance was inadequate—like me. His "teaching technique" tended to be lining us up, selecting the two best athletes to choose teams from among their peers—I'd always end up being the last one picked—and then tossing out a basketball/softball/whateverball and letting us go at it. Standing on the sideline, he never spoke unless it was to admonish a poor player for being a sissy/idiot/klutz/throwing like a girl, which was better, I guess, than his shouting "Kill the beast! Cut his throat! Spill his blood!" which seemed to be what he really wanted to say.

The nadir of my junior high years came at the hands of Mr. Cultrou. One day we were doing a unit on wrestling, a sport I wasn't all that into as it primarily consisted of some larger boy crushing my face into a rubberized mat for what seemed like hours on end. We were in the school auditorium for some reason, with the stage outfitted with a bunch of wrestling mats for us to use, around which we formed a circle while Mr. Cultrou explained the complicated and arcane scoring system for the sport. The auditorium was dark, with only the lights of the stage on, so that I felt, both literally and figuratively, on stage.

On stage or no, Mr. Cultrou's talk was boring me to tears. Of much greater interest was Gary, a classmate whose muscular body and feathered blond hair were disturbingly reminiscent of Andy Gibb (and we know the effect Andy had on me). I couldn't help but notice that Gary filled out his Winston-Salem/Forsyth County Physical Education t-shirt much better than I did or, in fact, than any of the other boys in the class. As my mind drifted, I began staring at him, something that, in his heterosexual obliviousness, he didn't notice. But, at some point in his lecture, Mr. Cultrou did catch on to the fact that my eyes were focused elsewhere and he stopped, fixing his gaze on me.

"Stop looking at his legs," he said slowly and clearly, enunciating every word, every syllable, with precision.

The entire class turned to gape at me. I think my heart actually did stop at this point. Here it was, my worst fear realized: being exposed as a boy who looked at other boys "that way," publicly, in front of a group of my peers. If God himself had spoken, I wouldn't have been any more horrified. With no hole to climb down into, lacking the ability to make myself invisible (both things I would have given one of my kidneys for at that moment), I sat there, the eyes of the world fixed on me, burning with shame. Mr. Cultrou took care to let the moment linger, probably ruing the fact that he left his brand at home that day and couldn't burn a scarlet *H* on me. After letting my humiliation sink in for what felt like hours, Mr. Cultrou resumed his lecture.

Looking back three decades later, what strikes me is how odd the whole incident was. I spent ten years teaching high school and, in my classes, there was way too much going on for me to care about who was making goo-goo eyes at whom. Why was Mr. Cultrou so attuned to my nascent same-sex attraction? Was he a fundamentalist who saw himself as a guardian of morality, who felt he needed to call out sin when he saw it? Or a closet case, struggling with his own feelings, who projected his self-hatred onto me? Who knows? Having been a teacher, I can't help thinking how odd it is that he noticed where I was looking in the first place.

Whether it was intended or unintended, the chief consequence of Mr. Cultrou's auto-da-fé of my young soul was that the campaign of harassment by my peers now blossomed into full flower, seemingly endorsed and blessed by a teacher. I began to avoid unstructured settings like the lunchroom, as these were the places where I heard the word "faggot" and "queer" the most. I took to eating my lunch in the hall, to arriving twenty minutes early to school in order to check in with my homeroom teacher and then go sit in the library so I wouldn't have to endure mockery during the fifteen unstructured minutes of "homeroom," to becoming nauseous whenever the bell rang and I had to run the gauntlet of the hallway to my next class. Even French class became a forum for harassment: when one of the cheerleaders, Martha, was asked to use the adjective *trop* in a sentence, she turned, pointed to me, and said, "*Il est trop gros*" ("He is too fat"). The teacher, as usual, said nothing.

The hardest part was feeling like there was nowhere to turn. Teachers like Mr. Cultrou joined in the harassment; others stood by and let it happen; no one spoke up. In ninth grade I finally got fed up enough to go to a guidance counselor and report how often I was harassed, thinking he would do something about it. Mr. Schiessekopf was a stocky, forty-something man who saw his paid job as guidance counselor an annoyance that got in the way of his "real" job as football coach. He listened to my report with skepticism, leaning back in his chair, body language radiating disbelief.

"I find it hard to believe this stuff happens and teachers do nothing about it. What kinds of things get said?"

Not wanting to compound my humiliation by saying the worst words out loud, I told him the "*trop gros*" story.

"Oh, come on, Kevin, kids say things like that all the time. It's what they do. It's just teasing."

"But they say worse things, too."

"Like what?"

"Mean things," I stammered, now looking down at my feet.

"Like . . . ?" he asked, impatient to get this over with.

"I get called things like 'faggot' and 'queer' all the time," I said in a hushed voice, face flushing red and hot, the victim blaming himself.

"Who calls you that?"

I listed some individuals, many of whom were the popular kids, the jocks and the cheerleaders.

Mr. Schiessekopf was unimpressed. "I know those kids. They're good kids. I don't believe they'd do something like this." With that, our meeting was over.

Mr. Schiessekopf's message was clear: you're on your own, kid. I became convinced that things would get better only if I took matters into my own hands, and I resolved to do so. My biggest tormentor was Mike, a popular tennis player whose dad was the athletic director at a local university, making his son a minor celebrity in our small town. Mike and I were in the same homeroom, first period, as well as the same English class, last period, so that his relentless daily mocking of the school "faggot" was the alpha and the omega of my school day. If I were forced to pinpoint a single reason why I hated ninth grade, it would be easy: Mike.

It was a spring day when I decided I'd finally had enough. I don't know what Mike said at the start of English class—Oscar Wilde he wasn't, so I am sure it wasn't all that witty or memorable. But whatever it was, it pushed me over the edge. I sat through the class, plotting how I was going to jump Mike as he walked past my row when the bell rang. I'd never been in a fight, and I grew more and more scared as the clock ticked down and my first one drew near. Then the bell rang and we all stood to go. I waited, heart pounding, blood rushing in my ears so loudly I could hardly hear, until Mike came past my row. As he did, I stepped forward and shoved him with all my might. He flew into a bunch of desks, knocking them over, landing sprawled and stunned on the floor, looking up in amazement at the faggot who had been taking abuse for an entire year but who, like the cowardly lion, had at last found his courage. Whether because of shock or fear, Mike made no move to get up, and soon our teacher flew between us, saying "Okay, boys, let's stop this right here, before we all end up in the principal's office." Mike got up and, without a word, walked out of the class.

I wasn't feeling victorious at this point. Instead, I was more scared than ever. I was sure Mike and his buddies would be waiting in the hall, in the parking lot, somewhere, to exact their revenge. So I went to the library and waited for an hour, figuring they might have given up and gone home by then, and it would be safe to leave. Sure enough, no one was waiting to jump me when I left the library. Curiously, no one bothered me the next day either, and Mike never again gave me homophobic lip.

I wasn't over my shame yet, but I was learning some important lessons. I'd better not count on the authorities to do the right thing because they tended to side with those who had power already. I *could* stand up for myself and I'd better do so, because no one else was going to do it for me. And if I did, it just might make a difference.

CHAPTER 5

Tests of Allegiance

I'm not quite sure how I started down the path to becoming an activist. It wasn't like activism ran in my family. Mom and Dad were apolitical people who didn't vote and were deeply suspicious of any involvement in politics. As opposed to today's Falwell-inspired politicos, they were traditional fundamentalists who thought that engagement with worldly affairs like politics was a dangerous temporal distraction from focusing on your immortal soul and the afterlife. Dad thought that ministers in particular had no place in politics. Whenever he was asked his views on a political issue, he would reply using the story from Matthew of when the Pharisees tried to trick Jesus into making a seditious statement against the Roman government: "Is it lawful to give tribute unto Caesar, or not? But Jesus perceived their wickedness, and said, why tempt ye Me, ye hypocrites? . . . Render therefore unto Caesar the things which are Caesar's; and unto God the things that are God's." If it was politics, it was Caesar's and, as a man of God, Dad felt he had no place in that world.

Mom didn't much care if she voted or not, although she was

definitely an old-line "yellow dog" Democrat, as were most white Southerners of her generation, so dubbed because it was said they would vote for a yellow dog if it was the Democratic nominee. One of her few comments on politics, though, proved remarkably prescient: "I'd never vote for a Republican. They're the party of the rich people."

The few things I heard about activists early on were negative. The first political issue to enter our home, when I was four or five, was the Vietnam War. Evening newscasts were filled with war stories, and every Friday the nightly news broadcasts would announce the weekly casualty totals for the U.S. and North Vietnamese forces, with the always-greater number of North Vietnamese dead —a number we didn't know at the time was largely fabricated— reinforcing the idea we were "winning." With two sons of draft age, my parents were keenly aware of the war, and their great fear was that one of their boys would be drafted and sent away. When Alan and Mike each drew draft numbers that meant they were unlikely to be chosen, my parents rejoiced. This joy also undoubtedly planted the seeds of the rage that would explode when Alan enlisted in the Marines voluntarily when I was six and dropped the news on Mom and Dad shortly before shipping out to Parris Island for boot camp.

But that didn't mean my parents were against the war or on the side of those who were filling the streets in opposition to it. I was watching the evening news with Dad when I was six or so and a segment on an anti–Vietnam War protest came on. One protester had been tear-gassed and footage of her washing her eyes out using a garden hose came on the screen. I felt bad for her and said it was terrible what those mean police had done to her. Dad turned to me and snapped, "She got what she deserved." The message was clear: people shouldn't buck the system, and those who do deserve to be punished.

But I was also getting a different message, one that taught me that some people were unfairly treated by the world, and that we had an obligation to do something about it. One source of that teaching was, ironically—given its origins as an institution dedicated to the enslavement of blacks—the Southern Baptist Church. The central story of our religion—the execution of an innocent man by corrupt leaders—implied that injustice existed in the world and that the authorities were often wicked and unfair. And then there were the realities of our own lives. The Southern Baptists of my childhood generally were near the bottom of the economic ladder. But the Church hardly taught us to "look up" to our "betters," emphasizing instead sentiments like those in Matthew 19: 23–24, where Jesus said, "Verily, I say unto you, that a rich man shall hardly enter into the kingdom of heaven.... It is easier for a camel to go through the eye of a needle, than for a rich man to enter into the kingdom of God." There was a definite implication that the rich were wicked, had ill-gotten riches, and would "get theirs" in the afterlife. We Southern Baptists, who worshipped Christ and disdained the goods of the world, *we* were the ones who would be rewarded with eternal riches, while theirs would last only a short while.

The flip side of disdain for the rich was an obligation to help the poor (Matthew 19:21, "If thou wilt be perfect, go and sell that thou hast, and give it to the poor, and thou shalt have treasure in heaven"). Having grown up so poor herself, Mom had a particular concern for the unfortunate, and throughout her life would try to find ways with her meager means to help those with less than she. She had her own favorite story from the Bible, one that would take on particular resonance after Dad died, the story, called "The Widow's Mite," from Luke 21:1–4:

> And He [Jesus] looked up, and saw the rich men casting their gifts into the treasury. And He also saw a certain poor widow casting in thither two mites. And He said, "Of a truth

> I say unto you that this poor widow hath cast in more than they all: for all these have of their abundance cast in unto the offerings of God; but she of her penury hath cast in all the living that she had."

Mom loved this story, and would tell it to me over and over and over again during her cigarette-and-coffee marathons at the kitchen table. The moral was clear: you will be judged on what you do to help the less fortunate, not on how much you have.

The second source of my awareness of injustice in the world was equally ironic: the Civil War, a war that, in the white, Southern version of history, was about fighting injustices done to *us*, not injustices we did to blacks. Mom grew up hearing stories of her great-grandfather, a Confederate soldier who spent much of the war in a Union prison camp, tales of his mistreatment at the hands of his captors, like being forced to kill and eat the rats that besieged the camp because the prisoners were given so little food. Our weekends trips to battlefields further convinced me that heroes were men like my great-great grandfather, like Robert E. Lee, like Stonewall Jackson, who (like Jesus) stood up against overwhelming odds for what they knew was right. Their emblem, the Confederate flag, was *the* symbol of being a Southerner, and I festooned my room and our car with them.

This was the history I learned growing up: that we, poor white Southerners, were an oppressed people; that the authorities, the rich, the system, were often wicked; and that I had an obligation to stand up for Lost Causes. I burned to avenge this history. Fortuitously, circumstances seemed to give my generation its chance in the form of the battle over integration. My family held the typical attitudes of poor white Southerners of our time. Blacks were at the same time both inferior and threatening, like wild animals, stupid but capable of great savagery, and hence they needed to be segregated away from us as they might contaminate or harm us if we mixed. The "outside agitators" who were trying to change these arrangements were a threat and had to be stopped. The word *nigger* was used casually, without any particular animus, simply an ordinary word that meant "black person." We saw the battle over integration as a replay of the Civil War, of Yankees once again invading our homeland, foisting their alien ideas upon us, using their superior force to compel us to do something profoundly wrong. I hated them for it.

My first political hero was Alabama's segregationist governor, George Wallace. In a time when we had no voice, Wallace spoke for us; he was a redneck who stood up to the System, to the Northern agitators who were forcing their way of life on us. The 1972 presidential election was the first I followed. Wallace was running for the Democratic nomination, and I lived and died with each primary, reading the newspaper intently, watching the nightly news every evening, hoping against hope he would win and then bring down the evil Richard Nixon who stood with the Yankees in forcing integration on us. When he was shot while campaigning in a Maryland shopping mall and had to drop out of the race, my entire family went into mourning.

Although Wallace was disabled, I still had other heroes, ones closer to home, chief among them the Ku Klux Klan. At an early age, my family's sympathy for the Klan became evident to me. The Klan was always spoken of as the uncompromising heroes who would do anything to stop the Yankees and the integrationists, who provided a counterweight to the unjust authorities in Washington who were foisting miscegenation and integration on us. Even though we couldn't ask him about it—it's supposed to be an "invisible empire" after all, with hoods worn to conceal identities —I knew Uncle Fred was somehow involved in the Klan. While Dad had refused to join the Klan when my uncle asked him (a fact I didn't learn until adulthood), we still saw the Klan as the good guys who would protect us from the blacks. I was intensely proud that my family was doing its part.

The threat from blacks became more pressing when, during my

elementary school years, the news came down that the courts had ordered bussing to integrate the Winston-Salem/Forsyth County Public Schools. My brothers, cousins, and uncle were all outraged and muttered ominously about things they were going to do to stop the busses the first day of school. Plans for a white boycott were soon spoken of, and it appeared that integration was going to come to Winston-Salem at a cost, if at all. As the first day of school approached and the rumblings grew into a roar, Mom was quiet, though of course I knew she shared the "right views."

Charlotte, North Carolina, about an hour south of us, was under a similar court order and started school before we did. Mom, my brothers, and I watched the news reports on their first day of school, sitting in our double-wide, adjusting the rabbit ears so we could pick up WXII Channel 12, the only TV station in Winston-Salem. When the newscaster announced that Charlotte's first day of school had been disrupted by vandals who slashed the tires of many of the school system's buses, my brother Paul and I cheered the news, which may, of course, have been less a political statement than an expression of delight at the possibility of not having to go to school.

My mother snapped back, "I don't know why you're cheering. Those people are only hurting themselves."

We looked at her, confused. Didn't she understand these people were heroes? That they were standing up for us, against the niggers and the Northerners? But we knew enough not to question her, so our lips remained sealed. The next morning came and she packed us off to the bus stop. I huddled on the floor of the bus all the way to school that day, as I had heard that the KKK was going to shoot out the windows with sawed-off shotguns. There was plenty of room: we were the only white kids on my bus route to get on the bus that day.

I didn't yet understand my mother's determination that we were going to get an education no matter what, even if it meant sharing a classroom with blacks. Whatever her personal views on school integration were, nothing was going to stop her kids from going to school and getting that education. So she loaded us up on the bus on the first day of school and not another word was said on the subject.

Mom was definitely not a closet integrationist. Shortly before my dad died in 1971, Alan came home. Alan had already disappointed my parents by joining the Marines (what was the point of a good lottery number if, like an idiot, you volunteered?) and putting himself in harm's way in the midst of the Vietnam War. But he was serving his country, so this was grudgingly forgiven. When he came home in early 1971, he brought completely horrifying news, that he had done something that would be far more difficult to forgive: he had fallen in love with and was planning to marry a black woman named Claudette.

I found this out late one night because of a shouting match between my parents and Alan in our trailer's living room/eat-in kitchen. We'd only been in North Carolina a few months and were living in a small rented trailer, so their shouting woke me. I went to my bedroom door and peered into the area where the fight was taking place. My parents were angrier than I had ever seen them, which was really saying something, and a fact made doubly terrifying *(when people get mad, they hit you)* because they were mad at Alan, who had always been Dad's favorite, the oldest son who could do no wrong.

Perhaps it was Alan's status as the favored son that brought down the intensity of this wrath from my parents, who couldn't imagine how he could engage in such a fundamental betrayal of their values. Their debating styles reflected their spanking styles: Mom was unpredictable, quiet and then shrieking wildly, "Why? How?" while Dad would try more rational arguments—you'll be outcasts, you'll never be able to come home again, your children will be mixed race pariahs with no friends, how can you do that to them? Alan, the quiet one, the composed one, never shouted back, just kept repeating that he loved Claudette and they were to be married. As livid as they were, my parents couldn't get him to back down. When it became apparent that Alan was going to stand his ground, Dad spluttered, "You can do what you want, but that woman is never going to step foot in my house."

Alan took the bus back to the Marine base in Norfolk the next day, leaving my parents steaming and me a very confused seven-year-old. Fifteen years older, Alan was the brother I looked up to. He had always made time for me and affectionately called me "Champ." He was the one whose exploits my parents extolled. He was the role model. It didn't make sense: how could he marry a nigger?

(Decades later, Alan and I would discuss this question, albeit phrased in a more politically correct way. He explained that he had grown up with the same racist beliefs as we all had. But his experience running on track teams with black athletes and then serving alongside black soldiers in the Marines had taught him that these beliefs were all lies, that black people were fundamentally no different than he was. In other words, he testified that integration worked and that the Klan's worst fears—that when white and black people mingled, the barriers between the races would be breached forever—were in fact true.)

Dad died two months later, but his passing did nothing to soften my mom's opposition to the marriage. Alan moved to Connecticut following his discharge from the Marines, as he wasn't welcome in our small Southern town. For all practical purposes, he disappeared from my life for years after Dad's funeral—the years when I needed him most.

The fact that I had a black sister-in-law was a source of shame that we did not talk about outside the family, another secret to keep. My cousins chortled over the misfortune that had befallen our branch of the family. One bright summer day, in the yard outside our double-wide, my cousin Nathan, a heavyset, vociferous fan of the Klan who was more than a decade older and at least 150 pounds heavier than I was, began to taunt me in front of some of our other cousins about Alan's marriage. With each taunt, I grew more and more enraged.

"God, think how fat her nigger lips must be! It must be disgusting to kiss them."

"Does Alan 'axe' people questions now or does he still 'ask' them?"

"Alan must be eating chitlins for dinner every night now. I bet his stomach is *full* of chitlins!"

Finally, Nathan had gone too far. This was an offense to the honor of my family that I could not tolerate: eating chitlins—the intestines of young pigs, cleaned and stewed and then frequently battered and fried, something of a delicacy among Southern blacks—was the lowest thing black people did, proof they were indeed animals, that they'd eat anything, like dogs. Chitlins were things no self-respecting white person would ever touch. I charged at Nathan, who simply laughed and flipped me over his shoulder to the ground. I landed with a thud on the grass, the wind knocked out of me. But my family's honor was at stake, so I rose and charged at Nathan again and again, like a small, enraged bull. Nathan, matadorlike, flipped me aside at the last minute each time, cackling along with our younger cousins at the little boy whose brother ate chitlins and who stupidly ended up on his back every time he charged. Exhausted, I finally collapsed on the grass, allowing Nathan and the others to walk away in triumph. My shame was complete: my brother had married a nigger, and I could do nothing to defend my family's honor.

It took adultery to bring my family back together. Although he couldn't visit, Alan stayed in touch with Mom by phone during the years he lived in Connecticut. In 1974, on the eve of the birth of his first child, he called Mom and confided in her that he was having an affair and thinking of leaving Claudette. It must have triggered something in Mom—perhaps her own memories of living in the North as a young bride three decades before, stuck in an unsatisfactory marriage, pregnant and with no place to go—all of the sudden, Mom was on Claudette's side.

Maybe Mom remembered the role her own mother-in-law had played in her life. Mom and Dad moved to Taunton, Massachusetts, the year they were married, 1946. But it was a bad time in Massachusetts: there were no jobs because the state's economy was literally "going South" as the textile mills were all relocating to union-free Southern states. Dad worked odd jobs and they lived in a summer cottage by a lake with no weatherproofing. They tried to stay warm by the woodstove during the frigid New England winters when both the lake and the water in their toilet froze and my mother bore my three older siblings.

Mom hated the North. She hated the cold, she hated the way the Yankees made fun of her accent ("Like *they* talk normal?" she would later say to me dismissively, "hell, they can't even pronounce an *R*!"), she hated how Dad would stay out late drinking and come home to smack her around, as she had a mouth on her and wasn't shy about using it to tell him he was a no-good bum. She was overwhelmed, with three kids under the age of five whose diapers she had to wash by hand in the tub. She must have felt like it was all a terrible mistake, that her life was turning into a horrifying replay of her own mother's, locked in a bad marriage with too many kids and no way out.

Her only source of support was her mother-in-law, Merilda Ora Carmel Jennings. Merilda was a short, stout woman who did her best to make her daughter-in-law feel at home. Merilda had known hard times; through her own childhood and immigrant heritage, she knew what it was like to feel alone and out of place. She lost her father as a child and was then taken away from her mother, who was judged to be incompetent. She grew up in a Darwinian, state-run orphanage where she literally had to fight to get enough to eat. Her older brother rescued the family when he turned fourteen and took custody of his two younger siblings, getting them out of the orphanage. Merilda married early, and the marriage was no piece of cake; Marlitt never got one of the good factory jobs that paid union wages and instead worked at a variety of jobs throughout his adulthood, meaning there was little money to go around.

Maybe it was these experiences that made Merilda feel such empathy with Mom. She went out of her way to make Mom feel at home, and even tried to make grits, a noble failure that Mom loved to retell. Having eaten grits two or even three times a day as a kid, Mom missed them sorely and bemoaned to her new mother-in-law that no one in this land of Cream of Wheat and oatmeal seemed to know what they were when she asked for them in stores. Merilda searched the stores in Taunton for grits, which were not commonly stocked in Northern groceries in the forties, finally found some, and decided to make a test batch, with the idea of surprising her new daughter-in-law with this special treat. The test batch went poorly, generating rocklike nuggets that seemed more like sand than food to Merilda, making her wonder why Alice made such a fuss about these things in the first place, so she decided to come clean and ask Alice how to prepare them. When Merilda asked Mom why they had come out so hard, Mom asked how long she had cooked them. Merilda replied three minutes, like oatmeal, which made Mom howl with laughter as, in those days before instant everything, it took a good twenty minutes to cook grits. Through her good-hearted ways, Merilda endeared herself to Mom, who would refer to her as "Ma" for the rest of her life.

The incident that would forever bond Mom to Ma happened one cold winter's night, early in her marriage. Dad had come home after a few too many and knocked Mom around again. Desperate and with nowhere else to go, she packed up her infants and fled to Merilda's house, swearing never to return. At Merilda's insistence, my grandfather Marlitt went over to the lakeside cottage where his son and family froze out the winter and told him that if he ever again hit this pretty little woman from the South, so small, so far away from home, with no family of her own to turn to, he would kill him with his own two hands. Having laid down the law, Marlitt returned home and took Mom back to the cottage, where an uneasy truce ensued.

So maybe Mom saw a bit of herself in Claudette. For whatever reason, Alan was summoned home for his first visit since Dad's death.

I was breathless with excitement over Alan's visit, the first in three years. I lurked in the living room of our double-wide while he and Mom talked, pretending to watch TV. Mom was stern with Alan: she would have none of this. "You got that girl pregnant, Alan, and you're going to stand by her," she informed him. It was nonnegotiable. Chastened, Alan returned to Connecticut, and he and Claudette stayed together.

The slight warming in our family's cold war led to our first meeting with Claudette. I don't know whether it was concerns about safety or shame at having a black daughter-in-law, but Mom decided we would go to Connecticut rather than have them come to North Carolina. That summer, as we drove north up I-95, I spent hours imagining what Claudette might be like. Would she have an Afro? How big *were* her lips, exactly? How black *was* she—really, really black, like Hershey's chocolate sauce, or sorta black, more like Mom's coffee after she put evaporated milk in it? Would she serve us chitlins for dinner? If so, what should I do? Would I be able to eat them without throwing up? So many questions; my mind spun.

Fourteen hours later, we pulled into the parking lot of the public housing project in Norwich, Connecticut, where Alan, Claudette, her two daughters from her first marriage, Neeky and Charis, and my infant nephew, Dwight, lived. I was torn between feelings of excitement—I was going to get to see Alan!—and trepidation—what if Claudette was mean? What if she *was* a real nigger, "axing" me questions and all? We knocked, and the door to their den of miscegenational iniquity swung open. Claudette, this great source of mystery, turned out to be a rather ordinary-looking person. She *was* dark-skinned, closer to Hershey's chocolate sauce than to coffee with evaporated milk, and she *did* have somewhat big lips, but otherwise she wasn't overly pretty or overly plain, just kind of average. This secretly galled Mom, who had chalked up Alan's marriage to his having been swept off his feet by some ravishing beauty, a Delilah-like creature against which her young Samson was powerless, which Claudette clearly was not. But more importantly, Claudette was gracious and welcoming and kind, an achievement that in retrospect is amazing, considering she was hosting the people who had basically disowned their own son and brother because he had married her. She invited us in, asking if we were hungry. When we said yes, to my relief I got a cheese sandwich. We were never offered chitlins or much hot food of any kind because, I later learned, Claudette hated to cook.

One thing was unexpected about Claudette: she had blonde hair. I'd never seen a black person with blonde hair and wondered how she got it. Did she dye it, like Grandma Johnson and my sister, Carol, dyed theirs? Was she some kind of genetic freak, a kind of hair albino, so that she, unlike other blacks, had this unusual feature? Was she embarrassed by it? Did others tease her? It was all so confusing.

I was still wary and at first kept my distance, observing Claudette and her daughters like they were beings from another planet whose ways I must understand so I could uncover their secrets. I kept waiting for her to slip up, to reveal her "real" self. Days went by and instead I found she had an easy laugh, an infectious good spirit, and would lustily sing along to her favorite songs, like "Midnight Train to Georgia," on the radio. She took a genuine interest in her new little brother-in-law. She seemed like she was actually *nice*, which was confusing, because she was also *black*, and those two concepts had, until that time, seemed mutually exclusive to me.

Her two daughters from her first marriage, Neeky and Charis, were close to my age. While technically I was their uncle, they functioned more like cousins and were a ton of fun to play with, which was a welcome relief to a lonely boy like me. Being girls, they had little interest in kickball, so we could do more-fun things instead, like play Candyland or the Game of Life or Operation, shrieking with glee when we'd hit the side and the "patient's" nose would light up and the buzzer would go off. Occasionally they would venture outside, where they would skip rope and do something called "double dutch" which, because I was both white and a boy, I wasn't expected to be able to do. They never called me weird but took me at face value, treating me like I was normal, which I hadn't felt in years. I spent most of the week in their room, slowly letting my defenses down and, by the end of the week, I loved them. My view of black people had been turned on its head. They weren't monsters who spent their days gobbling down chitlins and trying to figure out how to hurt white people. They took showers and played games and watched soap operas and did all the things white people did. I realized I had been lied to.

As our trip drew to a close, I finally mustered the courage to ask Claudette the question that had been plaguing me from day one: how did she come to have blonde hair? "Oh, honey, it's a wig!" she replied with a big laugh. "This isn't my hair!" Relieved that my new and beloved sister-in-law was not some kind of freak of nature, I got into the car with Mom and prepared for the fourteen-hour drive back to North Carolina, this time concentrating on how many licenses plates from different states I could spot between Norwich and Winston-Salem instead of how big-lipped and dark-skinned my new family members might be.

Having substantiated that Claudette was not a monster and that Alan was not eating chitlins for dinner, Mom decided it would be okay for me to visit them. Each summer during sixth, seventh, and eighth grades, Alan would fly me up to Connecticut and we would go off to a rented cottage in New Hampshire or Vermont.

I didn't understand at the time the financial sacrifice Alan and Claudette must have made to fund these trips. Alan was in his late twenties, with three kids of his own to support. They still lived in a modest apartment in a public housing project, which was what made it possible for them to make ends meet. But somehow they found the money to fly his little brother up each summer and take him on a vacation. And these vacations were among the happiest times of my childhood. Alan and Claudette would always rent a house for a week. We would hike Cannon Mountain and drive up Mount Washington and visit the Polar Caves. I fell in love with New England, with its white birch trees (trees with white bark! amazing!) and its rushing streams, its small towns with their picture-perfect churches. I started thinking this would be where I'd want to live someday.

But the biggest surprise was this: Claudette ended up becoming my favorite family member. She didn't seem to think I was weird or odd—she thought I was great. She loved that I read a lot and would listen to me prattle on about history and politics ad nauseam. I would tell her all my crazy ideas and dreams, which she would take seriously rather than laugh at. She'd announce with definitive finality that, yes, my dream that I would someday be president was going to come true, no doubt about it. She always found a way to make you feel better rather than worse, to see your good points and minimize your weak ones. I loved her for it.

My favorite childhood memory is one I don't remember. When my paternal grandfather, Marlitt Jennings, died in 1976, we came North for the funeral. It was the first time Claudette had come to a family function and, even though this was the "liberal" Northern wing of the family, this made it a momentous occasion. According to Claudette, the funeral home visit was excruciating. No one knew what to make of her, so no one spoke to her. Apparently this upset me, and I proceeded to take Claudette by the hand and introduce her to each member of my extended family. "It struck me," she told me years later, "that there were all these grown-ups in the room, but the only person who knew how to behave like an adult was this little kid." I don't remember him, but I like the little kid in that story.

Returning to North Carolina after my visits "up North," I began to look at things in a new way. Integration in the Winston-Salem/Forsyth County Schools worked like this: black and white students were bussed to the same schools, where white students proceeded to sit on one side of the classroom and black students the other, never speaking to or acknowledging each other. It wasn't a conscious decision on my part, but I began to cross that invisible line after meeting Claudette. When white kids said racist things, I would sometimes turn and tell them to shut up, that I knew better because I had a black sister-in-law. This news was greeted with incredulity by my classmates (it would have been better if I'd said my brother had married an axe murderer or a cannibal) and was taken as further evidence of how weird I was. I "managed" a black classmate named Dante's successful campaign for black school vice-president in fifth grade (we had both black and white school officers), making his posters and helping write his speech. On Valentine's Day in fifth grade, when we made our little Valentine's Day cardboard envelopes for our classmates to put valentines in and posted them on the bulletin board, I gave valentines to *all* of my classmates (typically white kids gave to the other white kids and black kids to the other black kids, maintaining segregation even in card distribution). I stopped buying into the racial divide.

This evoked a special fury from my white classmates. Being a sissy was bad enough: being a "nigger lover" was even worse. Black students were also clannish and suspicious in most cases (understandably: their experiences with whites to that date would leave any reasonable person suspicious), so I found myself in a racial no man's land—sometimes even in my own family. When I would play records by my new favorite groups, like Gladys Knight and the Pips, my brother Paul, a devotee of Lynyrd Skynyrd and other Southern rockers, would snarl, "Whenever you come back from up North, all you like is nigger music." I began to learn that taking a stand against prevailing mores didn't win you many friends, and there was a price to pay for doing so.

My Southern Baptist background came in handy here. We were constantly told in church that we would suffer for standing up for the truth, and thus my suffering for doing so did not come as a surprise to me. Verses like Matthew 10:22—"And ye shall be hated of all men for my name's sake: but he that endureth to the end shall be saved"—and Matthew 5:10–12—"Blessed are they which are persecuted for righteousness' sake: for theirs is the kingdom of heaven. Blessed are ye, when men shall revile you, and persecute you, and shall say all manner of evil against you falsely, for my sake. Rejoice, and be exceeding glad: for great is your reward in heaven: for so persecuted they the prophets which were before you"—had prepared me for this. My mistreatment at the hands of my classmates confirmed my righteousness and the evil of those who were cruel. I felt comforted that I, like our Lord Jesus, was being persecuted for taking up a righteous cause. They, the little white-trash rednecks who tormented me, could and would all go to hell.

I began to realize that the things we accepted as "normal" and "natural" in society were often of human creation and often grossly unfair. And nothing came to seem as unfair to me as my mother's lot in life. I knew Mom was smart—smarter than just about anyone I knew—but, lacking an education beyond sixth grade, she never had a shot at a decent job. The types of jobs she could get were always beneath her intelligence, but she worked at them with a furious dedication that only someone who grew up in poverty would have, determined to maintain her dignity in workplaces that were just as determined to strip her of it. I began to understand that Mom hadn't gotten much of an education because she had been unlucky enough to have been born both poor and a woman in Appalachia, and that luckier, dumber people who didn't work as hard as she did often made a lot more money.

I also began to see how differently she was treated because she was a woman. Mom busted her tail at McDonald's, but somehow was consistently passed over for promotion to manager in favor of men who weren't as good as she was. She was keenly aware that, at all the McDonald's franchises in Winston-Salem, none had women managers, and it burned her. She wasn't afraid to tell the franchise owner, Mr. Halverson, what she thought of this, and soon enough she was promoted to manager (whether this was prompted by her merit or fear of a lawsuit, I can't say).

But even this proved to be a bit of a hollow victory. Mom soon learned that the male managers were paid more than she was and, seething, she went back to Mr. Halverson. He listened to her and said, "Alice, these are men who have to provide for their families! Of course I have to pay them more!" Mom barked back, "Provide for their families? What the hell do you think *I'm* doing this for?" She then stormed out of his office. She never got that raise.

Mom's being a woman got her less pay, but it didn't protect her from all the risks of being a manager. As a new manager, she often got stuck with the night shift, which went until the restaurant closed at eleven and then for another hour or two while the crew cleaned up and she did the daily revenue count and product inventory. One night Mom heard a knock at the back door and, thinking it was one of the crew trying to get back in after having gone out to the parking-lot dumpster, opened it without looking to see who it was first. Two masked and armed gunmen greeted her. One forced the crew to the ground and the other put his gun to Mom's head, ordering her to open the safe and give him all of the money inside. Mom's hands were shaking so badly that she failed on her first two attempts to get the safe open. The gunman cocked the gun he had placed against the back of her head and said, "Three strikes and you're out, lady."

Miraculously, she got the safe to open on the third try. The gunman then shoved her to the ground, preparing (she thought) to kill her, but instead scooped up the cash and ran out. After waiting until she heard their car pull away, Mom got up, rushed to lock the door, and made sure all her "boys" (the teenagers who worked for her) were okay before calling the police.

This was hardly her last encounter with guns. The next one I got to witness firsthand. Shortly after we moved into our new trailer in sixth grade, my brother Paul, freshly married at age nineteen, got one for himself and his bride, Sharon, on the other side of the trailer park. One night in the midst of some domestic quarrel Sharon called her father in tears, and Mr. Bedford, who'd been hanging out with Jack Daniels that night, decided to take matters into his own hands. He showed up at their door packing some heat and started squeezing off rounds as Paul fled through the trailer park on foot toward our trailer. He pounded on our door, screaming, "Let me in!" which Mom did. Out of breath, he had just managed to tell us what was happening when hot on his heels came Mr. Bedford, who pounded on the door next.

"Alice! I know he's in there! Open up! I am going to kill the goddamned sonofabitch."

To our amazement Mom flung the door open. What was she thinking? This guy had a gun!

"*What* did you just say, Mr. Bedford?" she demanded in her steeliest tone, only the screen door between them.

"I said I am going to kill the goddamned . . ."

Mr. Bedford got no further. Mom flung open the screen door and stepped out onto our little porch, standing on tiptoe and thrusting her finger into the face of Mr. Bedford, who was over a foot taller than she.

"You will *not* take the name of the Lord in vain in my house, Mr. Bedford! I am a minister's widow and there are children here and you will *not* show up at my door drunk, using that kind of language, in my family's presence. Do you understand me?"

The change in Mr. Bedford's demeanor was immediate. He was reduced from pistol-packing redneck to guilty little boy. "Miz Jennings, I am so sorry. It was wrong of me to take the Lord's name in vain and I sincerely apologize."

"Well, good. Now you git on home and don't you darken my door again tonight." With that Mom stepped back inside and slammed the door in the heathen's face.

Shamefaced and sheepish, Mr. Bedford departed.

I was enormously proud of Mom, who could face down gunmen in a crisis, just like Barbara Stanwyck in *The Big Valley*. I would brag about how my mom was the first woman to be a manager of a McDonald's in Winston-Salem, making her something of a feminist trailblazer in my eyes. She went away to the McDonald's manager-training school, Hamburger University, at the corporate headquarters in Chicago for a week, and I proudly wore the belt buckle with the golden arches and the "HU" emblazoned on it that she brought me back as a souvenir. Other kids made fun of me—"what, you love McDonald's or something?"—but they didn't get that my mother was making history for women in Winston-Salem, so I didn't care.

It was Mom's nascent feminism that led to our final break with Robinhood Road Baptist Church when I was in middle school. Our church attendance had begun tapering off as Mom had to work more nights and weekends, but we were still regulars at Sunday morning services through my junior high years. I was secretly happy to go less often to a place that made me feel evil and dirty, even though I felt guilty for feeling relieved and knew that God could read my thoughts and was chalking up my passive resistance to churchgoing as yet another sin to read back to me on Judgment Day.

By the mid-seventies Mom became convinced that the Equal Rights Amendment, which would amend the Constitution to guarantee equality based on sex, was necessary—because she so manifestly saw how sex discrimination played itself out in her life,

I suppose. But this wasn't the prevailing attitude among Southern Baptists, so her point of view marked her as a dangerous woman. One Sunday we were in our usual place, in a pew near the front, when Pastor Brown began his sermon after we'd sung the Doxology. Sermons have no set length in the Baptist Church: the pastor might go for twenty minutes or thirty minutes or three hours, depending on how the spirit moves him.

For some reason that Sunday, Pastor Brown was moved to talk about the state of society today, something that was not often spoken of from the pulpit in these pre–Moral Majority days ("render unto Caesar the things that are Caesar's"). I was tuned out—it was hot, Pastor Brown wasn't the best speaker, and I was beginning to be afraid that we might be stuck there so long I'd miss the opening kickoff for that afternoon's NFL games. But then Pastor Brown worked himself into a fever pitch about the evils of the ERA, about how it would upset the natural order of the sexes and would force us all to use unisex bathrooms, and I could feel Mom tense next to me. Pastor Brown was in full, anti-ERA rant when he glanced at my mom. I half expected Mom to stand up and say something, but she didn't. Instead, her eyes burned a hole through Pastor Brown's head. I don't know if looks can kill, but I learned that day that they can definitely stop a Baptist preacher in his tracks. Pastor Brown stopped in midsentence, was silent for a moment, and abruptly changed the subject. Mom was in a cold fury when we left the church and refused to greet Pastor Brown or shake his hand. We never went back.

(In 1998, the Southern Baptist Convention passed a resolution telling women that a good wife should "submit herself graciously to the servant leadership of her husband." Mom, who hadn't set foot in a Southern Baptist Church for twenty years by then, was furious. "This is why I left in the first place," she fumed. "Submitting to men is what ruined my life.")

In America, we're taught to think of failure as an individual's own doing. We're the land of the free, where anyone can be whatever he or she wants to be, so if you don't make it, there must be something wrong with you. I was convinced as a child of our nation's goodness, of our moral superiority over the wicked Communists. I believed that we were indeed a society where, just as we pledged every morning in school, there was "liberty and justice for all" unless—like niggers, or genuine white trash who drank Jack Daniel's and couldn't hold a job—you didn't really deserve it. By junior high I was starting to see this for the lie that it was, that American society wasn't an even playing field, that factors like race and gender and class often dictated the course of your life, and that working hard didn't necessarily mean you got ahead or that those who got ahead really deserved to be there. My allegiance to the idea of America was tested when I came to question the idea that we were poor because there was something wrong with us or because we deserved it: I began to understand that we were poor because there was something wrong with our society. I began to get angry.

And so I began to try to do something about it. My first act was to form my own political group—Students for the ERA. I wasn't the most popular kid in our junior high—okay, maybe I was the *least* popular kid in our junior high—and feminist activism was hardly something young Tar Heel boys got involved in, but I defiantly wore a homemade button to school every day announcing my group and its formation. We had one meeting—I think three girls came—but the lack of response did not daunt me. I began to write letters to the editor to the *Winston-Salem Journal* on the subject, which drew infuriated responses from other readers. I was delighted to provoke such a response, because at least these people took me seriously, so I wrote more letters, on more topics, provoking more and more outraged responses from the generally conservative population of Winston-Salem. My letter writing became so notorious that the paper sent out a reporter to do a news story on the junior high boy who, as they put it, "can cause more frothing and fulmination with one letter to the editor than can a rabies epidemic." While at school I was derided and ignored, outside of it I was someone whose views commanded an audience and who even got covered in press articles. I liked the attention. Mom didn't know what to make of it, but it was a good cause in her eyes and, if it was what her boy wanted to do, then he could do it.

I was also beginning to understand how the political system worked. Our local state representative, Mary Pegg, was opposed to the ERA, which was then being bottled up in state legislatures, just a few states short of the three-quarters required for ratification. I decided to organize a protest march outside her house to highlight her hypocrisy in opposing a measure that would guarantee her, a woman, equality. I was learning to be a savvy organizer; I had contacted the *Journal* first to let them know we'd be there. The three girls and I showed up with homemade signs on a crisp fall day and began marching in front of Ms. Pegg's home, which was in the nice part of town, leaves crunching underfoot. To my surprise, a *Journal* reporter and photographer showed up, interviewed and photographed us, and we ended up on the front page of the metro section the next day, with a large picture and an article above the fold. When asked for her response to the protest, Ms. Pegg replied something to the effect that I seemed like an odd young boy with strange ideas whose mother maybe should keep a better eye on him. Infuriated, Mom dashed off her own first letter to the editor, saying that she was a taxpaying, hardworking citizen who shared her son's views and that her son was a very smart boy who was entitled to express them, and that Ms. Pegg should stop criticizing *her* child and worry about her own kids. Suddenly, I was a political figure.

I started working on my first political campaign that year, in 1976. Meyreesa Schoonmaker, a local attorney, had chosen to challenge a fossil named Carl Totherow for his State Assembly seat, and was backed by the local chapter of NOW, the National Organization for Women. I signed up and became her most dedicated volunteer. I was generally the only male around, and the only person under twenty, but, being used to being an oddball, this didn't faze me. While all the other boys were out playing baseball or hunting or working on cars, I spent the evenings of the bicentennial summer of 1976 in Ms. Schoonmaker's campaign headquarters (that is, in her basement). With lists of voters by precinct in hand, I called county residents one by one, asking if they supported Ms. Schoonmaker, hoping they'd say yes (then we'd make a note to call again the day before the election to remind them to vote) or at least hoping I could get them to pronounce her name right and that they wouldn't hang up first. It was tedious, tedious stuff, but the women who were working on the campaign, mainly young feminists, thought I was fantastic, and made me feel like a million bucks for doing this work. I felt like I belonged in this campaign, whereas I rarely felt like I belonged anywhere else, and I felt I was making a difference. When Ms. Schoonmaker took first place in a multicandidate Democratic primary, forcing Mr. Totherow into a runoff, I was delirious. We had challenged the system and its Pharisees, and we could *win*. Ms. Schoonmaker lost that runoff and never ended up in the State Assembly, and the ERA never became law, but I was hooked and well on my way to a life devoted to changing the world.

CHAPTER 6

Getting Out

When the first day of tenth grade came, I made it clear: there was no way I was going back to school. Wild horses weren't going to drag me back to Mount Tabor High School. I simply wasn't going to be treated that way anymore, and if the school wouldn't do anything about it, then I would just stop going to school. The night before the first day of school, Mom asked me if I was all set for the next morning. I dropped the bomb.

"I'm not going back to school tomorrow," I said.

Mom was livid. "What do you mean, you're not going back to school?"

"I mean, I am not going back to school. What's unclear about that?"

"You have to go back to school."

"Well, I'm not going to."

"You're under sixteen. The law requires you to go to school. You have to go back to school."

"Okay. Let the police come and try and make me, then."

I had never dug in my heels in quite this way before, defying Mom so openly. I'd always been "the good boy." She was baffled.

"What's going on here? You've always done so well in school. Why don't you want to go back?"

I was uncertain how to proceed. I had never told Mom about how, for years, I had been harassed at school; the reason why might prompt her to ask questions I didn't want to answer. Plus, she had it so hard already, and I didn't want to burden her any further *(What are you trying to do? Kill your mother like you killed your father?)*. I decided to go halfway, telling her about how the other kids treated me, but taking care to excise the fact that it was antigay harassment. I told her how I had gone to guidance counselors who had done nothing, and that this all had made me so miserable that I just didn't want to go to school anymore.

The news that her youngest had long been the victim of persecution, that school officials had done nothing about it, and that his education was in jeopardy as a result, had Mom steaming. Her lips grew tight. "Okay, then. I won't make you go back to that school. But you have got to stay in school and get your diploma. So what are we going to do?"

I explained to Mom that there was a "gifted and talented" program at Paisley High, that I wanted to be transferred there, and that I wasn't going to school until this happened. "Okay. I am going to go down to that school tomorrow and clear this up."

Now that we had a plan, Mom turned her fury on the school system. If getting me transferred was what it took to keep me in school, well, by God, they were going to transfer me. She marched me down to Mr. Schiessekopf's office and explained that he needed to arrange a transfer to the "G&T" program at Paisley for me.

"Well, Miz Jennings," he said, oozing unctuousness, "that's just not possible. You have to take an exam to get into that program, and the exam date has passed."

"Then, you'll just have to arrange a special time for Kevin to take the test."

"Well, ma'am, I don't think that's possible and, even if it were, the G&T program is full."

Mom fixed him with her most imperious stare. "Make room."

Now Mr. Schiessekopf was a bit discombobulated. "Uh, Miz Jennings, I don't think you're grasping the situation here."

"I grasp the situation just fine. I don't think *you* grasp the situation, Mr. Schiessekopf. My son isn't coming back to this school. When he came to you last year and told you about how he was being mistreated, you did nothing about it, but now you're going to. He needs to finish high school, so you're going to have to arrange a transfer to Paisley High so he can."

"Miz Jennings, Kevin is under sixteen, and he doesn't have a choice as to whether or not to come to school. It's required by law."

"Well, he isn't coming back to *this* school, and I'm not going to make him, so arrest us, or get moving on the transfer," she replied. "Let's go, Kevin. Sir, you call me when you've set up a time for Kevin to take the test."

The call came the next day, and I took the test. Apparently I passed, and a few days later I was at Paisley High. It turned out you could make the system give you what you deserved after all.

Going to Paisley involved some hardships. The school system did not provide transportation for those in the gifted and talented program, which wasn't a problem for most of the students in the program, who were affluent and had parents who could cart them to and fro. For my mom, this wasn't possible, so I took city buses to get to school. Winston-Salem had no mass transit to speak of and busses ran infrequently, so I had to catch a bus at around 6 AM, wait for half an hour downtown at an outdoor bus stop, exposed to the rain and the cold once winter came, and transfer to a second bus. All told, my daily commute was more than three hours round-trip.

But it was worth it. Paisley wasn't heaven, but neither was it the hell that Mount Tabor had been. The gifted and talented program segregated its students from the general population and placed them in accelerated classes. Apparently they took segregation quite literally: of the approximately eighty students in the program, only two were black. Virtually all of the students were from affluent, white families, indicating that the program had been created as much to stem the white flight that followed the advent of busing as it was to help "gifted and talented" students.

I wish I could report that I was outraged, but in reality all I felt was relief. For the first time in my school experience, being smart wasn't something that brought the scorn of my classmates upon me, as the G&T students had all chosen to go the "smart" route. While I wasn't one of the "cool" kids, at least the cool kids spoke to me. And I had a new love: the debate team. I joined the debate team sophomore year, and was soon immersed in the index cards and "disads" (disadvantages of your opponent's plans) and NFL tournaments (National Forensic League, not the football people) that would come to dominate my high school years. The discipline of debate taught me how to write, built my skills at making arguments and giving speeches, and generally gave me a place where I felt like I belonged. And I won a lot and got to bring home cool trophies, so my brothers' football and track prizes weren't the only ones on display in our house anymore. I had a place where I could be "Champ" again.

I began to remember my name was "Kevin" and not "faggot." And I decided I was never going to be the class faggot again. I became obsessed with finding and keeping a girlfriend. Showing up at school dances with a date became critical to me. Now that I finally had social status, I wanted to make sure I kept it, and a girlfriend seemed the best way of warding off any accusations of faggotry.

But denial was getting harder to pull off, because I had finally acted on my same-sex feelings. Mom became a kind of second mother for many of the teens who worked at McDonald's, who would often drop by our apartment to talk with her or ask her advice, so I got to know a lot of them. One girl, Tammy, became one of the "girlfriends" I took to a school dance my sophomore year. But the one who would have the biggest impact was a kid named Mike.

Mike was a year or two older than I was, as he had a worker's permit, which you had to be sixteen to get, allowing him to work at McDonald's. He was an average-size kid, five feet, seven or eight inches tall, average build, curly brown hair. There was something about him, I don't know what, perhaps it was his slightly effeminate characteristics, perhaps it was his attentiveness to me, but my proto-"gaydar" went off whenever Mike was around. Apparently so did his. One night during the summer between my freshman and sophomore year, he dropped by our apartment and knocked on the door, supposedly looking for Mom. I said she was working the night shift, that he knew she always worked the night shift on this day of the week.

"Duh! I forgot! Well, how about I come in anyway?" he replied.

Our eyes locked. I knew on some level what he was asking and that I was crossing a bridge with my response.

"Sure," I said, not feeling so sure at all.

Mike came in and we sat in the living room and talked for a while. Adrenaline pouring through my veins, heart pounding like a jackhammer, in a state equal parts excitement and panic, I have no memory of what we talked about. I can't recall exactly how we ended up in my bedroom, except Mike saying something like, "Wanna try it?" I nodded yes and, like a robot, got up and followed Mike to my room.

I pulled down my shorts and lay on the bed, unmoving. Mike kept his clothes on. While it was happening, I was in heaven. I couldn't believe how it felt. But as soon as it was over I went to hell, filled with shame at what we had done. Mike obviously thought it was his turn now, but I pulled up my shorts and told him to go—go now. I was filled with disgust at the faggot who had lowered himself to do this "to" me. Confused and probably hurt, Mike left.

Mike and I would have several more encounters during my sophomore year, probably because he didn't have many other options. The pattern was always the same, although we did take our clothes off eventually. Sexually speaking, it was always a one-way street, a street only Mike traveled down, which allowed me to imagine on some level that *I* wasn't gay, only Mike was. When, two decades later, the T-shirt "I'm not gay but my boyfriend is" came out, I would remember Mike with a rueful smile.

Rationalization intact, I managed to stuff these feelings way down inside and instead focused on having friends for the first time I could remember. I learned to party from my friend Jimmy, with whom I took German. Our teacher arranged for us to do Christmas caroling in German in Old Salem, a restored, colonial Williamsburg-like section of the city built by German settlers in the 1760s. It seemed innocent enough, so Mom gave me permission to go out at night to do this. But Jimmy and I had other plans. Jimmy was a bit more of a redneck than I liked—he reminded me uncomfortably of John, my nemesis from junior high—but he had a driver's license and had taken a liking to me for some unknown reason. He suggested we tell our parents we were going caroling but go "have some fun" instead and then return home at the hour when the caroling was supposed to be over, so they would be none the wiser. "Fun" turned out to consist of two six-packs and a couple of joints for us to split—a lot for a boy who had never drunk or smoked before—a little too much, in fact. By the time I got home, I was weaving like a proverbial drunken sailor.

"What's wrong with you?" Mom said, alarmed. "Are you sick?"

"Yeah, I don't feel so good. I just want to go to sleep. Goodnight, Mom."

Mom's antenna started buzzing: she had four older kids, remember, and hadn't been born yesterday. "Come over here."

I knew this would be a bad move. "No, Mom, I just want to go to bed. Good night." I headed toward the bedroom.

I never made it. Mom sprang up from the dining table and cut me off at the pass.

"I, I, I don't believe it," she sputtered when she got up close and the smell of alcohol overpowered her. "You're DRUNK!" (She didn't know how to recognize the smell of pot, thank God.) "How did this happen?"

Stoned as I was, this struck me as a hilarious question, as the answer—"Well, I drank some alcohol, Mom"—seemed fairly obvious. I started laughing. Mom was not so amused.

"Oh, so you think this is funny, do you? Well, I'll show you how funny it is." With that, she wound up and took out my nose with a mean right hook. It made a rather sickening crunch as it broke, leaving me with a severely deviated septum, causing such chronic congestion that people still routinely ask me if I have a cold twenty-five years later. This had the effect of making it all seem neither fun nor funny anymore. Switches and slotted spatulas were one thing: right hooks were a new addition to Mom's repertoire.

The next morning Mom informed me I was never, ever to speak to Jimmy again and that I was grounded for a month. But that didn't matter. I had discovered that the road to popularity ran through a distillery, and I resumed partying and going out as soon as my grounding ended. I quickly developed my skills at hiding the evidence—I personally boosted sales of Binaca by double digits in the late seventies, I am sure—so Mom wouldn't know.

I got my driver's license in the spring and generally reveled in being out of the hell of Mount Tabor High. The one thing I didn't want was any intersection between my old life and my new one. My new friends lived in Sherwood Forest, the ironic name of the wealthy neighborhood in Winston-Salem—I guess the developers didn't get that Sherwood Forest was where people who *robbed* the rich hid out—in homes whose square footage could house entire African villages. Mom and I lived in a perfectly acceptable but certainly not plush two-bedroom apartment now, on the outskirts of the south side of town, not quite the wrong side of the tracks, as her manager's salary had us living better than ever before, but absolutely, positively not on the right side of them. My new friends' parents were lawyers and doctors and executives, not managers at McDonald's. To the shame I felt about being gay, I added a level of shame about my family background, about our class. So I had a new recipe for success: pretend I wasn't who I was. I wasn't the fat little faggot who had grown up in a trailer park with a Mom who worked at McDonald's. I was a cool kid who wore a pink alligator shirt (somehow, pastel Lacostes were the symbol of preppy masculinity) and had cool rich friends and a girlfriend. The misery of the years when I had been the former made me all the more determined to cling to the latter, no matter how much denial that involved. I wasn't going back to being a miserable outcast. I started to become embarrassed by, not proud of, Mom.

So I was horrified to come home on my sixteenth birthday and find that Mom had invited some of my friends, who previously had just been disembodied names to her, over to our modest apartment for birthday cake. It was my worst nightmare. Bruce, the coolest of the cool, Tripp, the studly jock whom I was secretly in love with, and a host of other "cool" guys whose names Mom had heard me mention were gathered outside our apartment building, waiting for me to get home. Not only was it hopelessly uncool (we had already planned a drinking excursion for my birthday: cake was *so* junior high) but they also now knew where I lived, something I'd always been intentionally vague about. They knew I wasn't really one of them. Bruce arched an eyebrow, looked around, and said, "Nice place," in a way that perfectly expressed the exact opposite of the literal meaning of those words. Mom was confused as to why I was so withdrawn, so unexcited. All I could think was, how quickly could I get these guys out of here? They were no more excited to be there than I was, fortunately, so the cake was quickly wolfed down and off they went.

As soon as they were gone, I wheeled on Mom. "Why did you do that?"

Confused, she replied, "I thought it would be nice to have a little surprise on your birthday."

"Well, don't ever do that again. It's embarrassing."

Her mood began to turn. "What's embarrassing?"

"Mom, all those guys live in big houses. I don't want them to see where we live. It's embarrassing."

Furious (a fury that must have masked her hurt; how sharper than a serpent's tooth had this thankless child become), Mom snapped, "Fine. I'm *so sorry* our apartment embarrasses you. But I work my ass off to provide you with this and if it isn't good enough, you can go get your own place, buddy boy." And she stormed off to her room.

I was too young, too self-absorbed, to know what a jerk I was. I was too young to understand that forces larger than we were at work, forces going back to the Puritans, when prosperity became associated with goodness and poverty with evil. I didn't yet realize that I lived in a nation where class was an invisible but unmistakable dividing line, a line that education was enabling me to cross but at the cost of leaving behind everyone I knew lest they betray that I did not belong in the new land. All I wanted was to fit in with my new friends, because they were the life preserver that had been thrown to a teenager drowning in his own misery and loneliness. I didn't care who got hurt in the process. But when I think about the things I have done in my life that I am most ashamed of today, that would top the list.

At the end of my sophomore year I was accepted into a state-funded summer program called Governor's School, where academically gifted tenth and eleventh graders go away to a college campus for a six-week residential program. Those six weeks at St. Andrew's College in Laurinburg, North Carolina, were the happiest of my young life. Surrounded by other smart kids, safely away from Mom, I reveled in my new freedom and new persona. I learned to play racquetball and began the process of losing the pounds I had packed on in junior high. I stayed up all night playing Risk in the dorm. A social studies major, I thrived on the intense political debates we had in class. I came home, ready for my junior year at R.J. Reynolds High (where all the cool kids went), with a network of friends across the state, feeling on top of the world. And then the bottom fell out.

Exhausted by the struggle to support a family working at McDonald's, Mom had decided while I was gone to take my sister, Carol, up on her offer for us to move in with her family. This meant that we'd first have to move to Charleston, South Carolina, where Carol's husband, Tim, was stationed on a Navy submarine, for the fall of my junior year, and then to Honolulu, Hawaii, where Tim was to be transferred at the end of the calendar year. Perhaps the typical kid would have leapt at the idea of moving to Hawaii, but I was devastated. I finally felt like I belonged and now I was being dragged five thousand miles away from all my new friends. I was furious and scared: my grasp on happiness was so tentative, seemingly such an accident, that I couldn't imagine that lightning could possibly strike twice. When I thought of my future life in Hawaii, I pictured a future that looked very much like the past, one of loneliness and isolation.

But just getting off the plane in Hawaii blew my mind, a process that would continue for the next two years. From the terminal I could see Diamond Head, previously only a feature on *Hawaii Five-O*, could look out over the ocean, could see the sharply rising peaks clad in rich greenery behind Honolulu. It was a world that was completely foreign to my prior life. The malls had trashcans that said "*mahalo*" instead of "thank you" and white people were a minority on streets filled with Asians ("where were all the black people?" I kept wondering). Strange foods, fish with names like mahi-mahi and side dishes like poi, were found on menus, and McDonald's even served rice in addition to the obligatory french fries. I would learn in Hawaii that North Carolina, which had always seemed the alpha and the omega of the world, was but one culture, that there were myriad others, ones that lacked the baggage and bigotry of my native state.

The first day at my new school, Radford High, was an anxious one, a test of whether the "new me" would take or I would slide back into the misery of ninth grade. I had carefully planned to increase my chance of success by losing thirty pounds before we moved, so that I would now be both thin *and* cool, I hoped. Radford was totally unlike any school I'd been to: taking advantage of the climate, it did not have hallways but instead had covered walkways that connected buildings, and people wore shorts, T-shirts, and flip-flops to class, instead of the khaki pants–Lacoste shirt–Sperry Topsider uniform of the preppies in North Carolina. Radford was almost all "military brats," with new students coming and going all the time, so everybody was from somewhere else, and being the "new kid" was neither unique nor did it put me at a disadvantage. The fact that everyone was somehow tied to the military meant that the income range was fairly narrow, meaning I had no "Sherwood Forest" crowd to worry about. I again made a point of immediately finding a girlfriend to ward off accusations of faggotry. I joined the debate team, where my experience on the "mainland" gave me a huge advantage over the local kids, and began winning tournaments regularly. I made sure to make friends with popular kids and ran for student council, getting elected school treasurer at the end of junior year. I breathed a huge sigh of relief, as my plan seemed to be working. For a while.

The problem was, my feelings for guys hadn't gone away. I often had sleepovers with my guy friends, unconsciously hoping that something would happen, but it didn't—until spring of junior year. His name was Peter and he was on the debate team as well. Blond, preppy, and smart, he was kind of dreamy to me, reminding me of Andy Gibb and Gary and all the other blond guys who had drawn my eye before I even understood why. We made plans for him to stay over the night of the state debate championship. When I came in second, I was crestfallen, and a bunch of us made plans to go out drinking.

When we got back to my house, we went to bed and a conversation started. Maybe it was the alcohol, maybe it was our teenage hormones, but soon we were admitting our attraction to guys, then our attraction to each other and, soon after that, we were acting on that attraction. Peter rolled over and kissed me passionately (something I had never let Mike do) and said, "Well, I guess we've both screwed up our lives now," and then we went at it. But it didn't feel like I was screwing anything up. The old cliché "it felt so right" was true: for the first time, I was having a sexual experience with someone I was both attracted to *and* cared about. This was no one-way street. Peter was so cute and I was so turned on, soon all of our clothes were off and we "did it all," in a night that I can honestly say, twenty-five years later, was one of the most exciting ones of my life.

When I woke up in the morning, I knew I was in love. This didn't feel wrong, like what I had done with Mike had felt. What I did with Mike was dirty, just sex, confirming what I believed—that being gay was dirty and just about sex. But with Peter there were *feelings*. I never associated "gay" with "feelings" before. "Gay" was two animals humping: love was something between a man and a woman. Now I was feeling what felt like love toward a boy and realizing that gay didn't have to be "dirty." It was a revelation.

But for gay teenaged boys, first loves don't often end happily. The problem was, Peter felt differently in the sober light of day. He didn't want a boyfriend, didn't want the stigma that came along with being gay, and didn't want to ride off happily into the sunset with me. I was devastated and desperate: I would tell Peter I loved him and he would pull further away and I would become even more intense, scaring him even more and causing him to pull back even further. This all happened in secret, of course, as there was no way I could tell anyone about the relationship, as that would mean revealing my deepest, darkest, most shameful secret. Peter was in the same boat and, trapped in a pressure cooker of shame and secrecy and isolation, there was no chance we would make it. Our "relationship" sputtered along for a few weeks, except now I was the one who "did the deed" and Peter was the one who wouldn't kiss me or reciprocate. With every encounter I sank lower: I was truly a faggot (no denying it anymore), a dirty little perverted faggot. Every time I was with Peter confirmed that. But I wanted to be with him so I badly that I hung on by my fingernails, until he finally cut it off.

Now I sank to my lowest point. The affair with Peter had annihilated my self-deception about my sexuality. Because of the intensity of my feelings, I truly knew, *knew* deep down, that I was gay. Like any teen, I was also convinced that this, my first love, would be my only love. I made a last call to Peter, begging him to reconsider, to no avail; he let me know that if I didn't leave him alone, he was going to tell everyone I was gay. At the end of the call I looked at my life: I was gay, had lost the only person I would ever love (I was convinced), and was about to be "outed" so that I would return to the miserable days of my childhood. I walked into my family's bathroom, took out the economy-size bottle of aspirin, and took 140 of them.

Obviously, I didn't die. Instead I spent about twenty-four hours retching until I dry heaved, which I later learned is a typical reaction to aspirin overdose (thankfully, my family didn't have anything more lethal). I told Mom I had a stomach virus—I could hardly tell her, "Oh, I'm gay, the boy of my dreams has dumped me, and I tried to kill myself with a bottle of aspirin, that's why I'm throwing up." Luckily, school was ending and a few missed days didn't mean anything. Peter never followed through with his threat to "out me," perhaps having figured out that his evidence of my gayness was a tad self-incriminating, and he moved away during the summer when his dad was transferred to another military base. No one found out and I gave thanks that I had dodged a bullet, in more ways than one.

And having dodged the bullet, I began senior year with a determination not to make the same mistake. My best friend, Rich, was a blond-haired, blue-eyed, state-champion wrestler and a born-again Christian, and he and his younger brother, Ron, a fellow state-champion wrestler, also adorable, with red hair and blue eyes and freckles, kind of a hot Opie, became like a second family to me during senior year. Partly because of Rich's washboard abs, but more because of my own desire for a fresh start, I was desperate to be near him. I confessed to him that I thought I might be gay, and he told me that Jesus would save me from same-sex temptation, if only I would put my trust in Him. Once again I turned to the Lord in hopes He would be my salvation. Rich introduced me to Audrey, a good-looking, smart, blonde, Christian girl (all adjectives that described my type; the noun was the problem) who he thought could be a big help in my salvation, and we started dating. I felt an enormous relief that God was coming to my rescue, that this curse would be lifted from me. It was going so well that I even managed to stop masturbating for a while; God must indeed be almighty if he can achieve that miracle in a seventeen-year-old boy.

The healthy lifestyle of the Arnold boys seemed to be a path to salvation so, a couple of weeks into my relationship with Audrey, I accepted Ron's invitation to go lift weights with him and his best friend, Brian, another wrestler. Ron and Brian were justly proud of their perfect physiques—they'd be Abercrombie models today—and when we came home, they whipped off their shirts and did a pose-down in the mirror to show them off. I couldn't breathe: never had I been so close to two such hot guys in such a state of undress before. Years later, I would learn that this scene was fairly standard in gay-porn movies, but it didn't have a porn-movie ending for me: once Ron and Brian left, I rushed to the bathroom and "polluted myself," as the Victorians would say, and then sat alone with the knowledge that, yet again, God's promise of salvation had proven to be an empty one. However willing my spirit might be, my flesh was too weak to resist such temptation.

I developed a new attitude toward God as a result. Before, I was the one who was failing God; now I decided He was the one who had failed me. I had tried to please Him, had placed my faith in Him, had prayed for Him to lift this cross from my shoulders, and He had repeatedly let me down. Why put faith in Him? God hadn't saved my dad, hadn't saved me, had done nothing but cause me pain and anguish through His inaction and malevolence throughout my childhood. I decided I had done nothing wrong: *He* had, by promising to "set you free" and never delivering on His promise. What *had* He done for me, other than make me feel shame and guilt? Squat. Screw you, buddy—I don't need you around anymore, I decided. The Baptist Church had left me only a legacy of self-hatred, shame, and disappointment, and I wanted no more of it or its Father. The long erosion of my faith was now complete, and I, for many years, reacted violently to anyone who professed any kind of religion. Decades passed before I opened a Bible again.

I started spending a lot more time with my friend Troy after that, getting stoned on the hill behind his house, chowing down on the leftovers I'd snag from my after-school job at Taco Bell when the munchies hit. Troy was gorgeous, too, dark haired, wiry, but unencumbered by the fundamentalist baggage of the Arnold boys, so I could talk to him in a different way. I opened up to him about my struggles with my sexuality and he just listened. When stoned, I'd always suggest he should give it a try himself, and he'd always just put me off. He may never have put out, but he never put me out of his life, either, for which I was eternally grateful.

Aside from a taste for weed, Troy and I also shared a common musical taste for the angry punk music that was crossing the pond from England to America in 1980. We would listen to the Clash for hours, and their incandescent rage at the class system of Thatcherite Britain mirrored my own growing fury at American society. We had to be the only boys at Radford High School in Honolulu, Hawaii, who were more likely to listen to the Clash than AC/DC or Van Halen, but that just made me feel all the more superior to the unenlightened masses of my classmates.

Now I was all the more determined to get away from the unenlightened mass of my classmates. My sister, Carol, had given me a copy of *Barron's Profiles of American Colleges* for my seventeenth birthday, and I studied it with the devotion of a Talmudic scholar, seeking the answer to the riddle of my future in its pages. Wanting to get literally as far away as I could, I settled on Maine as a good place to go to school, as five thousand miles seemed like a safe enough distance to put between me and my family and past. I decided that a place called Bates College looked like a good bet. When I approached my advanced-placement United States history teacher about a recommendation, Mr. Ginoza suggested I aim higher, that maybe Harvard was in my grasp. So I eagerly applied early, rushing to the twenty-four-hour post office out by the airport on the evening of November 1 to make sure my application got postmarked before midnight. And then I waited.

The letter came in mid-December. It was a thin envelope, and I knew this was a bad sign: my studies of the Holy Book of Barron's had taught me that thick envelopes meant acceptance, as they contained all kinds of forms to fill out, and that thin ones were rejections, so I couldn't even bring myself to open the envelope for several hours. Finally, I did. Expecting the form letter that rejections normally involve, I didn't at first catch the meaning of the words, "Dear Kevin, I would like to congratulate you on your admission to the Harvard College class of 1985." Then I reread them, and their meaning sank in: I was getting out after all.

I didn't care much what happened after that during senior year. I stopped going to classes I didn't like (yes, Mrs. Kono, I still feel no regret over my 140-plus absences from your pre-calculus class, which stands out as the least valuable use of classroom time I experienced in my nineteen years of formal education), for which I was punished by the administration by being passed over for the honor of "ram of the year" at commencement. (The eventual winner, Bill, was matriculating to the Naval Academy and probably a much better fit for our military-oriented school than an angry, punk rocker, Harvard-bound homosexual like me, anyway.) I got stoned more often and went out to the beach at Bellows, overlooking Honolulu Harbor and the lights of the city, to drink with my buddies on Friday and Saturday nights, spending hours watching the planes take off and land at the airport, which is actually quite fascinating when you are drunk *and* stoned. The only thing I cared about was the debate team. I won the state championship that spring, avenging my second-place finish the year before, and then went all the way to the semifinals of the national championship. ("*Semi*finals?" was Mom's reaction when I called her after being eliminated, as if national championships were routine in our family and thus my finish was a big letdown). Other than that, all I was doing was counting down the days until graduation.

Our home life didn't help. My sister had always been an unpredictable person, so perhaps we should have expected something would go wrong. By the beginning of my senior year her marriage to her husband, Tim, had deteriorated and he moved out. Carol then began staying out all hours and even disappearing for days at a time, leaving Mom to play mother to not only me but also her granddaughter Pyper and her grandson Timmy, ages thirteen and nine. Money became tight and Mom went back to work, running a hotdog stand on the Pearl Harbor naval base for minimum wage, working in the hot Hawaiian sun eight hours a day to make ends meet. Mom hated Hawaii, felt she'd made a terrible mistake, and announced she was planning to pack up and move back to North Carolina the day after I graduated.

So I showed poor judgment when I decided to tell Carol I was gay. The problem wasn't her reaction to the news—she honestly didn't care. Carol had always been the liberal in our family, supporting Alan in his marriage to Claudette when everyone else abandoned him (they even lived with Carol and Tim briefly when they first moved to Connecticut), sporting a McGovern bumper sticker on her car in 1972, and openly doing things that scandalized Mom for as long as I could remember, like smoking pot and sleeping in the nude and talking about having had an abortion. Her husband, Tim, was similarly open minded, telling me his best friend in the Navy was gay and that he often was accused of being gay for hanging around this guy, but he didn't care what people thought and neither should I. But as Carol's marriage dissolved, she started dating the older brother of one of my classmates (a predictably age-inappropriate choice for a thirty-four-year-old mother of two who was running away from those facts), with whom she shared my secret. He then told his younger brother, Mark, who then told the entire school.

My worst nightmare had come true. But with cool jock friends like Rich and Ron, a position as a student-body officer, and a girlfriend, I was insulated somewhat from the consequences of Carol's actions. Most of my peers simply refused to believe the rumor, especially as I told them it was untrue and that Mark was just trying to get back at me because Carol had dumped his older brother. Yeah, there were kids who muttered "faggot" when I passed them in the hall, but they were the burnout losers I despised anyway and the cool kids didn't believe them, so I didn't really care. But now my countdown to graduation began in earnest; I truly wanted to get the hell out of there.

When the big day finally came, giddy with excitement over my future, it rolled off my back when my name was called at graduation and a couple of my peers shouted "faggot" in response. All I could think was, "Screw you, losers. I'm going to Harvard." And with that thought, I left twelve years of public school—twelve years of never feeling quite normal, twelve years of never feeling like I belonged, twelve years about which I could muster precious few pleasant memories but had countless ones of isolation and sadness—behind.

CHAPTER 7

Harvard Boy

The summer before I went to Harvard was one of anxiety and anticipation. Mom had skedaddled back to North Carolina shortly after my graduation, moving in with my brother Mike and sister-in-law Donna while getting settled. I followed within a few weeks, to sleep in their basement. I got a job working the graveyard shift in an icehouse. I lived that summer in a bizarre, parallel universe to that in which everyone else was living: while they were working all day in the intense heat and humidity of a Carolina summer, I would sleep all day and, vampirelike, awake at sunset, bundle up in several layers of clothing and, from 11 PM until 7 AM, fill and close the ten-pound bags of ice you buy in your local convenience store. It only heightened my anticipation of going off to Harvard in the fall, when I could at last leave behind the North Carolina I hated.

But I was anxious about Harvard for a very simple reason: I had no idea what to expect when I got there. Since we didn't have any money, I hadn't done a college tour and my sole guide for what to expect was the Harvard admissions handbook. I studied it intently, trying to figure out what the students in it were wearing, determined that I would look the part when I got to Cambridge. When that source of information proved insufficient, I turned to *The Official Preppy Handbook* and virtually memorized its contents, unaware that it was a parody. Thank God, I thought, now I know what to wear—always an important thing for a gay boy to figure out. I spent my hard-earned icehouse wages on Sperry Topsiders and a blue blazer and crewneck wool sweaters and other accoutrements that Lisa Birnbaum recommended in her holy book. Mom made sure that I also bought some thermal underwear: scarred by her own experiences in New England thirty years before, she convinced me that Massachusetts in the winter was somewhat akin to the Arctic tundra and that I'd better have some long johns if I wanted to survive.

In late July the freshman mailing came and, hungry for information, I devoured its contents. Amidst the various flyers and forms describing the many, many opportunities that awaited me at Harvard, so many that my head swam, was one that stood out: the one-pager from the Harvard Gay Student Association. If the mailing had contained a live snake, I would have been less surprised. Not only were there *gay* people at Harvard, they *admitted* they were gay, and they even had a whole "association" (whatever that was). I decided to use this news to test out my family and, while nonchalantly going through the mail in front of them, I pulled the flyer out and said something like, "Would you look at this?" passing it to my brother Mike. Mike started reading it, and the veins began to bulge out in his forehead. "Can I answer this?" he snarled when he was through. Well, one thing was clear: nothing had really changed during the two years I had been gone from North Carolina. It just made me all the more eager to get the hell out of there.

When September finally rolled around, I flew north to Connecticut to spend a few days with Alan and Claudette before heading up to Harvard. They drove me up to Cambridge on a stereotypically beautiful New England fall Sunday, a little bite in the air, leaves just starting to turn, and we pulled up in front of my nineteenth-century dorm, Weld Hall, in the heart of Harvard Yard. My first thought was that this old building must have once been a tenement house, like those I read about in history books, it seemed so worn and dilapidated. I sprinted to my room, Weld North 35, briefly met my roommates, and bid Alan and Claudette goodbye. Claudette smiled and said, "Well, I guess you'll be crying into your pillow tonight, your first night away from home at college," and, although I smiled and nodded, I thought, you're crazy: I've been waiting for this my whole life.

Throughout Freshman Week, I couldn't believe my good fortune: I was at *Harvard*, the pinnacle of American education. I knew how both lucky and unusual I was; the Andover kids of the Harvard Class of 1985 had a reunion during Freshman Week, when seemingly hundreds of them gathered on the steps of one of the dorms in the Yard, but I was the only person from my high school. My clothes were a little preppier than most—the prep school kids all wore ripped jeans (I had yet to learn that only rich people can afford to wear old clothes)—but so far I seemed to fit in. It was a dream, and I was terrified it would somehow come to an end, that somebody would figure out that I didn't really belong here and I'd be sent packing back to a trailer park in North Carolina, where I *did* belong. It didn't help that, at the Freshman Week opening ceremony, the Dean of Freshmen repeated the famous aphorism, "Look to your left; now look to your right; in four years, it's likely that one of the three of you won't be here." We all laughed, but I was sure that I was that one. I was also the only one who didn't know it was a joke.

Having passed several Advanced Placement tests in high school, I was eligible to skip freshman year and enter as a sophomore. Nervous that my scholarship would somehow be taken away before I could finish four years, I elected to do so, which meant I had to choose a major my first week of school. I decided to stick with what I was good at, with what my mom had taught me to love, and chose history. My history classes were a revelation. I enrolled in Simon Schama's nineteenth-century European history course, when he was at the start of his career, long before he was narrating BBC documentaries. His lectures—brilliant, erudite riffs replete with facts and stories about events I'd never heard of and places I'd never been—left me in awe. I read not only the required but also the suggested readings for each class, fearful that somehow my ignorance would be exposed, sure that I was the only one who didn't know everything he was saying because everyone else laughed and nodded along during lectures, like it was all a review for them. When I sailed through my midterms with an A-, I heaved a sigh of relief. It looked like I did belong there after all.

But the ultimate test awaited me: the Fifteen-Page Research Paper.

It was a pro forma requirement of every history class at Harvard that you had to do a Fifteen-Page Research Paper on a topic of your choosing, which your tutor would approve. The Andover kids, seniors, and graduate students in Professor Schama's course just noted the due date when the requirement was announced, like it was something they'd already done many times (which in fact they had), but I'd never written anything of this length and complexity before. I might have been able to fool them on the mid-terms, I thought, but the Fifteen-Page Research Paper would surely expose my ignorance.

I wracked my brains for a topic and eventually decided to explore the Schleswig-Holstein question, a dispute over two German-speaking provinces of Denmark that Bismarck used as a pretext to provoke a war with the Austrian Empire as part of his master plan for German unification in the 1860s. It seemed sophisticated enough to fool people: we sure didn't talk about the Schleswig-Holstein question in *my* high school. I thought I'd better check it out before going to my tutor to get her to approve the topic, so I trudged up the steps of Widener Library, an imposing edifice housing ten million volumes, the second biggest library in the United States. I checked out the card catalogue, which was how you found books in that precomputerized era, found the Dewey decimal number for my chosen topic, and headed off into the Stacks, where the millions of volumes threw off that musty smell that I associated with libraries, the refuge of my youth, an aroma I equated with safety and knowledge and contentment.

My heart sank. Virtually all of the books on the Schleswig-Holstein question were in either Danish or German. My high school German ("*Ich bin krank*"—"I am sick"—is all I can recall of it today; if we wrote that on the test, Frau Caldwell would let us off and would forget to administer a makeup later and you'd end up, inexplicably, with an A on your report card) proved inadequate in deciphering those books, and I didn't speak Danish at all. I was in despair: our topic choices were due the next day and I simply didn't have the skills to do the research I needed to do. I was a fraud, and now everyone would know. Depressed, I headed to my tutor Betsy's office the next day to report my failure. She listened sympathetically as I explained the difficulties I was encountering, and I held my breath after asking her what I should do. Deadpan, she replied, "Hmmm. You don't speak Danish?" Crestfallen, exposed as unworthy of being at Harvard, I croaked out a shamefaced "No." Betsy threw her head back and roared. "Kevin, *nobody* here speaks Danish! I'm not even sure people in *Denmark* speak Danish anymore! Don't take me so literally!" She offered me some research tips, gave me an extension on my paper (it had to be postmarked by Christmas Eve, and she gave me her home address to send it to), and sent me off.

I headed home for Christmas break, typewriter in hand, suitcase heavy with research volumes, my heart in my throat, and spent the first few days feverishly trying to write my paper. I finished and then had to sit down and type it (common use of computers lay in the future). I was afraid it wasn't long enough, and I was right: I only had thirteen pages. To add insult to injury, I had made my margins obscenely wide to try to stretch it out, which only made the meager text in the middle seem even smaller, an archipelago of type in a sea of white. Mom had the brilliant idea that we should trim half an inch off each page by hand, which would make the margins seem more reasonable and, as the hours on Christmas Eve dwindled, she took out her scissors and methodically trimmed each page. We rushed to the post office, literally the last customers on Christmas Eve, and I sent off my first Fifteen-Page Research Paper, making the deadline by a nose.

When I returned to Cambridge after the break during the first days of 1982, I got a call from Betsy. Knowing how scared I was, she decided to personally call and reassure me, to let me know that my paper was excellent, that I was getting an A. I couldn't believe it: I did belong after all. When I got through finals of my first semester and got my first report card, with an A- average, I finally began to settle in.

My initial excitement about the Harvard Gay Student Association turned to dismay upon arrival in Cambridge. There weren't any gay people that I could identify in my class, so I decided to keep my secret hidden. I did know when and where the GSA met, though, and I made absolutely sure to never, ever be anywhere near the Phillips Brooks House on those nights. I was going to fit in. I was going to be normal.

My roommates were not really my kind of guys, but the guys next door were. One of them—Steve, a three-time state-champion diver from New Jersey—was *especially* my kind of guy. A blond jock with a killer bod (sound familiar?), Steve not only was gorgeous but also was the "nice-guy jock" who took me on as his friend, just like Rich and Ron had done. He even forgave my stupid questions, like how he could be both blond *and* Jewish, and we became best friends. If somebody like Steve liked me, I must indeed have value, I thought, unable to believe that I had it all on my own. When it came time to pick roommates for sophomore year, Steve and I decided to room together, along with some of his current roommates.

Once again, I was in love. But this was not part of the plan. Having managed to somehow fit in at Harvard, I had been given a rare second chance. I was on the fast track away from my past, and my homosexuality was part of the baggage I planned to jettison to lighten the journey. I had gotten myself a girlfriend (at the safely distant Smith College, all the way at the other end of Massachusetts) and thought maybe, just maybe, it was going to work.

But Steve's abs did me in. I couldn't deny the effect he had on me or what it meant. With summer drawing nigh, I decided it would be best to go back to Hawaii. The idea of working in an icehouse in North Carolina just didn't float my boat, so I swallowed hard and asked Carol if I could stay with her. I took my work-study grant and headed to the Bishop Museum in Honolulu, eager to put my new skills as a Harvard historian to work. It wasn't quite as exciting as I'd hoped. I was stashed away in an attic workroom, given a cache of documents, mainly maps, that the museum had never catalogued, and told to make heads or tails out of them. It was nearly as odd as my previous summer job, except this time I was stuck all day in a musty, dark attic within shouting distance of the beaches of Waikiki.

It was a lonely summer. My high school was composed largely of military brats who moved every couple of years, so few of my classmates were around. My experiences at Harvard had given me a new vocabulary, a new set of concerns, a new worldview (a new snobbery?) to which few of those still around could relate, so renewing these friendships was a challenge. More disappointingly, my homosexuality didn't go away as I had hoped it might, even though I'd put five thousand miles between temptation—that is, Steve—and me. I channeled my frustration and energy into losing the "freshman fifteen" pounds I had gained, determined to gain control over my body on some level, somehow, some way. Convinced I wasn't yet thin enough when I had lost the fifteen pounds that was my initial goal, I then cut my calorie intake to fifteen hundred a day, then to one thousand, then to five hundred (five hundred calories being equivalent to an apple, a banana, and an English muffin with a smear of jam), punishing my body for wanting things—food, sex—that were natural to want but that I had long equated with evil. On the occasions when I gave in to my natural desires and ate something that put me over my five-hundred-calorie ceiling, I'd calmly go into the bathroom, stick my finger down my throat, and vomit. I was not going back to being the fat gay kid: I hated him and I channeled that fury into paring pounds, as many as I could, before going back to school that fall. I started the summer at 165 pounds; when I returned to Harvard that fall, I weighed 128, having lost thirty-seven pounds—25 percent of my body—in twelve weeks. My class ID from sophomore year shows a face so gaunt that I can't believe that no one intervened. Unable to control my sexuality, I was determined to control my body in some way, no matter the cost.

For sophomore year, Steve and I were assigned to Mather House. Harvard's system was that you lived in one of the old dorms in Harvard Yard, where everyone was required to live during freshman year, and then moved to a larger "house" (fancy word for dorm), where you'd live for the next three years. There was a lottery system in which you listed your top three choices; if you got a high enough number, you were sure to get one of your choices. This was a momentous decision and freighted with great social significance, as each house had its own character: Kirkland was the jock house, Eliot was the preppy house, Adams was the "artsy" (translation: gay) house, and Leverett was the black people house. We listed Quincy as our first choice because it was known as the party house; we put Mather as our third. Mather was the only one of the river houses to have been built in recent history (it was a concrete monstrosity that made many of the nearby public housing projects look cozy by comparison) but at least it was better than the old Radcliffe dorms to which one commuted by shuttle bus. The letters telling us which house we'd gotten were slid under our dorm room doors the day before spring break of freshman year. I remember the rage and frustration we felt when we got Mather, a rage so great that Steve tore up and ate our letter, literally chewing and swallowing it.

So none of us were thrilled when we checked into Mather House for sophomore year, and were less so when we found out we'd been "crowded," that is, that the six of us had been assigned to a five-bedroom suite, meaning that two of us would have to share a room. Since Steve and I were known to be the best friends among the six of us, it was logical that we were elected to be the first ones to share. Mather House or no, I was so happy to be back at Harvard, to be back "home," that I actually let myself start eating again.

Living in a house had its advantages. In Harvard Yard there were graduate student proctors who kept an eye on you, but in houses there were subject tutors who didn't care much how we behaved. In fact, they were more like buddies and would drink and get stoned with us, unlike the proctors we had to sneak around. I became pals with some of them, especially a guy named Andrew, a Canadian of Chinese descent who hailed from Montreal and was studying architecture at the Graduate School of Design. One night after dinner I dropped by Andrew's and was sitting around his living room (tutors got suites with a kitchen, a living room, and a bedroom), perusing some of the magazines on his coffee table. As I rifled through one, it became clear to me: this was a *gay* newspaper. Rube that I was, it had never occurred to me that Andrew might be gay (an architecture student? Gay?) and, as I was trying to absorb the meaning of his having this newspaper (there were gay newspapers?), he glanced over and said casually, "Oh, do you ever read that? It's a great paper."

Shocked, I replied, "But this is a gay newspaper!"

"Well, yeah."

"Are *you* gay?"

"Well, yeah."

I took a deep breath, and said, "I think I might be gay, too."

"Well, yeah, I thought you were," he replied.

This was not the response I wanted; I had everybody fooled, or so I thought. I interrogated Andrew as to what gave it away, and he said it was just a "feeling" he had. I flung questions at Andrew, the first openly gay person I'd ever really talked to, asking if his family knew, if his friends knew, if the college knew, and got yes, yes, and yes. Despite being the most awful thing in the world, he seemed well adjusted and happy and just fine with himself. My little mind was blown. Misery was not necessarily the lot in life of my kind of people, it seemed.

Liberated by this revelation, I was determined to now be out. Coming out was much more of a nonevent than I had expected. My roommates were cool with it. Steve told me it meant a lot that I trusted him enough to tell him; Joe said it didn't make any difference in our friendship; and Robert told me his girlfriend's roommate was a lesbian, that he was busy with a physics problem set that was due in an hour, and could he please get back to it as this really wasn't a big deal as far as he was concerned. I couldn't believe it: I had accepted myself, my friends were accepting me, and the long shadow in whose darkness I had lived as long as I could remember—the fear that I was doomed to a lifetime of isolation and loneliness because I was gay—was receding. I was going to be okay.

I ditched my preppy clothes and affected a new-wave look through items I bought at Cambridge's thrift shops. I immersed myself in the Harvard-Radcliffe Dramatic Club, directing and acting in a series of shows whose awfulness I now cringe to recall. (When I asked a friend what she thought of a production of Pushkin's *Little Tragedies* I had been in at the Experimental Theater, she replied, "Well, the name was accurate and the price was right," which, given that tickets were free, was hardly a ringing endorsement.) But most of all I made it my personal mission to educate the world about gay people, coming out as quickly as I could in every conversation (typical exchange while shopping at the Harvard Coop: "How much is this album? $6.99? Oh, okay. By the way, I'm gay."), filled with a fervor to witness similar to that of the recent convert who's just accepted Jesus as his personal Savior or the reformed addict who has just started climbing the twelve steps of Alcoholics Anonymous. I am sure I was annoying as hell.

The person who was most clearly annoyed was Mom. When I came home for Christmas break during sophomore year, I decided it was time she knew, and I informed her that I was gay.

"I don't understand. What about that nice girl you dated in high school, Peggy? What about that nice girl from Smith you dated last year?"

"Mom, I didn't really like them *that* way. I was just dating them."

"You sure seemed to like them to me."

"That's because I wanted you to think I liked them, Mom, and I really did like them as people, but, as hard as I tried, I didn't like them *that* way."

"Maybe you just haven't met the right one yet. This is a phase a lot of people go through. Have you talked with a psychiatrist?"

I exploded. "No, I haven't, Mom, because I am not sick; there is nothing wrong with me. I am gay, I always have been, and I am not going to change. You're just going to have to accept that."

A cold war now set in. Having been raised in the great Southern tradition of "if you haven't got anything nice to say, don't say anything at all," Mom refused to discuss it further. When I returned to Cambridge after break, our phone conversations got shorter and more hostile every time we talked. She was going to listen to me and accept me, I decided, and she just as fervently shut down and refused to give me her approval. Given that I was just getting by on my financial aid package and work-study job and Mom was not doing much better at her job as a graveyard shift medical-records clerk, long-distance calls were a luxury for us anyway, and I began to use this as an excuse to not talk to her very often. We were both secretly relieved: I didn't want to talk with her about my life and she didn't want to hear about it, either. I made it a point to get jobs far from home during summers and came back as little as humanly possible on vacations.

We reached the nadir of our relationship my senior year. In the fall of 1984, I was one of two students selected to direct a production on the main stage of the American Repertory Theater. I chose one of Tennessee Williams's last and most autobiographical plays, *Vieux Carré*, which deals with his coming-out experience as a young man, a story with special meaning to a Southern gay boy like myself. Mom wanted to come, so I saved my work-study pennies and flew her up. She invited Aunt Merlyn, my dad's younger sister, and her husband, Uncle Larry, who lived less than an hour from campus, to the opening. We hadn't discussed the play's theme and, as the drama onstage progressed, the drama in my family did as well. I could feel Mom seething with anger as the play wore on, but she said nothing. When it was over, my aunt and uncle congratulated me and left (seeming a bit stunned, I must say) and then Mom let me have it.

"Why didn't you tell me what this play was about?"

"Why? Would you not have come?"

"I didn't say that. But you could have warned me. And then I wouldn't have invited Merlyn and Larry."

Now it was my turn to seethe.

"Why? Do I embarrass you, Mom? Are you embarrassed by who I am?"

"I didn't say that. I just don't think it was appropriate for them to see."

"Why? Because what I *am* is not appropriate?"

A beat passed, filled with silence.

"I don't get this whole thing, anyway. Why are you gay?"

There. She finally asked what she'd wanted to ask for years.

"Because I just am. Why are you straight? Huh?"

Taken aback, she did not reply. And there our dialogue ended, with each of us glaring across the divide that yawned between us: she, fumbling, confused, angry, guilty; me, fumbling, confused, angry, guilty—more alike than we ever dreamed at the time.

By then, I was so disconnected from my family that the gap didn't register all that much. My Harvard experience had distanced me from them, had made me feel embarrassed and ashamed of them, their lack of formal education, their lack of sophistication, their lack of all the things that my "artsy-fartsy" friends at Harvard held dear. The fall of my senior year, around the time *Vieux Carré* was staged, I was interviewed by *Harvard Magazine* for a story on working-class students and the issues we faced. I talked about the difficulty of negotiating two worlds, about how I would have one kind of discussion in Cambridge and the impossibility of having that same conversation at home, where I was instead expected to "throw the football around." I had forgotten that *Harvard Magazine* was mailed free of charge to every parent of a current undergraduate, so that Mom got it and had read the article by the time I came home for Thanksgiving.

She thrust it at me accusatorily as soon as I walked through the door, snapping, "I don't think anyone has ever asked you to throw a football around."

Rolling my eyes, I replied, "It's a *metaphor*, Mom."

"Metaphor: is that a fancy Harvard word for 'lie'?"

"Whatever, Mom. It's not like I could expect you to understand." And with that, another silence descended and we retreated to our separate corners.

I now saw myself operating on a plane my benighted mother could never understand. I'd been extraordinarily fortunate when I was assigned to a junior tutorial led by Professor Patrice Higonnet, a tenured professor of French history. Tenured professors *never* lead small sections of five or six students, so it was a real stroke of luck, and the fact that Professor Higonnet took me on as his protégé was an even more astounding one. Most of my friends had never even spoken to a tenured professor for more than two minutes, and Professor Higonnet was inviting me over to his house for drinks with him and his wife and their child. As I sat in the backyard of his expansive home on Brattle Street, and he and his four-year-old daughter chattered away in French—she was learning Chinese, too, he let me know—and we discussed my prospects for doctoral studies in French history, I felt far, far removed from the trailer park where I'd grown up.

Following junior year, Professor Higonnet helped me win a traveling fellowship to go to Paris to do research on my senior thesis, and I went abroad for the first time. I landed on a Saturday evening in August and took a cab into the city to meet my friend Peter, who was spending the entire summer there. Peter and I strolled the streets and my mind boggled: I was in Paris, France. *The* Paris. I was amazed that the cars had yellow headlights. I was stunned to actually stand in front of Notre Dame and the Louvre and the Eiffel Tower. (I expected them to be roped off or something, with big signs saying DO NOT TOUCH.) These were the pictures from the *World Book Encyclopedia* that I had memorized as a child, except they were real, standing right in front of me.

On Monday I headed over to the Bibliothèque Nationale, where I had my first encounter with the actual French. Bibliothèque Nationale librarians set the standard for French snideness, and I have never felt like more of a redneck than on that first visit. Clearly unfamiliar with how the system worked, twenty years younger than anyone else there, speaking in halting, heavily accented French, I was a sitting duck. After hours of befuddlement, I overcame my embarrassment and approached a reference librarian for assistance. Peering down at me from the dais on which he sat, he harrumphed in disgust at the young American rube and snarled, "*Maintenant! Je vous fais une leçon!*" ("Now! I am going to teach you a lesson!"), at a decibel level just barely lower than that of the Concorde, so that everyone in the reading room looked up to see who the idiot was. *(L'idiot, c'est moi.)* I slunk away, traumatized and too terrified to use my classroom French again in an actual conversation with an actual French person the rest of the summer, so I basically spoke to no one except other Americans, which wasn't really a problem as all the Parisians were on vacation in August anyway. I spent my days poring over nineteenth-century documents in the Bibliothèque Nationale, bored, lonely, learning in the process I did not have the monastic qualities required of a true historian and researcher. I came back to Cambridge that September not sure what I would be doing with my life but knowing that a PhD in French history was not going to be it.

Just as I had decided I was too sophisticated for my family, I decided I was "too gay" for my roommates. Once my obsessive crush on Steve had faded away, I began to realize that we didn't really have that much in common—I was an artsy-fartsy, French-spouting, homosexual intellectual; he was a beer-drinking, pre-med, suburban, straight jock—and our relationship began to fray. When, during my junior year, Jake, the head of the Gay Students Association, put together a rooming group of five gay guys in Mather House and asked if I wanted to join them during my senior year, I accepted. Our banding together seemed to provoke great consternation among the college administration—Dean Epps said to Jake in a meeting, "Well, that's quite the little gay power elite you've got going there," with more than hint of disdain—but we reveled in it. Long before Queer Nation, we were ready to say that we were here, we were queer, and you'd better get used to it.

In fall of senior year, our in-your-face attitude provoked a confrontation with some of the new sophomores who had been unlucky enough to get bad lottery numbers and get assigned to Mather, just as we had two years before. While the luck of the draw had put a disproportionate number of the class of 1985's homosexuals in Mather, Mather's class of 1987 for some reason seemed disproportionately composed of young jocks, who were clearly uncomfortable with the very out, very defiant gay seniors. Each suite shared a bathroom with a neighboring room, and the sophomores who were assigned to share our bathroom were horrified to have a group of gay guys "across the bathroom." One, an ROTC cadet, was particularly obnoxious and vocal about his displeasure until, late one weekend night, fortified by some alcohol, I backed him up against a wall and told him that, if he didn't shut the fuck up, I was going to kick his ass. Just like it had with Mike my freshman year at Mount Tabor, it worked again, and the harassment abated. My roommates favored channeling their concerns through more appropriate vehicles and went to our house masters, Professor and Mrs. Herlihy, a kindly Irish couple with ten to twenty children of their own, and told them of the ongoing harassment. The word came down swift and hard—can it, sophomores—and we felt vindicated.

Shortly after that, my friend Suzy asked if I would be interviewed for the house newsletter's "Bachelor of the Week" series. They'd never done a gay bachelor before and she decided it was high time to include one. It was a silly little column—six or seven stock questions, a sidebar that took up less than half a page—so I was silly in return. I answered her questions—like "What are your favorite foods?"—with answers like "Oh, carrots, hot dogs, anything with that kind of shape is fine by me." Apparently the answer that really set the sophomores off was my play on the word "endowment," in reference to the Endowment for Divestiture, which encouraged alumni to give to a special fund that would be released to the university only when it divested its holdings in companies that did business with the apartheid-era South African regime: when asked what I looked for in a date, I replied, "Endowment—and I don't mean for Divestiture, honey." Suzy laughed and said it was her best interview yet.

The day the newsletter came out, the disgruntled sophomores, by now nicknamed "the straplings" by my friend Nan ("They think they're strapping young men, but they're really just little saplings, so let's call them 'the straplings' "), stormed the Herlihys' office. They said that I and the other homos were giving the house a bad image and that the Herlihys needed to do something about it, starting with making me apologize for my interview, as it had offended so many people. Mrs. Herlihy apparently asked to see the offending article, read it right there under the watchful eye of the straplings, then looked up and said, "Well, personally, I think it's very funny." And that was the end of that.

As comfortable as I might have seemed with my gayness on the outside, inside it was a different matter. Years of learning to hate myself didn't just slip away because I came out, and I still struggled with my feelings of self-loathing, feelings I would later come to understand as internalized homophobia. Unlike other traditional minorities in American society (Jews, people of color), gay people aren't raised by people like themselves and aren't connected to a community of people like themselves when growing up. As a result, we internalize the typically homophobic attitudes of those around us, and devaluing and demeaning homosexuality becomes part our own self-image. This voice in your own head—the voice that constantly tells you that you are worthless—is the real enemy. Like a lot of gay people, I found that other people sometimes accepted me long before I had completely accepted myself.

Comfortable as I might have been confronting and educating straight people, I was too scared of other gay people to go to a place like a gay bar. So I was restricted to meeting guys at Harvard. It was a shallow singles pool to swim in, to say the least: the number of out guys was pretty small and the closet cases would never get near me, as that would be too incriminating. (I found out years later that they generally had much better sex lives than did those of us who were out.) I relied on meeting guys at the "house parties" the dorms had each weekend. Typically I would have to have a few drinks in order to lower my inhibitions. If I was lucky enough, another out guy would be there, I'd swoop in, and soon we'd be sucking face on the dance floor. Before long we'd be back in one of our rooms, sucking more than face, before falling asleep and awakening the next morning with a crick in our necks from twisting like pretzels to both fit in one of the single beds Harvard provided. The next morning I would profess I was in love—if I was in love, then the sex wasn't dirty and wrong—and over the next few days or weeks I'd cling to and try to "marry" the guy. Inevitably this wouldn't work out, as I am sure I came across a little like Glenn Close in *Fatal Attraction* to my potential spouses ("I won't be *ignored*, Will/Stephen/Tom/Erick..."). I was more comfortable agitating for social and political change than I was dealing with my own feelings.

As senior year wore on I did all the things I was supposed to do, like my senior thesis, a project I had basically lost interest in due to my experience at the Bibliothèque Nationale and which I would grow to forever hate when I accidentally erased it from my friend Miriam's computer three days before it was due. I had to reconstruct it from a rough draft, leaving it so full of typos that I was downgraded from summa cum laude to magna cum laude and did not graduate at the top of my class as a result. My deeper concern was a mounting panic about becoming an adult and joining the "real world." The real world for gay people in 1985 was still a grim place. Anita Bryant's antigay "save our children" crusade in the late seventies, which had repealed many of the laws gay rights activists had gotten passed at that time, had morphed into the broader-based Moral Majority, whose favored candidate, Ronald Reagan, was ensconced in the White House, having just won forty-nine states in his reelection campaign. AIDS was sweeping the community and gay people were becoming even bigger pariahs than before, with the more unenlightened straight people refusing to use drinking glasses gay people had used. No treatments for AIDS were available and people routinely disappeared and died almost overnight. Only one state—Wisconsin—banned discrimination based on sexual orientation. My few ventures off the Harvard campus confirmed my impression that the real world was a scary and hateful place. Once, on Boston's subway, the T, a guy I was dating and I were surrounded by a group of teenagers screaming, "What are you, faggots? Who fucks who?" while onlookers did nothing, gazing with bovine obliviousness at our outnumbered terror. The prospects for a young homosexual like me seemed pretty dim.

And what was I supposed to do now that I was grown up? I joined the herd and did the corporate recruiting thing at the Harvard Office for Career Services, truly the most useless office on the Harvard campus, as its staff seemed to expect you to use Daddy's connections from St. Grottlesex to land yourself somewhere and didn't much want to be bothered by undergraduates who actually needed career services. My heart was so obviously not in it that not a single firm called me back for a second interview.

The real problem was this: I felt that work was supposed to be more than just something you did to earn a paycheck. It was supposed to *mean* something, it was supposed to make a difference, it was supposed to make the world a better place. I may have been in denial about it, but my Baptist heritage, coupled with my social conscience, wouldn't let me go after a corporate job with a full heart, which was just as well as it wouldn't have worked for me anyway. But what would? I knew the answer: teaching. I had spent the summer of '83 working at a camp for emotionally disturbed children called Wediko in rural New Hampshire and the summer of '84 as a teaching fellow in the summer program at a boarding school called Northfield Mount Hermon and had loved both jobs. I saw how I was making a difference in the lives of these young people. I remembered how isolated I had felt at their age, and I was thrilled when I was able to make their burdens a little lighter. I relished doing for them what I wished someone had done for me.

There was one problem: people didn't go to Harvard to become teachers. Not yet having the confidence to follow my own heart, I continued my search for a more prestigious thing to do. Like all liberal arts graduates with big-name but essentially useless degrees, the answer seemed clear: law school! Problem was, I had no money. Then I found a posting at the Office for Career Services for a law firm in Washington, D.C. that had a program where they'd take on a Harvard graduate as a legal assistant who would work for them for two years, be sent to law school at the firm's expense, and then return to join the firm's partner track. It seemed that my prayers had been answered. I sent in my résumé, interviewed, and was chosen. It was May 1 and graduation was barely a month away. Saved by the bell.

I headed down to D.C., where I was to spend a day at the firm and learn the ropes. If I took the U.S. Airways shuttle that morning excited about my future, I flew home that evening in despair. A law firm, it turned out, was just as stultifying as the Bibliothèque Nationale, but with none of the intellectual challenge or cachet. I was to be assigned to a case involving natural-gas deregulation in Louisiana, which had been going on for several years with no end in sight. Instead of poring over nineteenth-century French government documents, I'd be poring over twentieth-century U.S. government documents and working for the bad guys, a big energy corporation, to boot. This, I could see, was not going to work, even if I was being bribed with a free law school education.

That evening I went to an orientation reception for Harvard Summer School, where I was to be a summer proctor (resident advisor) for high school students. I was relating to a friend how depressed I was over my day in D.C. and she said, "Well, just meet some people here and take your mind off of it. Go talk to the assistant deans—they're really cool." So I marched over to one of them and struck up a chat. He asked what I was doing after graduation and I related my disastrous day to him, ending with the fact that I thought I was going to have to turn this job down even though I had no other prospects. He asked, "So what would you really like to do?" I said I thought I really wanted to be a teacher, and he asked what I could teach. I said history. He asked what I could coach. The honest answer would have been "nothing" but, knowing that this was the wrong one, I said squash, as I did play some for fun at Harvard. He asked if I could do any extracurriculars and I said I'd done a lot of drama. He said, "We're looking for a history teacher who can coach squash and maybe do some drama productions at our school. Can you come down for an interview?" Three days later I was at the Moses Brown School in Providence, Rhode Island, for an interview, and the following morning, a Saturday, the headmaster called and offered me a job. It was three weeks till graduation. I took it.

Graduation Week came and so did my mom. The requisite parental functions brought me great anxiety. I was still ashamed that my mom was an uneducated Southerner with a thick accent who worked for barely more than minimum wage while my friends' parents were lawyers and doctors and businessmen, many of whom had an Ivy League lineage or at least a line of college graduates that stretched back several generations. It didn't help that Mom and I were still in a cold war over my sexual orientation, which remained the love that dare not speak its name in our conversations. She arrived and seemed a bit in awe of the whole thing, raising my hopes that she might just keep her mouth shut the whole time, but things soon deteriorated.

Mom seemed to be just as ashamed of my career choice as I was of hers. Early in Graduation Week the Herlihys threw a reception for graduating seniors in their residence. Mom and I went, where she met many of my friends' parents for the first time. Making conversation, Mrs. Rock, the mother of one of my friends, asked me, "Kevin, what are you going to be doing next year?"

"I am going to be a high school history teacher at Moses Brown School in Providence."

"How wonderful!"

"But he's not going to do that for long," Mom interjected.

I glared at her.

"Oh, he's not?" Mrs. Rock replied, glancing over at me, sensing something was up.

"Oh, no. He's going to go to law school or get a doctorate soon," Mom answered. "He's going on to something more important than teaching."

I was ready to kill her, and Mrs. Rock could tell.

"Well, I think teaching is a very important thing, too. Good luck, Kevin, and nice to have met you, Mrs. Jennings."

Once again, just as she had when I made the semifinals of the National Forensic League championships in high school, just as she had at *Vieux Carré*—at a moment of triumph for me—Mom had me steaming and feeling like what I did was just not good enough. When we got outside, I let her have it.

"What was that about?"

"What?"

"That crap that I was going to do something 'important' like go to law school."

"Well, you are, aren't you? You're going to do something bigger than being a teacher with your life!"

"You're unbelievable. Do I embarrass you or something, Mom? Are you embarrassed by who I am?"

"Not at all. I am very proud of you."

"Then why, for once, can't what I am or what I do be good enough for you? Your other kids didn't even fucking go to college, and yet you make me feel like I'm the one you're ashamed of."

And, with that, another silence descended, and we retreated to our separate corners.

My ultimate moment of triumph was still to come, on Class Day, the day set aside for undergraduates during Graduation Week. During the Class Day exercises, one male student and one female student, chosen by a committee of their classmates, give what are called the Harvard and Radcliffe Orations respectively, and I had been chosen to give the Harvard one. I was a bit surprised to have been chosen, as my speech was not a laudatory one. Disgusted by the headlong flight of so many of my classmates into yuppiedom (it was the mid-eighties; greed was good), I had written a strong speech denouncing that choice as irresponsible for those who had been given a privilege like a Harvard education, which, to me, carried with it the responsibility to help those less fortunate than we. "For unto whomsoever much is given, of him much shall be required," as it says in Luke 12:48. (You can take the boy out of the Baptist Church, but you can't take the Baptist Church out of the boy, something I hadn't quite accepted yet.)

Class Day dawned gloomy and a downpour gathered force as the day wore on—not good news for an event to be held outdoors. But worse news came that morning when I found out that three of my friends were going to have their diplomas withheld on the next day, Graduation Day, for participating in a demonstration where students had seized control of the president's house to protest the university's continued investment in firms doing business in South Africa. My friend Kathy broke down crying when she related how disappointed her parents were going to be. We all felt powerless. Then it dawned on me: I, for one, had a platform, and I decided I was going to use it. The university was not going to get the last word on this one.

I was shaking by the time I got up to the podium to deliver the Harvard Oration. Partly it was because there were ten thousand rain-soaked people sitting in Harvard Yard waiting to hear me. Partly it was because my mom was in the audience and, if this speech was good enough for her, it would indeed prove there was a first time for everything. Partly it was because I was a boy who'd grown up in a trailer park, who was the first in his family to go to college, and here I was, the featured speaker on this Class Day, the fifth day of June in the Year of Our Lord nineteen hundred and eighty-five and in the Year of Harvard College three hundred and forty-nine. But mostly it was because I had a secret plan.

I started into my speech by sticking to the text that had been approved by the administration for me to deliver. But midway through, I departed from the approved text, talking instead about how Harvard supposedly taught us to stand up for what we believed, about how my friends were having their diplomas pulled for doing what the university had taught them, and how the university itself was being rewarded for its hypocrisy with continued support from donors even though it was investing in and supporting a racist apartheid regime. Many of my classmates started cheering and some alumni started booing. I then went back to my approved text and finished. I have no memory of how the audience reacted at the end.

But I certainly remember how Dean Epps, seated to my immediate right on the dais, reacted. When I got back to my seat, the dean conspicuously turned his considerable three-hundred-plus-pound body so that his back was to me as much as possible, a position he would maintain for the rest of the proceedings. Seeing this, and probably seeing the look on my face, my classmate Barry Ford, an African American football player I had never met, one of the "popular kids" who had been elected class marshal, walked across the stage and stuck out his hand. "That was a great speech," he said, earning my undying gratitude for standing by me. No one else spoke to me during the rest of the ceremony or afterward, but one of my friends told me he overheard an officer of the Alumni Association referring to me as "that militant homosexual monster." Mom said she didn't really understand why all these people had been making noise in the middle of my speech—wasn't that rude!—but it was a very nice speech anyway.

I could not have cared less. I was free and clear. Graduation Day dawned with a bright blue sky, and we marched to the main ceremony in Harvard Yard from Mather House after a champagne brunch where my friend Luis and I had a little too much and then took a bottle with us for good measure, which we downed en route. By the time we got back to Mather after the ceremony for our "House graduation," where we got our actual diplomas, we were pretty well snockered. I ended up sitting on my diploma after it was handed to me by Mrs. Herlihy so that the sheepskin bears wrinkles to this day. Furious that I had been drinking, Mom stormed back to the Holiday Inn in Somerville, where I had gotten her a room, taking a bit of the wind out of my sails at yet another moment of triumph. But that was a small distraction, for all I could think of was the words of the dean during Freshman Week: "Look to your left; now look to your right; in four years, it's likely that one of the three of you won't be here."

I was still here. And I had something no one else in my family had ever had before: a college diploma.

CHAPTER 8

Going Back In

My job as a proctor in the Harvard summer school program provided room and board for the summer after graduation. I didn't need much money, so I didn't get a steady job but instead did odd jobs occasionally through Harvard Student Agencies to pick up some cash. I spent most of my time hanging out and working out, having taken up weightlifting during senior year determined that, if I couldn't *be* a jock, at least I would *look* like one. In other words, it was a pretty lazy summer, the biggest event of which was meeting Bob, another openly gay member of the Harvard class of 1985, who I had somehow never managed to run into during our undergraduate years—rather an amazing feat since the number of openly gay guys in my class of sixteen hundred could be counted on one's fingers and toes. I got tricked into my first date with him. My senior-year roommate Jim worked with Bob, and Jim had told me Bob thought I was cute. I knew I was moving to Providence and had no desire to get involved with anyone, so I said thanks but no thanks to his offer to set us up. A few days later I dropped by the office where they worked giving Harvard tours, and Jim said,

"Hey, Kevin, what are you doing tomorrow? Want to see a movie?"

"Sure," I replied, upon which Jim turned to Bob and said, "How about you?"

"Sure," Bob answered, and I knew I'd been duped. We made our plans and I turned to leave, when Jim added insult to injury: "Oh, shoot, I just remembered I have something else to do. But you guys go ahead without me."

Annoyed, I was deliberately an hour late, knowing the movie would have started and thinking Bob would have given up and left. But he hadn't. We headed over to Chi-Chi's, known for its cheap margaritas and free chips, and soon were engrossed in conversation. Bob was a preppy, sweet, cute, all-American guy, who had graduated summa cum laude and Phi Beta Kappa in history and literature. His smile lit up his entire face, and I found myself getting lost in his blue eyes as the evening wore on. He even had blond hair, which turned brown when both the summer and his highlights faded but, by then, I was already in love.

Our second date was a trip down to the beach in Rhode Island. Bob had a car, a distinctly unsexy family station wagon he'd gotten from his parents, but the trip seemed hot enough to me. He'd pretty much been loafing a lot that summer, too, so that between his beach trips and his outdoor tours of the campus he had acquired a killer tan that made his teeth seem almost glow-in-the-dark white and his eyes seem bluer than the ocean we swam in. I kept looking in those eyes the whole day, wondering how I had gotten so lucky. That night we went back to his parents' house in Grafton, a small town in central Massachusetts. We fulfilled one of his fantasies by spending the night in his childhood bedroom (his parents were in Maine) and the next morning eating Rice Krispies out of the bowls he had eaten his before-school breakfasts in for twelve years. By the end of the weekend I had decided he was the One. Bob proved just as commitment-oriented as I, and the rest of the summer he fulfilled my fantasy of the perfect mate.

We were virtually inseparable. When the time came, in late August, to head to Providence to begin my teaching career, it was with deeply torn feelings that I made the move: I was excited over my new job but sad over the distance it put between Bob and me.

As I drove onto the Moses Brown campus for new faculty orientation, I couldn't help but be struck by how different the school I was to teach in was from the ones I had attended. Moses Brown, founded in 1784, was the school for the elite of Providence, which was by and large a traditional, conservative group dominated by Catholic Italian Americans. Its historic campus sprawled across many acres in the heart of the city's fashionable East Side, just across the street from Brown University, which had been founded by Moses Brown's brother John. These were privileged kids attending a privileged institution, paying a tuition that was more than half of my annual salary, and I was now to be their teacher. It was a daunting prospect.

From the point of view of Moses Brown School, the biggest event of my summer was that I had gotten an earring. In the mid-eighties, before they had become de rigueur among football players and rappers, earrings were still a countercultural statement, and I had known this when I got one. But I was careful not to use it to make a statement about being gay because I didn't think that would go over well in my new teaching career. I made sure to pierce my left ear, the "straight" side ("left is right and right is wrong"), so no suspicions would be raised. This failed as a strategy. The school year began with a full-day staff meeting in late August. At the end of the meeting, the headmaster, Mr. Forrest, asked me if he could speak with me for a few minutes. My heart skipped a beat (I was being called down to the principal's office? Already? But I'm a *teacher* now...) as I followed him out onto the yard behind the headmaster's house, where the opening meeting had been held. He didn't waste time. "If you plan on wearing that piece of metal in your ear when school opens tomorrow," he said, "don't bother coming in."

I was stunned and scared. I needed this job, I wanted this job, and I was in no financial position to lose this job. Plus, part of my excitement about Moses Brown was that it was a Quaker school, and its rhetoric about diversity and tolerance had seduced me. Although I had never for a minute thought that this tolerance extended to gay issues (that was simply beyond the realm of imagination in 1985), I thought it would be a generally progressive environment. I hadn't expected authoritarian dictates over what teachers could wear, aside from the expectation that the daily uniform would somehow involve khakis, a button-down shirt, and a tie, all of which I had bought out of the remainders bin at Keezer's in Cambridge. Somehow it hadn't computed that Mr. Forrest was an ex-Marine, that Providence in the mid-eighties was a cultural backwater in a small state where everyone knew each other, and that—once you were off the Brown campus—a tolerant viewpoint consisted of something like "we're nice to Jews (even though they killed Christ)." Cultural diversity at Moses Brown didn't extend to anything countercultural, and the earring had to go.

If I thought my heart had skipped a beat during my conversation with Mr. Forrest, it went into arrhythmia when I walked down the hall, *sans* earring, to my first-period U.S. history class the next morning. I had *hated* high school: what the hell was I doing in one again? Was I *crazy*? The site of so many traumatic experiences during my own youth, the high school hallway ranks as one of my least favorite places in the world. I tried to stride confidently, like the teacher I now was, but inside I was shaking, wondering if and when one of the kids was going to call me "faggot." I managed to get to the classroom without incident and heaved a sigh of relief when I got inside the door. This was an environment I could control and where I felt safe.

Until the kids arrived. The seventeen juniors in my first-period U.S. history class slunk in, eyeing their new, twenty-two-year-old teacher, barely five years older than they were, sizing him up to see if he was cool or a wimp. I felt as naked as a jaybird under their penetrating adolescent eyes. My section of U.S. history contained, for me, the Heart of Darkness of Moses Brown's class of 1987—the coolest, biggest, jockiest stars of the school's athletic teams had somehow ended up in my class. A couple of them played offensive line for the football team: they dwarfed my five-foot, eight-inch frame physically and, psychically, they were terrifying to me. It had only been a few years since kids like these had terrorized me, and now they were all sitting in my classroom. Arrhythmia accelerated into full cardiac arrest.

But I was going to prove I was cool, so I proceeded with my planned lesson. Determined to make history "relevant," I had made a cassette of various pop songs of the day (Madonna's "Material Girl" among them) and played them, asking students to analyze what they said about the values of our society. Still a punker at heart, I included the Dead Kennedys' anti-Reagan, antiracist screed "Nazi Punks Fuck Off," which undoubtedly was the first time the students had had a teacher play a song in class in which the singer told the president to fuck off. (Twenty years later, one question springs to mind: "What was I *thinking*?") The jocks were blown away and, being loyal Republicans, more than a little appalled. I could see that I had definitely gotten their attention.

I survived the first day, and the next, and the next, and began to feel more and more like I was a real teacher, at least until I was locked out of an interschool dance I was chaperoning and had to get one of my students to testify that I was indeed a teacher and not a senior before the chaperone from the all-girls Lincoln School would let me back in. I figured out how to be a teacher by thinking back to the worst teachers I had had in school—not a short list—and trying to be the opposite. Mr. Cultrou had used his power to humiliate students; I vowed to use mine to make students feel good about themselves. Mr. Schiessekopf had failed to take my needs seriously and to listen to me; I would always make time for a student who needed to talk. Mrs. Kono had proceeded to "teach" her material, oblivious of whether it interested her students or they actually absorbed it; I would make sure that my lessons were thought-provoking and comprehensible. In general, my teachers had been authority figures who didn't treat their charges with much respect; I would be the teacher who took my students seriously as individuals and thinkers, and who challenged and supported them in being their best. It turned out that teaching was indeed the right career choice for me and I loved it.

I invented a game called "family food" to help students understand why peasants supported the French Revolution, supplemented our dry U.S. history text with primary documents that showed how the people who experienced the events we were studying viewed them, and made sure that the stories of African Americans and women were part of our dialogue as well. I let kids call me Kevin and, despite the stern warnings from older teachers that this would mean they wouldn't respect me, found that they listened to me just as well when I was "Kevin" as when I was "Mister Jennings." By the time Parent's Night came in October, many of the parents who attended made a point of telling me how much their children liked my class.

Things were not going so smoothly outside of the classroom, however. The schools' faculty was dominated by a veteran old guard who showed little interest in new teachers and great disdain for educational innovation. I tended to huddle with one of the other new teachers, a lesbian named Monique, who also was the school's only black teacher. We were together so much that rumors began to spread among students, who were scandalized by what they saw as an interracial romance. One of the freshmen finally got up the courage to ask, "Are you and Monique boyfriend and girlfriend?" I couldn't resist answering, "The truth is far worse than you imagine," prompting howls in the classroom.

Monique was just as disappointed as I by the gap between the school's rhetoric and its reality, which was brought home to us very directly a few weeks after the start of the year when the school had a diversity training for parents, faculty, and board members. The local Quaker Meeting House (church) was a lovely, nineteenth-century building on the Moses Brown campus, in which we all gathered for the speaker. I found most of what he said fatuous and self-serving, seemingly intended to congratulate us all on how sensitive we were rather than challenging us to do better. During the question-and-answer session, I asked what I thought was a simple and pertinent question: "How can we claim to be such a diverse community when we have only seven black students out of a total of 360 in the high school, or about 2 percent of the total student body?" A silence fell, with the reaction from the audience making me feel as if I had just farted very loudly. I don't remember the speaker's answer, but I do remember an older trustee coming up to me afterward and barking loudly, "You know, we had a young teacher like you here in the sixties. He always mouthed off about things like this, too. You know what? He got fired." I glared back at him and snapped, "Is that some kind of a threat?" He just smiled and shuffled off.

When it comes to diversity, actions speak louder than words, and Moses Brown's actions spoke clearly and distinctly from the start. Monique had been hired to teach in the lower school, and had been up-front during her interview, saying that she was dyslexic and as a result would most likely make spelling errors on the board from time to time. She was assured that, given that she had a degree from a prestigious college and was moving into teaching from a career as a journalist, the school knew this was not a reflection of her ability or intelligence, and would explain the situation to anyone who was concerned. But, just a few weeks into the fall term, Monique told me she had been called in by the administration, who had informed her that parents were concerned about her spelling errors and that she needed to take more care, as the school was getting questions about why they had hired such an "uneducated" person to teach their children. Monique reminded the administration that she had forewarned them of this, but their only response was to tell her to try harder—as if trying hard can make dyslexia go away... a small sign of how out of touch with developments in the field of education this insular school was.

I was livid. I knew racist code language when I saw it: every time someone made a comment about this "uneducated" teacher, there should have been a subtitle saying "black" instead. These folks didn't have the balls to come right out and say they didn't believe black people were good enough to teach at Moses Brown, so they had found an indirect way to say it. And the school did not have the courage of its convictions to stand by its earlier commitment to Monique, lest it offend its paying customers. I made an appointment to see Mr. Forrest.

Mr. Forrest seemed a little startled to have a first-year teacher in his office ("Young teachers are to be seen and not heard" was, I was realizing, his unofficial motto), and asked why I had come. I got right to the point.

"I understand that Monique is getting some flack from parents and that she doesn't feel very supported by the school. This school makes a big deal about its commitment to diversity, and I think this gives you a chance to put that rhetoric into action. She's the only black teacher here, and whether she succeeds or fails is going to say a lot to black students, to the whole community, in fact, about the place of black people here. If you don't stand behind her and support her, and she fails, it is going to be a huge setback. So I am wondering why you haven't done more to support her."

"Well, first of all, it isn't appropriate for me to discuss personnel matters with one of her colleagues..." he began.

"Monique knows I am here. I'm sure she would be okay with you giving me an explanation."

"Well, parents have legitimate concerns about her making spelling errors on the board."

I interrupted. "She *told* you that would happen when you interviewed her. If you were concerned about that, you should never have hired her in the first place. You know she's qualified for this job. You should tell the parents that."

"You know, Kevin," he said slowly and clearly, looking me right in the eyes, "If I were you, I would worry a lot more about doing a good job myself and keeping my job than about what happens to others." The threat was unmistakable. Monique's career at Moses Brown lasted exactly one year.

Brave though I might have been on some social issues at Moses Brown, I was much more timid about challenging the status quo on sexual orientation. I came out to my department chair (the assistant dean from Harvard Summer School who had led me to Moses Brown) pretty early on and, while personally supportive, he indicated that talking about this too loudly probably wasn't a very good idea. Aside from Monique and I, the only other gay teacher I could identify was the dean of students, who clearly had established a "don't ask, don't tell" policy with the school. I didn't dream about telling my students who, because of my "relationship" with Monique, didn't seem to suspect anyway. I had some people so thoroughly fooled that when Passover rolled around, the Latin teacher invited me to her Seder. I eagerly accepted the invitation, truly curious to participate in this ceremony for the first time (would they serve the blood of Christian children?), only to have my enthusiasm dampened when I arrived to find that I was being set up with the only other single person over the age of eight in the room, a lovely young Brown undergraduate. She was just as bemused by the transparency of the gig as I was, though, so we ended up having a good time after all.

The signs from the administration were pretty unequivocal on the issue of sexual orientation. I had a student named Will, a sweet, lonely kid who had problems relating to his peers, who often seemed to be a half step behind the lesson or conversation that was going on. The other kids saw this and nicknamed him "Veg," short for vegetable. Will latched on to me, as he too liked the Dead Kennedys and couldn't believe that a teacher owned one of their albums, hanging around my classroom to talk about music or anything at hand, but really just wanting to connect to somebody. I became his unofficial champion on the faculty and tried to intervene with the kids who ridiculed him. Every week we had an evening staff meeting, held in the expansive living room of the headmaster's house, during which there was a segment where we would discuss students who needed a little extra support. I brought up Will, talked about how I thought this nickname was feeding into his poor self-image, and urged my colleagues to intervene if they heard kids using it. In response, Mr. Forrest quipped, "Well, better a veg than a fruit," and everyone laughed. Whether they were laughing with him or at me, I'll never know.

As the year wore on, my self-confidence wore down. Having been raised on the importance of telling the truth ("Thou shalt not lie"), and having found my voice during my years at Harvard, I was dispirited and depressed by living a lie every day at Moses Brown. Every day I wasn't truthful with my students and colleagues was one in which I accepted on some level that there was something wrong with me that needed to be hidden. I see now that I put up with this not only because I was afraid of losing my job but also because I didn't feel entitled to better treatment. A lifetime of having been taught I was wrong and bad had penetrated in a deep way, and the fierceness I showed around issues of racism—an issue that society had validated was wrong—was not matched by a same fierceness on my own behalf, as I wasn't sure I deserved to be treated as equal to straight people. Maybe I wasn't the strong person I thought I was, I began to think. Maybe Harvard had been a fluke.

What galled the most was feeling like I had to stand by while ignorance and bigotry toward gay people ran rampant in the school. I may not have felt confident enough to think I deserved better treatment yet, but I certainly knew that bigotry was wrong and that I, as a teacher, had an obligation to do something about it. But I felt too paralyzed to actually say anything, fearing that would lead to the ultimate question—"Why do you care? Are you gay or something?"—that I did not want my students to ask. It would have been logical for the students to ask such a question: my straight colleagues were by and large entirely silent on the subject, so an intervention of any kind would have stood out like a flashing red light, demanding explanation. So I too was silent when kids called each other "fag," and every day I hated myself a little more for doing so.

So here I was, back where I always seemed to end up when in a school: powerless, ashamed, and wanting out. By now I was spending most weeknights (and every weekend) up in Cambridge with Bob, arising early enough to do the hour-long drive back to Rhode Island in the predawn winter gloom. I was eager to escape the stultifying atmosphere of Providence, where a trip to the grocery store or gas station on the claustrophobic East Side inevitably entailed running into one of your students. It didn't help that I was hired as a replacement teacher to fill the slot of someone who had taken a sabbatical, meaning I wasn't guaranteed a job for the next year. I was nevertheless stunned when the teacher on leave announced he was not returning and, instead of my being given his job, the school let me know that they would interview other candidates. The fact that my classes were going swimmingly, that I had had nothing but positive feedback from students and parents, that I was diligently coaching my sports (the junior varsity soccer team had yet to figure out that I had never played the sport; somehow we had a winning record), all seemed to matter not at all. I found myself biting my tongue even harder, trying to be the "good soldier" so I could keep my job, hating the compromise more and more every day. By the time I was informed that they did want me to stay after all (following a humiliating parade of interviewees for my position that my colleagues and students all witnessed traipsing through the school), I think I had passed the tipping point into a level of anger and resentment from which I would never recover, feelings enhanced by the fact that Monique, my one ally, did not have her contract renewed.

I began to count down the days until summer vacation, just as I had when I was a student, and was delighted when my first year of teaching ended and I was still in one piece. I had gotten a summer job teaching at Upward Bound, a federally funded summer enrichment program for high school students who were to be the first in their family to attend college. I was excited to work with a population with whom I had so much more in common than those who could afford the steep tuition at Moses Brown. The kids in this particular group were all from the North Shore of Massachusetts, where depressed, dying mill towns offered little in the way of academic or economic opportunity. Unlike the lily-white population of Moses Brown, they were a multicultural stew, a majority of whom were students of color, African American, West Indian, Cambodian—a “We Are the World” mix of nationalities. The one downside was that the job required being in residence at the University of Massachusetts in Amherst, a prospect that did not thrill me because it meant six weeks away from Bob.

At first the Upward Bound kids threw me a bit. Many didn't possess the basic skills in reading and writing that I had been able to take for granted among my Moses Brown students and I had to adjust my teaching style accordingly. But they were hungry and curious and eager to learn, and the subjects I was covering in my self-designed curriculum—African American history, the Holocaust—were all new to them, as they weren't part of the standard curriculum in the public schools they attended during the school year. They ate it up.

Living together 24/7 in the dorm, we also got to know each other in ways more profound than I had gotten to know my students at Moses Brown. I would run into kids in the gym, kids like Carvel, an athletic African American kid who was there every day. We often spotted each other on the bench press and had a friendly competition going as to who could bench press more. I became a real person to him, he told me, because I didn't “seem like a teacher.” And the students' stories astounded me. When given an assignment to write the history of their families, one Cambodian student told of her family's escape through the jungle to Thailand after the Khmer Rouge had killed most of her siblings. She dutifully read it aloud in class, in a tone so flat it was as if she were reciting from the phone book. The hair on the back of my neck was standing up by the end.

I couldn't help but contrast their openness with how I withheld information about my life. I began to think it was time for me to come out. Given the low pay of the Upward Bound program, my colleagues tended to be younger, more adventurous types than the faculty of Moses Brown, and they thought it would be good for the students for me to come out. Plus, it wasn't my regular job, so, if it went poorly, there would be fewer consequences than there would have been at Moses Brown. I discussed the idea with the program's director, who I thought was a closeted lesbian, a suspicion confirmed for me years later when one of my colleagues said she had run into her, and her girlfriend, at a Holly Near concert. She was not only supportive but also said she would come to my class to show that support. I took a deep breath and decided to go ahead.

Classes at Upward Bound were small, eight to ten kids, and my students were arrayed in their usual semicircle of desks the day I decided to break the news to them. We were about two-thirds of the way through the summer, so they knew me pretty well at that point. The program director had come and was sitting in the back of the class, to offer her support if necessary, but she often observed classes, so the kids didn't think anything of her presence. But my stomach was churning; I knew it was the big day.

It's funny, but I can no longer remember what lesson I used as the basis for my "coming-out class," or how I brought the subject up. Whatever it was, the students seemed to take it in stride, and an interesting and thoughtful discussion ensued. Kids asked me typical questions—"When did you know? Does your family know? What do they think? Do you ever worry about getting beaten up?"—all of which I tried to answer honestly. Deep into the discussion, Inez said that it must be hard for gay people in America, that she could identify with my situation because it was much like hers as a young Puerto Rican woman. Carvel (who wasn't always the most attentive of students) awoke from his daze at this point and said incredulously, "Gay? Who's gay?"

Inez reached over and smacked his arm, saying, "Carvel, you so stupid! Don't you pay no attention in class? Kevin told us he was gay about fifteen minutes ago!"

Carvel was filled with disbelief. No one as "normal" as me could possibly be gay as far as he was concerned, and he simply refused to believe me. "You're just saying this to see how we react," he scoffed. "This is just another one of those weird things you do all the time in class."

Deciding to leave his critique of my teaching style aside for the moment, I replied, "No, Carvel, really, I'm gay."

"Oh yeah? Prove it then."

Nonplussed, I wasn't sure at this point how I was supposed to "prove it." The more obvious methods would have been inappropriate in a classroom, so I was momentarily at a loss. But then I reached into my wallet and took out a picture of Bob and me. "Look at this picture, Carvel. This is me and my boyfriend."

Carvel took the snapshot, glanced at it, and handed it back to me. "Naaah. This could just be a friend of yours. You're still just trying to see how we react."

Okay, now what, I thought. I turned to the program director and said plaintively, "Susan, I'm gay, aren't I? Tell them."

"Yes, Carvel, Kevin is gay," Susan, replied. "I came to class today because I knew he was going to tell you all this and I wanted to show that I support his decision."

Carvel remained unconvinced. "Naaah, y'all set this up before class, and he told you to say that, just to see how we'd react."

By now, Inez had had it. She reached over and smacked Carvel's arm harder this time. "What's your problem? The man said he was gay, so he's *gay*. Why you so stupid?"

Carvel snapped back at her. "He *can't* be gay. He don't walk funny." With that, his final answer, Carvel leaned back, folded his hands behind his head, and smiled, convinced he had incontrovertible proof that I was indeed straight.

Aside from Carvel, the students pretty much took the news at face value, although with their own interesting interpretations of it. My colleague Jules knew of my plans to come out and so was eager to talk with students when they returned to the dorm after class. She was particularly close to a Vietnamese girl named Thavra, whose English language skills were fairly limited. When Thavra got back to the dorm, Jules asked her, "So, Thavra, I hear Kevin had some interesting things to say in class today."

"Oh yes, very interesting," Thavra replied.

"What did you think? Do you have any questions about it?"

"Oh yes. Is Kevin going to have a baby?"

Surprised by this line of questioning, Jules launched into a lengthy explanation of how difficult it was for gay people to adopt children and that I probably wasn't going to have a baby as a result. Thavra looked confused.

"But he has two!"

"Two what, Thavra?"

"He has both!"

Now totally confused, Jules replied, "Both what, Thavra?"

"He has both parts! Can't he make his own baby?"

Suddenly it dawned on Jules. "Thavra, what do you think 'gay' means?"

"It means you have both parts—man and woman!" Thavra replied.

Thavra apparently thought it was pretty cool that her teacher was a hermaphrodite and only wanted to know if I could impregnate myself.

The rest of the summer passed, and it didn't seem to make a big difference to the Upward Bound kids that I was gay. But their reaction made a big difference to me. I realized that the problem wasn't the students—it was the adults. Adults, like those running Moses Brown at the time, often used students as a foil to demand that gay teachers stay in the closet, with their bogus claim that discussing sexual orientation is "inappropriate," all the while encouraging straight teachers to come out (their spouses were even listed alongside their names in the faculty directory). Discussion of *hetero*sexual orientation was fine—it was *homo*sexual orientation that was taboo. The confines of the closet began to chafe more than ever, and I returned to Moses Brown in the fall ever more frustrated at the double standard of the school, one where gay teachers were expected to lie and hide while chipping in to the faculty pool to buy wedding and baby gifts for our straight colleagues.

As the leaves fell, so did my confidence. The first semester progressed and the determination I felt at the end of the summer's Upward Bound program seemed as distant as the hot and humid days when I felt it. Moses Brown was still Moses Brown, and my sense that I could do something to change its culture faltered. I reverted to the same silent, closeted self I had been in my first year, except with the knowledge that I didn't have to be—making the taste of my sellout all the more bitter in my mouth.

The moment when I decided that I could no longer stay at Moses Brown came that fall. As a second-year teacher I was now eligible to be selected as an advisor by students and I became one of the most sought-after among the faculty. I had a full load of advisees, and having a chance to mentor these young people became my favorite part of the job. They often just wanted someone to talk to, which was a feeling that I certainly could relate to from my own school years. I loved being that sympathetic ear.

My favorite advisee was a kid named Jack. Yes, it's true, teachers do have favorites, which is inevitable—what they shouldn't do is *play* favorites, which I strove not to do. But any honest teacher will tell you that it's a kick when some kid idolizes you, and Jack idolized me. The fact that he was a soccer star, a center of the school's social set, one of the "cool kids," was ironic to me—these were the kids that ignored me when I was a student just a short time ago, and now here was one who hung on my every word. I learned through Jack that cool kids are people, too. When I was a student, I thought these kids had it made, but I learned through my many chats with Jack that they often had their own insecurities and problems that could be no less daunting than my own had been. Jack came from a large Portuguese family and his highly traditional, workaholic parents didn't have much time for (or much in common with) their prep-school-educated son. Jack was trying to figure out who he was, how he fit into the world, and I gave him attention and provided him with a role model as he tried to make his way in a world different from that from which he came. I got it: I had made the same journey.

The pivotal moment came that fall of 1986, when I was coaching junior varsity soccer. Jack was on the varsity soccer team, and had brought some of his buddies over to cheer on the junior varsity when his game was over. Caught up in the game, I didn't at first notice that a heated argument was brewing behind me among the varsity players, who must have thought they were out of my earshot. But soon I tuned in and, to my utter horror, realized they were arguing over whether or not I was gay. Jack was enraged at his teammates for suggesting such a heinous thing and finally shouted at them, "He can't be gay: he's too *cool* to be gay."

So there it was: they knew. I now know that students always know; teachers live in a glass closet at best, where students—especially today's students, infinitely more savvy than I was on issues of sexual orientation at their age—can see in quite clearly, even if you never poke your head out. By staying silent, I hadn't fooled them into thinking I was straight: I had simply confirmed that this was indeed something too shameful to discuss. Tragically, the students I had managed to convince the most thoroughly were the ones who looked up to me, like Jack. I had left Jack with an untenable choice: either his mentor was indeed someone worthy of being looked up to (and thus could not be gay) or he was gay (and thus someone who would not be worthy of being looked up to). Jack was yelling at his peers because he *admired* me and couldn't stand to see me "slandered" in this way. My silence had confirmed the most horrible lie of all: no one you admired could be gay.

From that day on, it was only a matter of time until I left Moses Brown. By spring I had found another job at a place called Concord Academy through a teacher I had met at a new teachers' conference. It was known to be a more liberal school and it was close to Boston, so I wouldn't have the two-hour daily commute. Having been shut out for two years, I was now getting out of Moses Brown.

Not that there weren't moments when I might have changed how the story ended. One came during a Quaker Meeting in the spring of 1987. For those unfamiliar with Quaker Meeting procedures, the basic idea is that the congregation meditates in silence on a theme and, if compelled by the spirit to speak, anyone can stand up and do so. Although few of the students who attended Moses Brown were Quakers, the school still clung to this tradition, holding school-wide meetings quarterly. The freshman class president, Adam, came to me that spring. The school's religion teacher had suggested that each class have its own meeting, as folks seemed reluctant to speak up when the whole school gathered, and that each class should pick someone they admired to start the meeting off with a short speech about something personal to get people thinking. Because I took them seriously and treated them with respect, the freshmen had adopted me as something of their class hero, and they wanted me to start their meeting.

I was touched and honored—and a little bit scared. It had been tough enough to keep silent about my sexual orientation already. But now I was being asked to get up and say something personally meaningful, and I couldn't really see how I could be authentic and honest if I didn't talk about this, the moral dilemma—whether to tell the truth or lie—that vexed my every day at Moses Brown. To be given this opportunity on a silver platter to educate, and to turn away, seemed to me to be the ultimate moral failure.

(Seventeen years later, I learned exactly how much of a golden opportunity this was. A former student, Bruce, tracked me down in New York. Bruce had just come out himself and wanted me to know that my presence at Moses Brown had made a big difference to him. He told me it had been widely known in the freshman class that I was gay and that I was leaving because the school couldn't accept that. The freshmen were devastated and had hoped—by inviting me to speak—that they could show me how much they liked me and that maybe I would change my mind. Who knows: perhaps some of them were even thinking I'd use this as the forum to come out. It was indeed a test.)

I failed the moral test the freshman class gave me.

I wasn't sure what I was going to say when I stood up that morning in the freshman-class Quaker Meeting. I was still pondering whether or not to tell my truth. But, as I looked out on those eager faces, my nerve failed, and I didn't. I have no clear memory of what I said—because I didn't say what needed to be said, so whatever I said had no real meaning. I do remember telling the freshmen how much the invitation meant to me, how much I cared about them and how much I would miss them. But I don't remember much else. Two decades later, I'm ashamed of myself. In all honesty, I was ashamed of myself then. Teachers are supposed to model integrity for their students and, on that day in the spring of 1987, I didn't meet that standard. I let my fears override what I knew was right and—by not telling them what they already knew to be true—I taught my students it was okay to lie. I was a bad teacher.

I'd have one last chance to tell the truth near the end of the school year. Having never dealt with gay issues in my classes during my two years at Moses Brown, I decided in my final weeks to rectify that. We wound up the year in my U.S. history class by studying recent events, such as the civil-rights movement. I decided to show the Academy Award–winning documentary *The Times of Harvey Milk*, which told the story of the election and assassination of an openly gay city councilman in San Francisco in 1978, and use the gay rights movement as an example of the movements that had changed America in the sixties and seventies. The students were clearly moved by what they saw on the screen. When it ended, I shut off the VCR and began discussion with a question that I hoped would get them to put this subject within the context of the other movements we'd studied.

"Okay, who can tell me why we'd watch this film as part of a class on modern American history?"

"Because you're gay," Paige, a junior girl, mumbled in the back of the room.

Everyone had heard Paige and a hush fell in the room. I had a decision to make. Would I pretend I hadn't heard Paige or would I address what she said? I looked at the class: never before had all eyes been fixed on me with this kind of intensity. I decided not to ignore her question.

"Paige, did you want to ask me something?"

Looking back, I'm sure Paige thought I was angry. But I was dying—absolutely dying—for her to ask me the Question. Then my decision would be easy: I didn't raise the issue—I was just answering a student's question.

But, fearing my reaction, Paige didn't ask.

"No."

"No, really, Paige, it's okay. You can ask."

"I didn't want to ask anything," she replied.

I guess I could have forged ahead anyway, but now that the pretext that I was simply responding to a student's question had been removed, I didn't. So I just went on with the discussion.

A couple of weeks later, the class of 1987 graduated and my days at Moses Brown ended, without my ever having been asked or having answered the Question. For two years I had lied, letting my students and myself down in the process. I vowed I would never do it again.

CHAPTER 9

Out for Good

Concord Academy looks like it stepped out of someone's fantasy of what a New England boarding school should look like. Founded in 1924, the school grew slowly, buying up the eighteenth- and nineteenth-century white clapboard mansions that line Main Street in the heart of the town where America was birthed by the minutemen and turning them into dorms and classrooms. The buildings that the school itself constructed were carefully calibrated to match this aesthetic, with the school having even purchased, dismantled, and reassembled on its campus a nineteenth-century New Hampshire church to add to the feeling of Yankee authenticity. Behind the campus a small river flowed down to the Old North Bridge, where the minutemen had made their fateful stand against the British on that historic morning in April 1775; up the road were the homes of Thoreau, Emerson, Alcott, the great thinkers and writers of nineteenth-century America. The place was steeped in history and I—ever the history buff—fell in love at first sight.

The school's history mirrored the town of Concord's reputation for nurturing out-of-the-box thinking. Started as an all-girls school, Concord Academy was known for its freewheeling ways and its outstanding arts program. The school had gone coed in the seventies, and when I arrived even had a senior house where boys and girls lived together—hardly standard operating procedure for a boarding school. Caroline Kennedy was an alumna, proving the school's liberal credentials. It seemed like the right place for me.

In August 1987, I did something that unintentionally would force the Question early in my career at Concord. Bob and I had gone to Provincetown for a couple of days in mid-August. Having been together two years (and having had a few too many one evening, I think), we impulsively decided to go into a jewelry store and buy wedding bands that we would wear as a sign of our commitment. Purchases in hand, we made our way onto a moonlit beach and exchanged them. Having grown up believing I'd never find love, I felt like I'd hit the jackpot.

But this small piece of metal would prove just as problematic for me at Concord Academy as my earring had at Moses Brown. A few weeks later the fall term commenced and I had my first Concord Academy classes. Students are always curious about their new teacher—especially if he's new to the school—so they naturally began to ask me questions. Spying my ring, one innocently asked, "Are you married?"

I froze. Why I hadn't anticipated this question, I don't know, but I hadn't. I stared back at her for what was probably only a few seconds, but the silence felt like it was expanding to fill an eternity. Mind racing, I decided to fall back on the safest (and from a legal point of view the most accurate) answer.

"No."

She was not to be put off so easily. Undeterred, she shot back, "Then why are you wearing a wedding ring?" pitching me another curveball for which I had not done batting practice.

I stammered, "Well, uh, I'm in a relationship."

"Oh," she replied. And the interrogation ended.

I was rattled and disappointed with myself. Here it was, barely a week into the new school year and the Question, the one I had prayed for someone at Moses Brown to ask, was put out there and I had dodged it.

I decided to seek the advice of some of my colleagues about what I should do, should the Question be asked again. Those I worked with most immediately in the history department already knew I was gay—I had been up-front from the beginning (once safely hired, that is)—so I began with them. My department chair, who would end up teaching at Concord Academy for more than thirty years, seemed mystified as to why the issue bothered me, thinking I had answered the Question in the only appropriate way and that my sexual orientation was something that should not be disclosed to students (he disclosed his own *hetero*sexual orientation with a messy public divorce that his children suffered through while enrolled at the school, but he thought that was appropriate, I guess). A couple of older, closeted teachers whom I sought out reacted with unmitigated horror to the idea that I would have answered the Question more directly. *Homo*sexual orientation, it seemed, was just out of bounds.

Everyone had been clear about one thing, though: whatever I did, Jim had better approve. Jim was the school's headmaster. Jim was charismatic, driven, and dedicated to making Concord Academy the best school it could be. He spoke often of the importance of diversity, served on the board of A Better Chance, a scholarship program that brought low-income youth of color to boarding schools, and seemed the polar opposite of Mr. Forrest, my old headmaster at Moses Brown. He had a severe stutter, a handicap he struggled with publicly and unapologetically, never letting it stand in his way. I was hopeful that he would "get it," and his personal and political example seemed to indicate he would. (He was also, I would learn, extremely controlling, with a leadership style that would more and more remind me of Richard Nixon as the years wore on. But I didn't know that yet.)

I made an appointment with Jim, and went in and explained my dilemma. I asked him how he thought I should answer the Question if it got asked again.

His reply was swift. "Why don't you just tell them the ring is a gift from someone you love?"

My high expectations came crashing down. I spluttered back, "Jim, do you call your wedding ring a 'gift from someone you love'?"

Jim laughed. "Of course not!"

"Then why should I?"

I don't remember much of the brief remainder of our meeting, but I did learn an important lesson: Jim didn't quite get it.

In October, Bob and I set off for Washington to join several hundred thousand of our closest friends in the second national march for equal rights for gay people. It's trite to say that the experience transformed me, but it did. A half million people turned Washington into an all-gay city that weekend, kissing on the subway, holding hands on the street, defiantly and jubilantly enjoying a freedom they were rarely afforded back home in Alabama and Montana and Utah and Concord, Massachusetts. When the massive throng gathered on Sunday for the march, stretching as far as the eye could see, some contingents waited for hours before even stepping off. The high was indescribable: here we were, marching hundreds of thousands strong past the symbols of our nation. We chanted "Shame! Shame! Shame!" at the White House, a building from which we had gotten only silence and inaction as over forty thousand Americans, mainly from our community, were killed by AIDS by the end of 1987. We chanted "Shame! Shame! Shame!" at the Supreme Court, which had ruled just the year before in *Bowers v. Hardwick* that laws criminalizing same-sex sexual behavior were constitutional. In this case, Justice Byron White memorably wrote in the majority opinion that claims of gay activists were "facetious," and Chief Justice Warren Burger stated in a concurring opinion that to invalidate sodomy laws would be to "cast aside a millennia of moral teaching" that was "firmly rooted in Judeo-Christian moral and ethical standards." (Huh? I thought we had separation of church and state... gotta revise my lesson plans when I get back to Concord.) We may have still been marginalized and vulnerable to being fired from our jobs in forty-nine states (good old Wisconsin being the only one with a state anti-discrimination law at that point), but on this October afternoon we were united in the knowledge that we could have power, a far greater power than we had ever understood before, if we only stood together and fought back. It gave me a new sense of confidence, and I returned to Concord ever more determined to live a life of honesty.

But the Question never got asked again.

I grew increasingly frustrated at the lack of opportunities to be honest with my students. It's curious how narrowly I defined what those opportunities might be. It never occurred to me that I could have answered a typical student question, say, "What did you do this weekend?" with a casual, "Oh, my boyfriend, Robert, and I went to the movies," the same way my straight colleagues would have said, "Oh, my girlfriend, Roberta, and I went to the movies." That level of privilege, the privilege to talk about your life as if doing so was normal and not a controversial political statement, was reserved for straight people. If directly asked, I thought, I could answer, but it would be inappropriate to disclose my sexual orientation otherwise. Having lived as a second-class citizen my entire life, I didn't yet feel I could act like a first-class one.

Aside from the issue of sexual orientation, however, Concord Academy was a dream teaching job. The students were incredibly smart, my colleagues truly intellectuals (I was something of an oddity as I had no graduate degree; MAs were expected, and PhDs were routine), and the atmosphere was one that encouraged and valued innovation. But for me, the best part of the job, as always, was being able to be an important figure in so many kids' lives. Fifty percent of the students were boarders, often living thousands of miles from home, so Concord expected its faculty to take a strong interest in their students outside of the classroom as well as within it. I collected a set of quirky, brilliant, and offbeat kids as my favorites, but I also became a favorite of the school's small collection of jocks. Still a regular habitué of the gym, I was one of the relatively few athletic male faculty in what was once an all-girls school—girls were still the majority—where athletics weren't highly valued. The school's biggest jock, a senior lacrosse player named Alex, had chosen me to be his faculty advisor. Alex had gotten special permission to take my Latin American history elective, which was reserved for sophomores, due to a special interest in the topic, and he stood out like a sore thumb in the class. Broad-shouldered and movie-star handsome, he could have easily passed for twenty-five and looked a decade older than the other students. I liked him from the first day, when I asked each kid to introduce himself or herself and tell the class something unusual about themselves, and Alex replied he had a pet boa constrictor, which made me laugh out loud.

Soon many of his peers were dropping by my office and I was bemused to be the favorite teacher of Concord's (very small) circle of jocks. One kid who especially tugged at my heartstrings was a sophomore named Max. Max's parents were going through a difficult divorce and he had a lot on his plate for a sixteen-year-old. Max started off talking about the Red Sox and the Patriots (both depressing-enough subjects in the late eighties) but ended up talking about how confused and angry he was by what was happening to his family, things he didn't seem to have anyone else to talk with about. Max was the kid with the proverbial heart of gold. He had forged a special bond with the one wheelchair-bound student at Concord, Amy, whose life was cursed by the ever-malfunctioning elevators on our aged campus. When the elevators were down, Max would often just carry Amy up the stairs and then carry her scooter up so she could get to class. Once he discovered that she'd never been on a canoe ride, he dragooned me into helping him get

Amy down to the river that ran behind the school and into a canoe so we could paddle her down to the Old North Bridge. I've never before or since seen a kid as happy as Amy was that day, nor have I been as proud of a student as I was of Max.

I loved going to work every day. Loving my job had a downside, though. The more I loved Concord, the less I wanted to put my job at risk by taking a stand over the issue of sexual orientation. Even more frightening was putting my relationship with my students at risk by so doing. I felt like the esteem in which I was held was built atop a kind of psychic fault, and that the earthquake of coming out would cause this esteem to come tumbling down. Like Sally Field, I desperately wanted everyone to like me, really like me, and my heart sank at the prospect of going from faculty favorite to pariah. The fact that I was the favorite of so many of the jocks, the same kids who had tormented me when I was in high school, made me even more sure that this would be my fate. I had nightmares that I would find my office or my blackboard or my car scrawled with "FAGGOT." I'd like to report I was brave and resolute, but I'd be lying. So the school year began to slip by, and I was no more out at Concord than I had been at Moses Brown.

But that spring, a version of the Question was finally asked and I finally answered honestly. One weekend I was at the school preparing for my classes, running photocopies of primary documents I was planning to use. I was in the basement of the darkened administration building, the only person around, so I was startled when a group of four senior boarding girls, most of whom I had taught in a fall elective, saw me in the copy room and dropped in. They had been a joy to teach, the kind of brilliant, outspoken girls Concord had been producing for decades. I loved their irreverence, sense of humor, and intelligence. Annabeth, their de facto leader, was a special favorite, a free-spirited student from Vermont, the rich kid who could afford to wear old clothes, old clothes that tried and failed to hide the fact that she was a blonde beauty who looked like she had stepped directly off the canvas of a Botticelli painting. They were surprised to see me on the campus on the weekend, as they knew I did not live in one of the dorms, and asked why I was there. I replied that I was just getting caught up on some prep work. One of them then asked, "Why don't you live in the dorm, anyway? Everybody loves you, and you'd be a great house parent."

I took a breath.

"I don't think the school would want me as a house parent."

They scoffed. "You're kidding, right? They're always desperate for house parents and you'd be great. Why wouldn't they want you?"

It was time to tell the truth. "Well, I'm gay, and I have a partner, and I don't think the school would want a gay couple running a dorm."

They were outraged. "The school won't let you live in a dorm because you're gay?!"

I backed off a bit. "I didn't say that. I've never really asked, so I can't say for sure. I just don't think they would."

Annabeth spoke up. "This makes me so mad. I'm going to go to Jim and tell him they should ask you and your partner to be house parents. My little brother and little sister are coming here next year and I would love for you to be their house parent."

Now I was panicked. "No, no, no, no, please don't do that. I'm not looking to pick a fight over this. Please don't do that."

"Well, if you don't want us to, we won't, but it still makes us mad," another one chimed in.

Then the conversation veered off into more typical adolescent-girl territory. "So, what's your partner's name? How long have you been together? How did you meet? What does he do? Is he cute?" I answered them all patiently, showed them Bob's picture (they all agreed he *was* cute), and at last had the kind of conversation with my students that my straight colleagues routinely had with theirs. Curiosity satisfied, soon the quartet was merrily off to its next destination.

So this is it, I thought. The cat's out of the bag. Everybody will know soon.

Coming in Monday, I expected that other students would ask the Question, as I was sure the rumor would have spread far and wide over the weekend. But they didn't. Days went by and it was radio silence on the subject, as before. Did they all know my secret and not care? Did they all know and were so horrified that they dared not speak its name? Did the girls not tell anyone else? What the hell was going on here? I was baffled. I didn't know what to do. My sexual orientation had fallen in the forest and it hadn't made a sound, it seemed. But an unexpected challenge would soon present itself in my office.

Robertson was one of the kids who ended up in my office on a number of occasions. He was bright and personable, a quirky kid who loved drama and literature and the Smiths (once again, my music tastes came in handy). He was also underachieving and prone to frequent absences. I didn't get it. But I liked him, and tried to let him know I cared. On this spring day, Robertson showed up at my office door in the tow of Christine, one of my official advisees. "Robertson needs to talk with you," Christine said, and practically shoved the young man into my office before closing the door behind her.

A brief, awkward silence ensued. "Have a seat, Robertson." Robertson did so. "You had something you wanted to talk with me about?"

"Well, actually, I'm here because Chris wanted me to come talk to you."

"Okay. Do *you* want to talk to me?"

"I do." A pause. "I met somebody..." His voice faltered. Another pause. "It's hard to talk about."

We stared at each other intently, and I suddenly knew what this was about.

"Let's start with the basics, then. What's his name?"

Robertson's eyes widened. "How did you know?"

After a lifetime of hiding myself, I thought, I know the signs. "Lucky guess," I replied. "So, who is he? Is he another student, or did you meet him somewhere else? And what's the problem? It's okay to be gay, you know."

Robertson soon told me his tale, about someone he'd met in Boston, how he thought he loved him, and how heartbroken he was that his calls never got returned. I suppressed a smile at his naiveté (this won't be the last time that happens, kid) and tried to look sympathetic about his lost true love—who, I didn't have the heart to tell him, had probably forgotten Robertson's name by now. Unburdened and relieved, he stood to go.

"Robertson, can I ask you a question before you go?"

"Sure."

"Why'd you come to me with this story?"

He looked at me quizzically. "Uh, because you're gay?"

I was taken aback by his matter-of-fact tone. "How did you know? Did the seniors tell you?"

"What seniors?"

"The senior girls."

"What senior girls?"

I paused. "No one told you I was gay?"

"No. It was pretty easy to figure out. You'd have to be kind of stupid not to have figured it out by now."

And with that, he was off.

Once again, I discovered that I was hiding inside a glass closet. I replayed my conversation with the girls now and was struck by the fact that they didn't react with any surprise at all to my announcement I was gay. Like Robertson, like Christine, like everybody else(?), they had already figured it out. I was the one who had instituted the "don't ask, don't tell" policy. They were apparently fine with my being gay and ready to talk about it. I was the one who had a problem.

Enough of this, I thought. With the school year winding down,

I decided to again use *The Times of Harvey Milk* as part of my lesson on the modern civil-rights movements in my junior-year U.S. history class. Once again, the film moved the students, which was visible when it finished and I turned up the lights for discussion. But this year, the discussion was going to be different.

"Before we start," I said, "There's something you should know about me that I believe many of you have already figured out. I want you to know this before we start the discussion, because I want you to be able to say what you think and not feel like you have to tiptoe around the subject because I have: I'm gay."

The reaction was mixed. Many of the students, mainly girls, looked on nonchalantly, like, "Yeah, so what? Tell me something I don't know." A couple of the jock boys, most especially Tony, a working-class Italian American kid who was one of those closest to me in the class, looked visibly stunned. "I know some of you may be surprised, and I want any of you who have a question to feel like you can ask it." Silence ensued. "Well, if there are no questions, let's get on with the discussion."

The discussion went just fine.

Graduation was only a few days away, and there were two kids who were leaving the school that I felt I had to come clean with before they left. One was my senior advisee Alex. In our final meeting, sitting at one of the tables in the dining hall, I broached the subject.

"Alex, I have really enjoyed working with you. But there is something I wanted you to know about me, as I feel like I haven't been totally honest with you this year. I'm gay."

He was unfazed. "Yeah, I know," he replied. "I figured that out a long time ago."

Here I was nonplussed. The school's biggest jock knew I was gay, had picked me as his advisor, and didn't seem to care?

"And it didn't make any difference to you?"

"Not really. Well, there was one thing..." he paused.

"It's okay. You can tell me."

"I never thought I could talk to you about problems I had with my girlfriend. I didn't know if you'd understand."

I couldn't help laughing out loud. "Well, Alex, I bet I would have. Relationships are relationships, and they all have the same kinds of issues whether you're straight or gay. But, if that was my only shortcoming, I guess I did an okay job."

"Yeah, Kevin," Alex smiled. "You did."

The other kid was Max, who was not being allowed to return to the school for his junior year. I had pleaded his case in many a faculty meeting, to no avail. Thinking back on our canoe trip with Amy, I thought if we couldn't make room for a kid like Max, that said more about us as a school than it did about him. But the decision was made and Max was out. He was taking it hard—it was yet another rejection just when he was feeling let down by his parents—so on one of the last days of the school year, a warm May afternoon when the rest of students were getting their yearbooks signed and saying goodbye and "see you next year," I took him for a walk around the campus. We ended up sitting down beneath a huge tree, a centuries-old beauty whose shade covered a large chunk of the yard in front of my classroom building.

"Max, I know this is a hard time for you. But I want you to know that you're one of the best kids I have ever had the privilege to work with, and that I know you're going to be okay. Right now, not coming back to Concord seems like a big deal, but someday it will just be an old memory. I hated high school myself, and I have found that life just gets better as you get older. Sometimes you just have to hang on and wait for this part to be over."

"You had a hard time in high school? You seem like you could handle anything."

I laughed. "Trust me, Max, high school sucked for me. But I am fine now and you'll be fine too, and that's what I want you to remember on those days when you feel down."

"Why did you have such a hard time in high school?"

Here goes, I thought. "A lot of reasons. My dad had died, my family didn't have a lot of money, and we moved around a lot. In fact, I went to five different high schools."

Max whistled. "Five? You're kidding?"

"Yeah, five, in three different states, so I know you can survive leaving one and going to another. Sometimes the change is even good for you. It was for me." I paused. "And I had a hard time for another reason. I'm gay, and I felt really out of place and lonely all the way through high school as a result." I paused to gauge his reaction. "Does it surprise you or upset you to learn that about me?"

"Uh, no, I already knew, so I am not surprised or upset. It was part of why I liked you. It made me think of you as more of a real person. I figured you must be pretty strong if you could handle something like that, and it impressed me."

Once again, the glass closet. "Well, Max, that means a lot to me. But I want you to remember you're really strong, too, that you can handle anything that comes your way."

"Thanks, Kevin. I don't think I would have made it through the year without you."

As my first year at Concord ended, I had to face a basic question: who or what was keeping me in the closet? I realized it was me and my own fears. Not that I didn't face the very real threat of job loss, but my deepest fears sprang from my own childhood, from the years when I was alone and isolated and friendless. I had projected onto my students those fears, sure that they would turn on me as my peers had when I was their age, and I was choosing to protect myself by not dealing with the issue at all. I had been so deeply scarred by my own childhood, so thoroughly trained that I was not worthy, that I couldn't envision a world in which I would be accepted for who I was. In the end, I was the one who had the biggest problem with gay people—beginning with myself.

Over the summer I spent a great deal of time reflecting on my first year at Concord and concluded it was time to be more forthright. The senior girls, Robertson, Alex, Max, the U.S. history class, had taught me that I was the one holding myself back, and that it was time to get over myself and do the right thing. If my schools and my teachers had failed me, I was now going to make up for it by making sure that my school and I did not fail the next generation. If no one else was going to step up, it was time for me to do so.

I didn't realize at first that I had chosen a collision course with the school's headmaster, Jim. Jim's ambitions for Concord were what drove him, and anything that threatened those ambitions was an obstacle he was determined to surmount. Once a top-tier all-girls school, Concord had slipped in the prep-school rankings once it went coed, while its formerly all-male counterparts had risen. (It's okay for girls to aspire to be like boys and to choose their schools, but for boys to go to a place identified with girls is suspect.) Concord had a largely female alumni base that was not as wealthy as those of the formerly all-boys schools and a feminine image that scared away many boys; this made fundraising and recruitment that much harder, causing the school to find it difficult to compete with the other top-tier schools. Jim was determined to raise the school's standing and had invested in athletics and other "boy" activities to change the school's image. Steadily the school's fundraising and admissions were improving; Jim's approach seemed to be working.

The first clue that my plans did not jibe with his came that summer, when *Independent School* magazine asked me to write an article about being a gay teacher. Having gotten the message, "Don't do anything without Jim's approval," I of course decided to tell him about this and showed him a draft of my piece to get his feedback. Jim's only reaction was, "They're going to change the names of the schools, right?" Looking back, I realize now that the content was of no interest to him: "protecting" Concord's reputation was his primary concern.

More ominous signs came later in the summer, after I sent a letter to Jim asking that Concord revise its nondiscrimination clause to include the category sexual orientation. I had first shown it to a number of colleagues, mainly ones I perceived to be sympathetic, but the vast majority were remarkably unenthusiastic in their response to the idea. I was mystified: since we talked so much about diversity, it seemed only logical to me that we would include sexual orientation as a protected class in our policies. I ignored these red flags and sent the letter anyway. Weeks went by and no letter came back from Jim. While the silence was somewhat unsettling to me, I thought this would be an easy yes, so I chalked it up to the summer break, when responses tend to be slower. Surely, I thought, this would all fall into place when school started in September.

Just before school reopened, I got a very noncommittal letter from Jim, saying this was a board decision that could not be taken up before their next meeting, which would be in October. This seemed like a reasonable enough response. Right after school started, I made an appointment with Jim to discuss my letter, thinking I might help him prepare for the meeting. He began by explaining, "Well, Kevin, as you know, Concord Academy does not discriminate based on sexual orientation. We've always had gay faculty here and it has never been an issue for the school."

I was relieved. "Great. Then you won't have any problem putting the policy in writing, right?" I replied.

"It's not quite that easy."

Here I got confused. If the school didn't discriminate, why wouldn't it just say that? "Seems easy to me."

Jim visibly bristled. "Well, it isn't. I need to talk with the board and..."

Yadda yadda yadda was all I heard. "Okay, I get that. So, when are you going to talk to the board? October?"

Jim virtually exploded. "You know, Kevin, there are a lot more important issues than this that I need to focus on. Every minute I spend on stuff like this takes me away from the important things I need to do, like fundraising. I'll deal with this when I deal with this."

His vehemence pinned my ears back and his rationale baffled me. Fundraising is more important than treating members of our school fairly and equally? I decided to leave that for now, but I should have had a clue that this was not the right time to pursue the next subject.

The school day at Concord started with a fifteen-minute talk in the school's chapel, which was in many ways the heart and soul of this secular school. "Chapel," the name given to the talks delivered there, was indeed a sacred time, a privilege reserved for seniors or faculty members who signed up to deliver a message of their choosing. It was the central ritual of school life. I had signed up to do one on October 11, 1988, the anniversary of the march on Washington and the first-ever National Coming Out Day.

When I told Jim of my plans, consternation fairly radiated off his body. "I'm not so sure this is a good idea, Kevin."

"Why not?"

"Well, heterosexual faculty don't give chapels about their sexual orientation, and I am not sure it would be appropriate for gay faculty to do so, either."

Now I was indignant. "Jim, heterosexual people don't *have* to give chapels about their sexual orientation. They talk about it all the time as a natural course of events. I mean, you talk about your wife and kids almost every time you speak. Why should I be expected to keep my mouth shut?"

"Kevin, I am not sure this is the right time for such a talk. What I'd like to ask you to do is postpone it while you and I work things out."

What do we have to work out? I wondered. This was going worse than I thought. I tried to explain that I had chosen October 11 for a reason, because of the anniversary of the march and National Coming Out Day, and that a delay would defeat the purpose. But Jim wouldn't budge. Discouraged, but still believing Jim was acting in good faith, I agreed to postpone and left his office, dropping a note off with the chapel coordinator that October 11 was now a free date.

Having bought the "we're committed to diversity" talk hook, line, and sinker, I was thrown by this exchange. My self-assurance wavered as weeks went by and Jim made no move to "work things out." I approached him again in October, only to be rebuffed again with the "this isn't the right time" remark. I began to have my doubts if the right time would ever arrive.

As the fall wore on, Robertson continued to drop by my office to chat, often updating me on his latest "adventures." Sometimes these startled me, and I began to underline the importance of safe sex to him. One day he snapped back, "Why should I use a condom? My life isn't worth saving, anyway."

Why, indeed? Hadn't I felt that way at his age? Weren't all young gay people taught that their lives were literally "worth less" than those of straight people? Robertson's question took me back to ten years before, when my own sense of despair was overwhelming, and forced me to confront the question: What are you going to do about it?

Later that day, I sat at a faculty lunch table with some of the younger faculty. I talked about my conversation with Robertson and how ashamed I was of my failure to do more to make sure that his generation had it better than mine did. I talked about my quandary over my chapel: clearly Jim was never going to give it a green light; did I dare cross him by doing it anyway? I was stopped in midsentence by Jefferson, a middle-aged English teacher who was seated a little farther away but still within hearing distance.

"You have to do the chapel, Kevin."

We all turned, a bit surprised. I mean, Jefferson was okay, but this was a bit startling to hear from one of the old guard.

"Wow, Jefferson," I replied, "I never saw you as a big advocate for gay rights before."

Jefferson's response was swift and unforgettable. "This has nothing to do with gay rights. But it has everything to do with your integrity. If you don't do this chapel, you'll never be able to look yourself in the mirror again."

There was nothing more to be said. I found the chapel coordinator and signed up for the next available date: November 10, 1988.

I found Jim later that day while walking across the campus. I explained to him that I was doing the chapel on November 10, that I had to do what I had to do, and that I understood that he would have to do whatever it was he thought he'd have to do as a result. He neither endorsed nor opposed my decision. "Everybody has First Amendment rights," he muttered before stalking off.

Jim tried one last strategy to get me to back off. He sent Julian, one of the old guard, a longtime and highly respected teacher, to talk with me. Julian was also gay, a screaming queen frankly, whose flamboyance put Liberace and Paul Lynde to shame and made Richard Simmons seem like Arnold Schwarzenegger. Julian had made the compromise that seemed to be the only possible one for teachers of his generation: talk about it with your friends at the opera but never, ever with the kids, and you can keep your job. He was "concerned" by what Jim had told him. He counseled me that Concord was a fine place to be gay, that no one had any issues with it, but that my chapel was going to upset the applecart and would jeopardize that acceptance. He said I seemed to be "using" the kids to push "my agenda," which was never appropriate for a teacher to do. I was filled with sadness for Julian, at his being forced to play this Uncle Tom role, but I also felt tremendous anger that the people who were supposed to be my role models were so craven in the face of their oppression. I thanked him for his consideration for my well-being, but told him my mind was made up. We did not speak again for the remainder of my time at Concord.

When I sat down to write my chapel, it wasn't as easy as I

thought. I didn't want it to be all about being gay because I wanted to tap into a universal message that would appeal to everyone in the audience. As I thought it over, the theme became apparent to me. I reflected on how, when I was young, I thought I had to obscure or efface the things that were different about me, as these were handicaps to be overcome. I wrote about how I had to come understand as an adult that what made me different was what made me special, was what made me *me*, and that I wouldn't "choose" to be straight now, even if I could, because then I wouldn't be Kevin. I chose my music—Bobby McFerrin's "Don't Worry, Be Happy" as my opener, figuring its upbeat tone would help set the right mood.

November 10 dawned a bracing, bright blue New England fall morning, and I approached the chapel, dead leaves crunching underfoot, literally shaking with nervousness. My college friend Pam had flown in from California to be by my side, and her presence helped me feel a little less like I was walking the plank. I was less nervous about losing my job than I was about how the kids would react. I'd never met a teacher who'd done what I was about to do, and had no idea how it would go over. I was indeed at sea.

The Concord Academy chapel is made of white clapboard, filled with hard, narrow, maple pews on which its original nineteenth-century parishioners could never have fallen asleep. It's a structure that could have been the subject of a postcard or on the cover of a tourism brochure or the stage set for a production of *The Crucible* or the actual church where the witch trials took place. It's a small building, so small that the school's three-hundred-plus students and faculty routinely spilled out into the vestibule on the days when everyone showed up. By the time I hit the chapel doors on November 10, the vestibule was already filled. News had spread somehow of what I was going to say, and everyone had shown up.

One played one's opening music on the chapel sound system

during the five minutes between the first bell, which rang at 8:15, and the second, which rang at 8:20 and signaled that chapel was to begin. I slipped in my Bobby McFerrin CD and turned to look out over the pews. It was a tradition that kids made signs wishing their friends good luck on the day they gave their chapels and posted them on the walls. When I looked up, I saw that the walls were covered with signs from kids. One had even spray-painted a good luck message on a sheet and draped it from the balcony. (I still have that sheet today.)

The second bell rang at 8:20 and it was time to start. I got right to the point:

> If I had Bobby McFerrin's vocal talents, I would express my message as beautifully he does but, lacking any gift but that of gab, I will be forced to talk to get my point across. Given that my only evident ability is that of speech, it is no wonder I am impressed by the power of language and particularly the power of names. The names we give to things can shape or even alter the meaning of the things named. The word that stands out as the one which has shaped much of my life is the word 'faggot.' I have spent years dealing with what it means to be this thing that society calls a faggot, trying to find a foxhole of self-esteem in which I could hide from the incessant negative bombardment gay people face every day in the United States.

No one screamed, no one fainted, no one sprang up and fled the building but, if I hadn't had their attention before, I could see I had it now. I continued, my confidence building, telling them my story of struggling to accept myself for who I was. There are times, when you're on a stage, that you can tell everyone in the audience is with you, that they're on your side, that's they're pulling for you. This was one of those times.

Just after I got started it seemed I was at my conclusion, where I was to share the lesson of my life and what it meant for theirs:

> My topic today has not been gay rights, although some will insist on seeing it that way. I've chosen my theme because we are all "gay" in some way. What I am referring to has nothing to do with sexuality. Instead, I am talking about a condition of the mind, an outlook on ourselves and our lives that we all share. We all have a cross of some sort that we bear. You might fall into one of the easily targeted groups in our society, for many are degraded—blacks are told they are inferior to whites, women that they are weaker than men, and so forth. If so, hopefully you can see that it is not that *you* don't measure up but that the yardstick itself is warped. Use that knowledge to make a difference in your own life and those of others. Fashion yourself a new yardstick, one that measures people for who they are, not what they are. Perhaps your pain stems for a more private cause: your parents could be divorcing, you might not be as attractive as you wish you were, or you might be the kid who couldn't play kickball and was always made fun of at recess. All of these things hurt, and they are all unfair. However, in each of them, there is something that made you into the special person that you are today. If your parents had stayed married, maybe you wouldn't have forged the strong friendships you rely on today; if you were thin and pretty as a model, maybe you would have pursued the fleeting pleasures of popularity instead of developing the intellectual skills you have now; if you'd been great at kickball, maybe you would have stayed outside at recess and fostered an ability to handle inflated rubber spheres with your feet instead of going to the library and developing the love of reading that sustains you today. Your cross may have also been your salvation, and someday

> you may be happy you didn't have the burden of a "normal" life. In actuality, no one is "normal," and the only reason life is interesting is because none of us is exactly alike. Treasure what makes you special, not what makes you like everyone else, and treasure what makes others different from you.

I had done it. I had made it through, and hadn't lost it. But, of course, as I closed with my thank yous, I did lose it:

> I'd like to close by offering a special thanks to the members of the Concord Academy community. One group I would like to single out is my students. I had always been afraid that, when students found out that I was gay, I would be rejected and the joy I find in teaching would disappear. Over the past year you have proved me wrong. You have given me the opportunity to be who I am and have judged me by my teaching, coaching, and personality rather than prejudging me on the basis of my sexuality. Your acceptance and affection means more to me than you will ever know.

At this point I got so choked up I had to stop. I realized that these kids, whom I was paid to teach, had been teaching me all along, teaching *me* the lesson of my life—that yes, the truth will set you free, that yes, you are a good person, that yes, the fact that you are gay doesn't change that. By accepting me, they had helped me finally accept myself. I was overcome. Fortunately, the 8:35 bell rang to indicate chapel was over, and all I had left to do was to gesture for them to leave.

But hundreds of them didn't. Instead, they rushed the pulpit of the creaky old chapel, hugging me, crying, a display of adoration that I would later joke was the only time in my life I felt like Madonna. It was the last thing I had expected, and it went by in a blur that left me feeling overwhelmed and breathless. And made me ten minutes late for first period.

Realizing this (and remembering the student's credo that, if a teacher was five minutes late, you were allowed to leave—a principle they viewed as a sacrosanct right), I was in a panic by the time I ran across campus and sprinted to the second floor of Russell Robb Hall to my classroom. When I got to the all-glass door and looked in, my heart stopped. Most students were seated at their tables, which formed a U around my desk (I routinely sat on, not behind, the desk), but a few were at the blackboard, scrawling on it. It was already covered with graffiti and I had to turn away. It had happened, I thought—they had written "faggot" and other epithets all over my blackboard, just like I thought they would; next would be my office and my car, I was sure. Only the kids who liked me had stayed behind to say congratulations: now the true feelings of the student body would be revealed.

Eyes down, I took a deep breath, opened the door, causing those still at the board to scatter like roaches do when the light is turned on, and strode purposefully toward the blackboard, ready to grab an eraser and wipe away the offensive language. Just before I did so, I decided to look up and see what they had written. In large letters, they had printed, "We love you, Kevin, and we're so proud of you." And every student in the class had signed the board. My face flushed with embarrassment. The 180-degree swing from what I had expected to be vilification to what turned out to be adoration left me even more befuddled than I was before, so I took the eraser and wiped down the blackboard, just like I was planning to. To this day, I wish I had taken a picture instead. Pretending all was normal, and that this was a school day like any other, I turned around and started my lesson. I have no idea what the lesson was about. And I cannot remember what Jim's reaction to the chapel was. It didn't really matter. The students had symbolically voted, and it was a landslide in my favor. One of my colleagues had refused to come to my chapel as a protest against its content, which only earned him the ridicule of much of the rest of the staff, who couldn't wait to tell him what he had missed. I came back to school on November 11, braced for the possibility that an avalanche of angry parental phone calls might have come in overnight and that I'd have a new fight on my hands, but such was not the case. The school year continued, my classes still met, and the sky did not fall.

A couple of weeks later, I was doing some grading in my office when a freshman named Faith came in. I knew who she was—she was an opinionated, outspoken girl who routinely wore a black-leather biker jacket, conspicuously made out with her senior boyfriend around the campus, and was adored by her classmates, who had just elected her freshman class president—but I didn't really know her. She wasn't in my class, wasn't my advisee, and wasn't on a team I coached, so I was a bit surprised by her sudden appearance. I asked her if there was something I could do for her.

"Yeah. I want to start a club to do something about homophobia at this school."

What? I thought. First of all, the idea had never crossed my mind. Second, because Faith was always making out with her boyfriend, I had never pegged her as a budding lesbian.

"Ohhhhkay..." I began, "I'm just curious, though: why do you feel so passionately about this?"

"Because my mother is a lesbian, and I am tired of hearing my family get put down around this school."

Another curve ball. I knew my coming out would help gay kids, but who knew we had kids with gay parents?

"Oh. Okay. That's interesting." I was stalling now. "Got a name for the club?"

"I dunno," Faith replied. "But since you're gay and I'm straight, why don't we call it the Gay-Straight Alliance. Whaddya say?"

Danger! Danger! flashed through my mind. I'd always heard the accusation that gay people recruit children, and knew how this claim was used to damn us as a community. Throughout history these kinds of accusations had been used to justify persecution of minorities—the pogroms against the Jews who supposedly drank the blood of Christian children in the Passover Seder, the lynching of black men who were supposedly after little white girls, and the denial of civil rights to gay people, whom Anita Bryant had sought to Save Our Children from just ten years before. The argument was always rolled out because it *worked*; people get irrational if they think someone is threatening their kids, and I knew its power and volatility. If I seemed to be "encouraging" kids to be gay *(the horror! the horror!)*, I would be dead meat. I also knew how easy it would be for Jim to say I was manipulating kids for my "agenda" and that such a club would play into his hands as prima facie evidence of my secret plans all along. But here was Faith, fifteen-year-old, high school freshman Faith, all of five feet tall, and she was ready to take on the system. How could I say no?

"Okay. I guess so."

"Great!" she exclaimed, and off she went.

The next morning, during announcement period, Faith and her best friend strode onto the stage. This provoked a murmur in and of itself—freshmen were to be seen and not heard, and rarely made announcements—but then her content practically silenced the place. "We're starting a new club to fight homophobia in our school, and it's called the Gay-Straight Alliance," Faith said in a loud, clear, confident voice. "Everybody is welcome to come. Our first meeting is..."

We were on our way.

CHAPTER 10

Getting Organized

The first call came as a total surprise.

It was from another boarding school, maybe twenty miles from Concord, one with a much more traditional reputation. "We've heard about your work," the administrator said, "and we'd like to begin to address gay issues at our school. Would you be willing to come to talk with our faculty?"

You've heard about my work. Huh? I thought.

A few weeks later I was in an oak-paneled library, in front of about seventy-five teachers, with the charge of educating them about the needs of gay students. Aside from being gay, I wasn't really all that sure what my qualifications were to be doing such a workshop, but good little boy that I was, I had prepared lots of handouts and questionnaires and readings, and fairly blasted them with information. At the end, an older teacher, who seemed like he could have been my grandfather, tottered over to me.

"Young man!" he barked.

"Yes," I squeaked in reply, sure he was going to tell me I was perverted or this was inappropriate or cast some other malediction my way.

"I think this was an excellent presentation. And I think you're a great person to be talking about this subject, because you don't seem gay."

"Thank you," I said, genuinely pleased at his reaction.

I look back years later and ask, "What the hell kind of compliment was *that*?" But I cast aspersions not on the giver of the compliment, but on the delighted receiver—me. Here I was, the person educating others about homophobia, yet I still had such a deeply internalized sense of worthlessness because of my own gayness that I somehow thought that not seeming gay (meaning what, exactly? Darren on *Bewitched* for men? Miss Jane Hathaway on *The Beverly Hillbillies* for women?) was better than seeming gay (again, meaning what, exactly?). I'd eventually come to understand how this self-loathing pervaded my gay brothers' personal ads: "straight-acting gay man seeks straight-acting gay man" (can you imagine "white-acting black man seeks white-acting black woman"?), and someday I'd understand that wearing shoulder pads was just as much a kind of drag as wearing a ball gown is—but I wasn't there yet. So I saw it as a compliment and took it as one.

After that, the calls began to multiply and I was soon speaking at more and more schools. The ways people found me reminded me of stories I'd heard about Russian dissidents communicating below the radar in a system that allowed them no official voice. It was always word of mouth, the friend of a friend of a friend who had "told them about my work," and would I come to their school? I never advertised and never marketed myself as a speaker. They always found me.

With my blue blazer and button-down collar, I was the perfect ambassador to these elite schools, ones so very, very distant from the kind I had attended myself as a child. I went to Harvard. I looked like them, I sounded like them, I made being gay seem nonthreatening. They liked me, they really, really liked me. And I liked doing the work.

For one such engagement, at a 1990 New England Teachers Conference sponsored by the Independent School Association of Massachusetts, I was paired up with a teacher at Phillips Academy Andover, Kathy Henderson, who had established a Gay-Straight Alliance there. I was somewhat shocked to learn I was not the only one doing this work. Finding Kathy was like finding an oasis in the desert. It wasn't that I didn't know other gay teachers, but they were usually sad cases, sometimes Uncle Toms like Julian at my own school, or more frequently folks who would come up to me after my workshops and whisper in my ear that they were gay, but they were terrified and could never, ever come out at their school. By contrast, Kathy was brash and unapologetic about her work. I was always careful to have just the right "look" and parsed my words to couch my message in ways the listener would find acceptable; Kathy could not have cared less what other people thought. She knew she was doing the right thing, and if others didn't like it, tough. I loved her energy and enthusiasm, so appropriate for a physical education teacher (did I mention she was a lesbian, or would that be redundant?), and we got along like a house on fire, as my mom would have said. Having been isolated for so long, Kathy and I were ecstatic at having found each other. "We've got to stick together," she warned me. "Neither one of us wants to be the only duck on the pond."

As we sat in a hotel conference room and waited for the workshop to begin, I confessed to Kathy that I was wondering if anyone would show up. The first few who poked in their heads were nervous, like little kids putting their toes in the water to see if it was warm enough to dive in. As the start time approached, however, the trickle turned into a torrent: all the chairs were taken, all the standing room was filled, people were sitting in the aisle, and the energy in the room was electric. There was a palpable sense among all the teachers present that, finally, we were going to talk about something we'd been silenced about for too long. I felt like a rock star. After the conference, I would get the news from the Independent School Association that ours was the highest-rated workshop of the entire event.

By now it had become obvious to me that we needed to organize. There were the gay teachers who'd whispered in my ear; the straight teachers with a gay brother or lesbian sister who'd tell me how they'd seen their siblings suffer and wanted to make sure that their students didn't endure the same humiliations; the committed educators of every sexual orientation who would tell me that they were fed up and couldn't idly stand by anymore as bigotry was propagated in their schools. Yet they were all alone, struggling in isolation, reinventing the wheel in their schools. I called Kathy and she agreed: we had to bring these folks together somehow, and we began to plan a conference.

I knew that if this was going to work, it had to be seen as a genuine education conference, not a gathering of gay activists. I'd been consistently surprised by Dick Barbieri—the head of the Independent School Association of Massachusetts—by how clearly passionate and committed he was on diversity issues, how he always included sexual orientation in his "laundry list" alongside race, religion, et cetera, which virtually no one else did in 1990. If he would put his organization's name on the event, I thought, there'd be no way it could be attacked. I thought we had a good chance—by now I had become friendly with Dick and his wife, Christine Savini, the diversity coordinator at Milton Academy, through seeing them at numerous conferences—but I also knew we were asking for him to put his organization's name behind something that had never been done before: organizing educators to fight homophobia in their schools.

I invited Dick and Christine to dinner with Bob and me at an Indonesian restaurant in Cambridge near where we lived. When we got around to what I thought would be the difficult part of the dinner, it was over fast. "Sure," Dick said. "We'd love to sponsor such an organization." With that, GLISTeN—the Gay and Lesbian Independent School Teacher Network—the Cro-Magnon ancestor of the organization that I work for today, was born.

We put together our little program for our first conference and sent it out. Dick insisted that we make it clear that this was a professional-development opportunity and that it was open to people of all sexual orientations, a condition that we were not only happy to meet but also one that coincided with our own philosophy. This was about making schools better places to learn, and the gay teachers could not do all that work by themselves. I asked Concord to host it and when they balked, I pointed out that they were proud to host other Independent School Association conferences, so what was the problem here? Having been raised with so much shame, I was learning how to use it as a weapon. They assented.

The week of the event, we had about thirty people registered. Not great, but not bad; like my workshop at the New England Teachers Conference, I had thought no one would come, so the fact that we had enough people to actually move ahead with the event was a victory to me. The conference was set for a Sunday (the only day boarding schools don't have games, maximizing our chances for a good turnout), and this Sunday in May of 1991 was one of those special New England spring Sundays when, after the long nightmare of winter, you actually begin to believe that the trees will leaf again and the temperature will break seventy degrees again and the Red Sox will win the World Series again sometime in your lifetime. I drove to Concord Academy with a flock of butterflies in my stomach: if it didn't go well this time, we might never get a second chance, and my hope of a movement to change schools would be stillborn.

I was confused by the large number of cars in the school parking lot when I got there. Was there another event on the campus, I wondered? I found a spot and headed over to the chapel, where the opening talk was to be given. There were all these people headed the same way. Who were they, I kept asking myself: what is this other event?

It turned out they were all there for our event. Over one hundred people—nearly four times as many as had preregistered—had crowded into the chapel by the time Kathy and I got up to open the day's program. Ever the history teacher, I gave a very somber intro about how important the work we were doing was, carrying on the American tradition of standing up for what was right that had begun here in Concord (blah, blah, blah . . .); Kathy, the physical education teacher, took the pulpit and led a cheer by shouting, "Give me a G! Give me an A! Give me a Y! What does that spell? GAY! GAY! GAY!" Jim, who had dropped by to see what was up with this event to which he was such a reluctant host, appeared to have swallowed his tongue.

I found out over the course of the day why so few had preregistered. Some were closeted and didn't want to risk putting their names on a "gay" list. Some were straight and didn't realize they *could* come until the preregistration deadline had passed. Some were from public schools and had somehow heard about the conference through the same underground that spread news of my work, but didn't preregister because they thought they might be turned away because they didn't work at an independent school. All were hungry—for the sense of community, for the tools, and for the inspiration they so desperately needed to believe that they could make a difference and that the prejudice that had forever been a part of the life of their schools could actually be combated. Most came imbued with fear; all left filled with hope.

By now, one would think I'd have noticed the pattern: I expected little, or the worst, and every time things went well. But we were in such uncharted waters that I couldn't trust this pattern. I'd never seen a successful model of organizing around gay issues in schools; I'd never seen a mainstream organization that welcomed us; I'd never seen that many straight people who cared. Was this all a fluke? A lifetime of being taught to expect disappointment, to expect rejection, kept telling me it had to be. I had a profound sense that I was a guest, that my invitation could be revoked at the slightest sign of bad behavior. I never relaxed.

And with good reason. While my "extracurricular activities" were going swimmingly, things at Concord were deteriorating. My chapel talk had seemed to be a watershed in terms of student attitudes. If anything, I became more popular afterward and students clamored to be in my classes, on the teams I coached, or in my advisee group. But it wasn't just me anymore: students themselves were organizing and taking action. Faith's announcement of the Gay-Straight Alliance had drawn a handful of students to its first meeting, but soon the group grew to have twenty to thirty regular attendees (pretty good for a school with 320 students), all of whom were deeply committed to its cause. On the second National Coming Out Day in 1989, the Gay-Straight Alliance decided to ask everyone to wear pink triangles as a sign of solidarity with the gay community, modeling themselves after the Danes who during World War II all donned yellow stars so the Nazis could not figure out who the Jews were. Their supply of two hundred triangles was gone by the middle of lunch, meaning that two out of three students were wearing them. For months after, students all around town, on the train to Boston, at the Friendly's ice cream parlor next to the train station, in the coffee shops on Main Street, trotted around with pink triangles on their backpacks. I always wondered what any closeted suburbanites who were around thought of this sudden proliferation of the symbol of gay pride in their midst.

But the institution itself wasn't budging. The October 1988 board meeting where the nondiscrimination clause was to be decided came and went with nary a peep on the subject. Despite my continued queries, meeting after meeting went by and nothing was done, and the 1988–89 school year ended. My exchanges with the administration became more and more adversarial: with every commitment they failed to keep, my faith in their good intentions waned, my patience dwindled, and my anger grew. Where once I would have accepted such mistreatment as the lot of a gay person and wouldn't have felt entitled to much better, the new me had no time for it.

By the fall of 1989, the students were beginning to sniff around the subject as well. They started asking why Concord didn't include sexual orientation in its policies. Now I was between a rock and a hard place: if I told them about the foot-dragging by the board and headmaster, I would be accused of insubordination, but if I didn't support them in their legitimate demand for answers, I would be betraying the very lessons I had taught them about standing up for what was right. Students finally told me they wanted to launch a public campaign to demand a change. I pleaded with them not to: "Jim and I are working on it," I said, "These things take time." It made me sick to my stomach to say these words. Had I been completely co-opted by the system? I wondered. Maybe I was the House Faggot after all, reduced to making apologies for the man in the Big House.

As 1989 melted into 1990 and there was still no action, I grew more and more tired of playing overseer to the students in the Gay-Straight Alliance. They devised a plan: a diverse group of students were going to stand up at announcement period and ask why the school did not have such a policy, and the student representative on the school's board, who was a Gay-Straight Alliance member, was going to ask about the issue point-blank in the next board meeting a few days later, as it had yet to make it onto the agenda. I sat in the Gay-Straight Alliance meeting and wondered if I should intervene, if I should talk them down once again. Weary, I decided I wasn't going to do that anymore. I kept my mouth shut.

When announcement period came the next morning, there was a murmur when an unusual group of students, a group that didn't usually hang out together, approached the stage. I had to smile: the Gay-Straight Alliance students had been very strategic in their selection of spokespeople. Each student said his or her name and role: "Hi, I'm Brad and I am captain of the boys' lacrosse team"; "Hi, I'm Rose and I'm the student body president"; and so on down the line, a line that ended with Robertson. When his turn came, he took a deep breath and said, "Hi, I'm Robertson and I am a gay senior." I got goose bumps: while everyone knew Robertson was gay, he was the first student in Concord's history to stand on a stage and say it aloud. I marveled: I never thought I'd see the day.

When they were done, Brad stepped forward. "We are here because we want to ask a question of the headmaster: if Concord really doesn't discriminate against gay people, why haven't you put that in writing?" And then they walked off the stage.

In the faculty section where I was sitting, a wave of shock reverberated. One or two teachers actually gasped. For students to directly challenge the head of the school was unusual but not unheard of: but for students to stand on a stage, with one of them saying "I'm gay," and demand policy change to protect gay people was unprecedented. The old guard alternately glared at me or avoided eye contact after announcements had finished. A line had been crossed, and I knew it.

Within minutes, I was summoned to Jim's office. He was apoplectic. Veins bulging, his voice approaching the decibel level of a jet taking off, he made his accusations. I had put the students up to this. I was using them for my agenda. I had betrayed him after he had tried so hard to work with me. I was "inappropriate," a word I would come to loathe over the next few years, as I heard it repeatedly but never got it clearly defined, so that it simply became the bludgeon with which I was struck by the administration whenever they didn't like something I did.

My responses were to no avail. I tried to explain that I had actually been reining the students in for months, not prodding them to action. Jim would have none of it and accused me of fomenting the whole thing. I found this especially ironic because, while the school touted the fact that it promoted independent and critical thinking in its students, when push came to shove, Jim seemed to think they were sheep I could herd into bleating during announcements. I acknowledged that I knew of their plan to make today's announcement, but that the plan was theirs and theirs alone—not a concoction of mine.

At this, Jim exploded. "You knew they were going to make an announcement and you didn't do something to stop it?"

"Jim, I knew they were going to make an announcement and I knew the topic, but I didn't know what, specifically, they were going to say."

"That doesn't matter. You're an adult; you're expected to support the school, and you had an obligation to stop them."

Now it was my turn to be hot and bothered. "Actually, Jim, you're wrong. I feel no obligation to stop them. I am a history teacher and my job is to teach these young people that they live in a democracy where they have rights and that we respect the right of free speech in America. Frankly, I was tired of restraining them and trying to convince them not to exercise those rights. You want to do it, you do it, but I'm not going to do it for you anymore. Plus, if you ask me, they asked you a completely legitimate question, and the real shame is that you don't have a good answer."

Beat.

This time, Jim spoke slowly and deliberately, quietly, no veins bulging. "I want to be very clear with you, Kevin. I expect you to support the school when we agree *and* when we disagree. I will accept nothing less going forward. Do I make myself clear?"

Beat. We glared at each other.

"So, basically, you're telling me that if I get out of line, you're going to fire me. Is that what I am to understand?"

Beat. We glared at each other.

"I said, I expect your support." Pause, eyes lock. "We're done here."

I left, enraged, intimidated, shaken. My guest pass into this world of elite private education was about to be revoked. You got to stay as long as you were well-mannered, and asking for your rights as a gay person was clearly very bad form.

But the student announcement and the student rep's challenge to the board a few days later had the desired effect: the school got off the dime. A board commission to study the issue was established and began working. I reached out to them and the first response I got was that they were "concerned" about putting sexual orientation into a legal policy because it was an "undefined" term. The board member who wrote me this was a senior partner at the prestigious law firm of Hill and Barlow, so I thought he must know something I didn't. I consulted an attorney to get an answer on this and found out that the term had been clearly defined in a series of court judgments stretching back many years in Massachusetts. She assured me this was something any competent Massachusetts attorney would know, providing me with citations to share with Mr. Hill and Barlow. Red flags went up in my mind: Mr. Hill and Barlow was either stupid or insincere and, as a senior partner at a major law firm, I seriously doubted he was stupid. Some patterns I was slow to recognize: this one, a pattern of prevarication and obfuscation on the part of the school's leadership, was very, very clear and by now I expected nothing more.

Toward the end of their deliberations, the commission agreed to meet with some students and staff. I sat in the reception room of the school's administration building, once the living room of a colonial-era mansion, on the early evening of a gray April day, with a small fire burning in the fireplace to ward off the chill. I watched as these brave and articulate young people from the Gay-Straight Alliance argued their case. I was proud of them and also sad, seeing that they had complete conviction that their passion and logic would carry the day, that right was predestined to win, a faith I no longer shared. I sensed that a decision already had been made and that their passion and hurt wasn't going to change it. When the policy came down two weeks later, I realized I had underestimated how bad it was going to be:

> Although clearly not intended, a shorthand statement assuring that students will not be discriminated against according to their sexual orientation could be misunderstood as permission to express their orientation through sexual activities. . . . While an adult's sexual orientation usually has become clear, there may be no such clarity for some adolescents. . . . Adolescence for many is a time of confusion over sexual roles and identities. Any official statement—or community culture—that encourages public declaration of specific, fixed orientation poorly serves the notion that adolescents should grow at their own pace and decide what, if anything, they choose to disclose about their orientation while at Concord Academy. . . . Given the realties of the world today, we believe students must consider the full consequences of any early public declaration of a homosexual orientation. . . . We want our students to make good decisions in their lives, and we owe them the candid acknowledgement that, however we may wish otherwise, a student's public declaration of homosexuality may limit future options. We think that in nearly all instances, before a student makes such a decision, professional counseling should be sought.

This was as bad as it could get, I thought. No one with any understanding or empathy for gay people could have written such a document—it fairly shrieked that no one who had ever walked in a gay person's shoes had played any significant role in drafting it. I read the document again, a running dialogue going through my mind as certain phrases leaped out at me.

"While an adult's sexual orientation usually has become clear ... adolescence for many is a time of confusion over sexual roles and identities." I knew this argument—it was a more politely stated version of the "it's a phase" argument that gay teens have heard since time immemorial, that they're "confused," that they're really straight and, given time, will come to understand that. The policy statement could not have been written by people who'd ever been told that their feelings weren't real, or that their deep-seated understanding of who they were—an understanding they'd had forever and in many cases had fought desperately to deny—was just "confusion."

"Any official statement—or community culture—that encourages public declaration of specific, fixed orientation poorly serves the notion that adolescents should grow at their own pace." This sentence pretty much defines heterosexism—an (often subconscious) assumption that everyone is heterosexual—as it fails to recognize that schools encourage heterosexual students to declare their "specific fixed orientation" all the time, through rituals like the prom. Nobody was saying here, "Don't say you're straight": they were saying, "Don't say you're gay."

"We believe students must consider the full consequences of any early public declaration of a homosexual orientation." What about the consequences of *not* declaring one's orientation? The depression, the loneliness, the substance abuse, the suicides, all prompted because you can't be honest about who you are? Having never experienced this, the writers couldn't know that the costs of the closet are always higher than the costs of honesty.

"A student's public declaration of homosexuality may limit future options." Honestly, did the writers think they needed to tell young gay people there are consequences for being gay in a homophobic society? That we don't know? That this is news to us? Why do you think people don't come out in the first place? And was this news suppose to "scare straight" young people who might be thinking of coming out? Telling us not to come out because we might get hurt denied the reality that the deepest hurt comes from being in the closet, from not being able to be who you really are.

"We think that in nearly all instances before a student makes such a decision, professional counseling should be sought." For so, so long, "professional counselors" had not been the friend of gay people. No one who knew the history of psychology and homosexuality—the electroshocks people were given in hopes of frying these feelings out of their minds, the "aversion therapies" with enforced vomiting designed to create an aversion to same-sex attraction, the decades during which homosexuality was defined as a "sickness" (a definition expunged by the American Psychiatric Association only in 1973, within the lifetime of most of the seniors in the Concord Academy class of 1990 who had met with the board just days before)—could have so blithely said, "Send them to counseling." No one who had ever been brought by his or her parents to a psychologist's office in hopes of a "cure" could ever have suggested this was the appropriate first response to a young person's saying he or she was gay.

I thought back to that meeting in the administration building, of the passion of the students, of how they bared their souls and spoke of their pain so honestly, so frankly, to try to educate the adults, and how it had all fallen on deaf ears. How could the administration be so insensitive, so ignorant? How could they do this to these young people, perpetuating the cycle that made them miserable in the first place? *How could they?* Now the school had drawn its line in the sand, and it was unmistakable. Back off now on the gay stuff, or else.

The students in the Gay-Straight Alliance were crestfallen. They had believed the school's rhetoric on diversity, they had believed that their voices mattered and would be heard, and now they felt used and betrayed. At the Gay-Straight Alliance meeting right after the policy came down, the students sat around in one of the house parent's living rooms, stunned, talking about how they had believed the "system" worked and that they'd never have that kind of faith again. But if the school's intention was to silence them, it played its hand exactly wrong. By betraying them so thoroughly, by discounting them so definitively, it merely hardened their resolve. The students spoke bitterly about their anger and how they were not going to be intimidated by the new policy. They started planning for new ways to raise awareness, new activities that would dramatize the issue for the school community, and their excitement grew. In retrospect, if the school had thrown the kids some kind of a bone, it would have saved itself a lot of trouble. Instead, it provoked an anger that would persist throughout my years at Concord.

The 1990 school year ended shortly after the new policy was promulgated, and Jim and the board went away undoubtedly thinking the issue had been resolved. In one of the first chapels when school reopened in the fall, a young lesbian student stood up, came out, and said, "Every day I come to this school and I am told that I can't be honest, that I have no right to be proud, that I am a second-class citizen. Homophobia is everywhere and bigotry is inexcusable. It's time to start showing you care."

Game on.

CHAPTER 11

Making History

There's an old saying, "When one door closes, another opens," and by now the nascent GLISTeN organization was absorbing more and more of the energy I had once put into trying to improve the climate at Concord. Following our successful conference in May 1991, the influx of new people began to take the organization in broader directions. The first thing to change was the name: wishing to make it clear that anyone from any type of school could come, we dropped the "I" and became the Gay and Lesbian School Teachers Network (GLSTN). The role model for public school teachers was increasingly my partner, Bob. When Bob graduated in 1985 he hadn't really known what he wanted to do with his life, but watching my excitement about teaching made him decide this was the right career for him, too. He went back to the Harvard Graduate School of Education to get certified to teach in a public school and in 1987 began working as a history teacher at Newton South High, an outstanding public school in a well-to-do suburb. Bob is generally a lower-key, less confrontational person than I, and his coming out was thus more deliberate and careful, timed to coincide with his being granted tenure in 1990 after his third year of teaching at Newton South. He also had the advantage of strong support from his department chair and his principal, Van Seasholes (who would serve on the founding national board of GLSTN years later), and perhaps of learning from my mistakes. Soon Bob started the first Gay-Straight Alliance in a public school at Newton South and another quickly followed at Brookline High. Our work was spreading beyond the small circle of private schools where we had started, and our name change reflected that. A network was beginning to grow, one of like-minded people all finding ways to address gay issues in their schools, and the solidarity that was emerging made each of us feel more emboldened on our own campuses.

In early 1992 I got a call from David LaFontaine, a man I'd never met. David ran a group called the Coalition for Gay and Lesbian Rights, which had thrown its support behind Republican nominee Bill Weld in the 1990 gubernatorial race and was credited with helping him win in a squeaker in this, Massachusetts, the most Democratic of states. David knew the governor owed him one and, when the moment came to cash in his political chit, he shared with the governor a recent study showing that one out of three gay teens attempted suicide, and said simply, "Do something to help our kids." Amazingly, the supposedly liberal and overwhelmingly Democratic state legislature rejected the governor's response, a proposed Commission on Gay and Lesbian Youth, so in the spring of 1992 Weld just decided to appoint one under his own auspices, and to call it the *Governor's* Commission on Gay and Lesbian Youth. David was asked to chair it. Having heard about GLSTN, he was calling me to ask me to run its education committee. It became quickly apparent that many commissioners had little or no knowledge of youth, and that the ones who did came mainly from social services and knew little about schools. Basically, I was being handed the school portfolio and asked what the governor should recommend.

I knew we had to do two things: first, prove there was a problem (most people still believed that there were no gay students) and, second, make very specific recommendations on how to fix it. Addressing the former, we decided to hold hearings across the state to document the conditions in the schools. The initial list of those scheduled to testify was way too adult-heavy, so I began working the GLSTN network to try to find students who would speak at the hearings. It was amazing how hard this was: even at Concord, the most "liberal" school *(Don't look too close! Pay no attention to the hypocrites behind the curtain!)*, we had only three openly gay students at the time, and it was hard slogging to find youth who had the courage to stand in the well of the statehouse and talk about the daily horror that school life was for them. But we persisted and eventually we got a critical mass.

The hearings in the fall of 1992 changed the tone of the debate, and changed me. Student after student spoke, putting a human face on the issue for the first time. When I reread the report we wrote based on the hearings, I see their faces again, and wonder at their courage as they stood in the statehouse, telling their stories to all who would hear.

They told us about learning to feel they were inferior, as eighteen-year-old Randy did: "Who could I talk to? . . . I had been conditioned into believing gay is wrong. . . . After years of conditioning, I lost respect for myself and wanted to die. . . . [At school] I was spit upon, pushed, and ridiculed. My school life was hell. I decided to leave school because I couldn't handle it."

They told us about how the places and people that were supposed to protect and shelter them—their schools, their families, public authorities—all failed in their responsibility to do so, as eighteen-year-old Troix did: "I couldn't handle being in high school living something that I wasn't, so I just dropped out and called it quits. I got kicked out of my house, and at that point there was violence involved. My mother went nuts and came at me with an iron, and I ran downstairs and I locked the door and she called the police. The police came and they asked what was going on. I told them, and my mother started saying that I'm always in Boston with the fags and that I'm doing this and I'm doing that. The police started cracking all kinds of gay jokes and telling me what he would do to his kids if they were gay, and he told me I should leave."

These brave kids told us about how they came to the decision to try to take their own lives, as eighteen-year-old Steven did: "I just began hating myself more and more, as each year the hatred toward me grew and escalated from simple name-calling in elementary school to having people in high school threaten to beat me up, being pushed and dragged around on the ground, having hands slammed in lockers, and a number of other daily tortures. Throughout eighth grade, I went to bed every night praying that I would not be able to wake up in the morning, and every morning waking up and being disappointed. And so I finally decided that if I was going to die, it would have to be at my own hand."

They told us about how the insensitivity of their schools played a role in these tragic decisions and how these decisions had affected their lives, as nineteen-year-old Stacey did: "My teachers and counselors labeled my 'confusion' as rebellion and placed me in the category of a troubled discipline problem.... I had nothing to identify with and no role models to guide me, to help me sort out this 'confusion,' and I began to believe I was simply alone.... A few weeks into my sophomore year, I woke up in the psych hospital in Brookline after taking my father's camping knife to my wrists.... I was placed in thirteen hospitals in two years. By what was supposed to be my junior year of high school, I had accumulated a 'résumé' consisting of five suicide attempts, four halfway houses, several high schools, and one family in shock."

In short, they let us know how we, the adults, were failing them.

Each hearing was grueling. I would look around, watching how my fellow commissioners were at times transfixed and at others had to look down because the pain on these young people's faces was simply too much to face eye-to-eye. It wasn't unusual to see people crying, sometime having to excuse themselves because they couldn't sit and listen anymore. With each hearing I could also feel a hardening resolve, born of outrage and anger, that we simply were not going to let this continue, that we would use our platform to demand real change.

While the hearings were grueling for the commission, they were cathartic for the students. They were transformed in the process, finding that they indeed had a voice and could use it to great effect. I had worried that I was putting them at risk by asking them to speak out: instead, they developed a sense of their own power through the experience of advocating for themselves. Time after time, they would testify that the harassment bothered them less than the indifference of the adults in their schools. "We knew we'd get harassed," they'd say, "But we didn't expect that the adults would stand by and do nothing." I realized that, going forward, the young people would have to be front and center in any work that we did.

While the hearings were underway, a working group of folks from the GLSTN network labored to fashion the commission's recommendations. We eventually settled on five major items: policies protecting gay and lesbian students from harassment, violence, and discrimination; training for school personnel; school-based support groups; school-based counseling for family members of gay and lesbian students; and age-appropriate inclusion of gay and lesbian issues in school curricula. With a clear direction in place, we set about writing the report for the commission, which was to weave together research and student testimony to explain the rationale and urgency behind these recommendations.

There was only one point of contention. What were we going to call the report? Here, I went head-to-head against another commissioner, who came to this work from a background as a family therapist. She insisted that it be called "Breaking the Silence."

It was 1992–93, the height of the AIDS crisis, and the slogan "Silence=Death" was everywhere, demonstrating graphically the cost of silence. To me, though, our goal was different. We weren't asking schools to break silence: we were asking them to take action and create a better learning climate. Plus, many people had no desire to see gay people break their silence and would much prefer that we remain silent forever. I proposed that we call the report "Making Schools Safe for Gay and Lesbian Youth." After all, that was what we were seeking to do, and who isn't in favor of schools being safe? We took our two potential titles to the commission, where my argument carried the day.

As we sent a draft of the report over to the governor's office for review, we nervously realized that we had probably gone far beyond our original mandate, which was to study the issue of gay youth suicide. Perhaps the governor would back away from our recommendations, which would mean they were dead on arrival. But we argued that you could only deal with the issue of suicide if you addressed the hostile climate that was its root cause, and the governor's staff seemed persuaded by the argument. Word came back: you can print the report as written, and the governor would publicly endorse four of its recommendations (policies, training, school-based clubs, and school-based counseling) but would say that curriculum issues should be left up to local school districts to decide. As a teacher, the curriculum loss was a bitter pill, but the sweeping endorsement of the others was far more than I had hoped for. We had the seal of approval from the governor to tell schools that they should incorporate sexual orientation into their polices, they should train their teachers, they should have Gay-Straight Alliances, and they should have counseling that helped families adjust to the fact their kid was gay instead of trying to convince the kid it was "just a phase." In other words, the governor was willing to tell schools to do everything that Concord Academy (of which his wife was an alumna) wouldn't do of its own volition. The irony was not lost on me.

When we released the report on February 23, 1993, it was front-page news in the *Boston Globe.* I was elated and had a copy in my hand in the faculty room, reading the stunningly favorable coverage from the state's newspaper of record. Curious to see what I was reading so avidly, one of the old guard picked up a copy of the *Globe*, saw my name in the article, and snorted, "I knew you did all this just to get attention" before walking out.

A few weeks later, the state board of education voted unanimously to make the four recommendations backed by the governor the official policy of the state of Massachusetts, and a line item was put in the education budget to create a program to implement the new policy. The program—Safe Schools for Gay and Lesbian Students—would be the first of its kind in the nation. Having no idea how to design such a program, the department of education turned to us for guidance, and a series of meetings ensued that were actually quite comical. Accustomed to drowning in a sea of their own memoranda, the department's bureaucrats wanted more "process" than the freewheeling GLSTN types did, and one shouted in frustration at a meeting, "We need paper! Paper, paper, paper!" After several fruitless meetings, they realized they had no expertise or ability in this arena and decided to bring my partner, Bob, on to develop and implement the program.

One thing was left. Policies are nice, but laws are better, so we turned our attention to the state legislature. We had the votes in the house, but the senate seemed like it might be a problem. Having learned our lesson from the commission's hearings, we reached out to the exploding GLSTN network to find students from Gay-Straight Alliances to make sure that each senator met an actual gay student from their district. I can remember one memorable meeting, where a senator told me and the student who was with me that he had "good schools" in his district, where teachers would never let anything like this happen. In a quiet, low voice, the young man with me related how he had once been picked up by a group of jocks in his school, shoved inside a locker that they then locked from the outside, and how he spent nearly an hour banging on the door of the locker until a custodian let him out. I have rarely seen a politician at a loss for words: that day, I did. As these meetings unfolded and each senator was confronted with the reality of what the students in his or her community's schools had to put up with every day, the tide began to turn. Following a massive rally in the fall of 1993 with hundreds of students in attendance, the vote came down quickly and overwhelmingly in the bill's favor. Soon Governor Weld had signed it, and what I had once tried in vain to get Concord Academy to do was now the law of the state of Massachusetts.

But by then, I was gone.

By the fall of 1993 I was a Klingenstein Fellow at Columbia University's Teachers College, having been given this honor because of my work on gay issues in schools. But I had wanted to get away from Concord as much as I wanted to go to Columbia. With such a long history of frustration and conflict, it's hard to pinpoint the exact moment when my trajectory began to take me out of the school, but the beginning of the end was probably the Dating Club.

In the winter of 1992, two well-meaning students, frustrated at the lack of social life among their peers, decided to start a Dating Club. Just prior to Valentine's Day, they thought it would be funny to do a skit during announcements to publicize the new club. They convinced Jim to play Cupid (complete with wings), and to run around the stage shooting arrows at pairs of boys and girls, who would magically become interested in each other and pair up. Most of the students found it uproariously funny—most, except for the ones in the Gay-Straight Alliance.

When I showed up for the next Gay-Straight Alliance meeting, the students were hopping mad. As far as they could see, the school's policy that it opposed declarations of "specific, fixed sexual orientations" had just been given the lie to. Jim was happy to go onstage and shoot arrows at couples—so long as they were heterosexual ones. He was perfectly fine with declarations of *hetero*sexual orientation and, in fact, had encouraged them. To the students, the facts had been lain bare. This had them steaming, and they were already planning what to do by the time I got there. One of the students hit upon an idea she felt would expose the double standard. They would make posters, saying things like, "Dear Jim: There's this girl in my math class I really want to ask out. Would Cupid come and shoot arrows at her for me? Sincerely, a Damsel in Distress." The other students loved the idea and immediately began making up other posters.

Once again, I was in the uncomfortable position of either using my influence to convince students not to voice their views or risk incurring the wrath of the administration for not snitching on the dissidents. Screw it, I thought: Jim should have known better than to do this, and he too should be held "accountable" for his actions, "accountable" being Jim's second-favorite word after "appropriate."

When I got to school the next day, the campus was abuzz. Students were gathered around the posters, talking about them, and a nerve had clearly been struck. Little did I know that, in their excitement, the GSA students had tacked a poster to the door of Jim's office so he would see it first thing in the morning. But also, little was my surprise when I was summoned to his office first period.

Jim was his usual apoplectic self, accusing me of "putting the students up to this." Wearily, I explained once again that the students were capable of thinking for themselves, that they themselves had conceived the idea, and that—if I was guilty of anything—it was of doing nothing to stop them. If possible, the last admission made the veins in Jim's neck bulge out farther than ever before (and I'd seen a lot of vein-bulging over the years), to the point where I was honestly afraid he was going to have a stroke, a heart attack, or become completely unhinged and take a swing at me *(when people get angry, they hit you).*

"You *knew* about this? You *knew* they were going to vandalize school property and you did nothing about it?"

"Vandalize school property? What are you talking about, Jim? Kids put up posters all the time around the school. I never knew we considered that vandalism before."

At this point, Jim snatched off his desk the poster that (unbeknownst to me) had been tacked to his door. It was the "Damsel in Distress" one. He literally screamed, "This was nailed to my door!!"

While I doubted it had been actually nailed (taped or tacked I would have believed, but nailed struck me as unlikely), the history teacher in me loved the idea that, like Martin Luther, the Gay-Straight Alliance students had nailed their Theses right on his door.

"Well, Jim, I didn't know they were going to do that. But don't you think we're missing the point here? Why don't we focus on the content of these posters? The fact is, you got up onstage and encouraged declarations of heterosexuality. Isn't that a violation of school policy?"

Having his own policy turned on him seemed to befuddle him, and he paused briefly. As had happened two years before, this time he came back calmer and more deliberate.

"My job is to hold people accountable for their behavior, Kevin. And if you can't support the school, I am going to have to hold you accountable."

Accountable. There's the buzzword again. I knew I was in trouble now.

"What are you gonna do, Jim? Fire me?"

Beat. We glared at each other.

"I'm going to have to think about all this. We'll talk some more soon."

With that, our meeting was over.

On February 19, 1992, I received my contract letter for the 1992–93 school year. I was told that I would not be receiving the customary salary increase that accompanied contract renewal, and that this would continue until I developed a "satisfactory approach to addressing disagreement." And what would that satisfactory approach be? As the letter made clear, a satisfactory approach would be silence on my part:

> You have rightly challenged Concord Academy to take a role in combating homophobia.... We are interested in your perspective on these issues, and we also expect your public support when we agree, and when we disagree. We do not want you to incite students to combat the institution or assist them with activities that run counter to the broader mission of the school.... We expect you not to include students or other teachers in the resolution of this challenge.

The trap had been laid: you must support us, and if you don't, or if you talk to anyone about this, you're gone.

Fortunately, a lawyer friend had suggested, when I first thought about coming out in 1987, that I document every meeting I had with the administration, that I save every letter and memo, and that I establish a paper trail attesting to my outstanding job performance in case a day like this ever came. That file was now six inches thick, and I took it down to Gay and Lesbian Advocates and Defenders (GLAD), where the incomparable Mary Bonauto counseled me on the next steps. I told her I saw this as the first step in setting me up to be fired, and she advised me that under no circumstances should I sign the contract, as that could be seen as an admission that I had indeed done something wrong that merited the withholding of my pay. I also reached out to the parent of one of my advisees (and a Gay-Straight Alliance member), whom I will call "the professor," a noted scholar at Harvard who had argued several cases before the Supreme Court. "Don't worry, Kevin," the professor said, "If Concord fires you, I'll represent you myself."

Bring it on, Jim, I thought. We'll see how your Hill and Barlow minions hold up against Mary, the professor, and my paper trail in court.

But it never came to that. I met with the associate headmaster, Clare, rightfully pointing out that the accusations that I was inciting students were figments of Jim's imagination. I detailed my many contributions to the school—the fact that my classes were among the most sought-after, that they consistently received the highest evaluations by the students, that I had never been given a negative evaluation by the chair of the history department, that I was the only teacher who coached all three seasons of after-school sports, that my boys' and girls' volleyball teams were among the few teams the school had that regularly had winning records, that I had the highest advisee load of any teacher, that I had been sophomore class adviser for years . . . the list went on and on and on. The advice by the friend who told me to put together a file—"Be so good they can't fire you"—stood me in good stead now. I told Clare that I refused to sign a contract that suggested I did not deserve a pay increase.

After that meeting, the issues were clear: if you get rid of me, I am going to be able to prove it wasn't because of my job performance. I have no idea what conversations transpired between Clare and Jim afterward, but the deadline for signing my contract came and still I refused. Eventually, I was given one with a pay increase.

But it was too late to salvage my relationship with the school. I knew from that day forward that it would be impossible for Concord ever to fire me. But I was out of there. I gave it a try that fall but finally decided to call the Klingenstein program, which had expressed an interest in my coming to Columbia for a year, and within a couple of months I was in Clare's office asking for a yearlong leave of absence. Even though I wasn't eligible for a sabbatical for another two years, Clare was practically giddy with relief and granted my request almost immediately. I am sure my absence made her life much easier.

The last few months of the 1992–93 school year felt a bit like a farewell tour. With the end of my time at Concord drawing nigh, I thought of how I had changed during my years there. While I had seen the effects of the Gay-Straight Alliance and GLSTN and the governor's commission and the battles over school policies on others—how it gave them new confidence, gave them a voice—I had missed how these effects had been even greater on me. When I had started at Concord in 1987, I had seen being treated equally as a privilege that, if the school were benevolent, it would grant me and other gay people on the staff and among the student body, and I would have felt enormously grateful for it. But by 1993 I saw it for what it was—a right—and I wasn't willing to settle for less. Not getting it made me angry which, I had finally come to understand, is the appropriate reaction to being mistreated. But I knew that many in the school saw me as unreasonably and needlessly angry, so (ever the educator) I tried in my final chapel talk to help people understand why they saw only my angry side.

Standing at the pulpit for the last time, I looked out over the student body assembled in the white clapboard chapel. The walls were just as festooned with posters as they had been in 1988, the pews just as hard and just as crowded, but these surface similarities were deceiving. Everything had changed: these students could not remember a time when Concord didn't have a Gay-Straight Alliance or openly gay teachers and students; they now lived in a state where discrimination against students based on sexual orientation was illegal, and the ideas that had seemed so crazy when I first voiced them had now become the law of the state of Massachusetts. I too was different, wiser perhaps, but having paid a high price for that wisdom in the form of tremendous disillusionment. But being my father's son, I tried witnessing one last time to help them understand what the world looked like from where I sat.

> This, most likely, is my last chapel, as my life's course will soon be taking me out of the Boston area. I decided I would speak to you about an emotion with which I have often been

closely associated during my years here. That emotion is anger.

"I know the anger that lies inside me like I know the beat of my heart and the taste of my spit. It is easier to be angry than to hurt. . . . It is easier to be furious than to be yearning."

When I first heard these words, written by the black lesbian poet Audre Lorde, I experienced a shock of recognition. Anger is an emotion I experience daily as a gay man in a homophobic society. I don't know if I need to explain to you why I would be angry as a gay man. But I am angry because in forty-two states you can be fired from your job because you are gay.

I am angry because there are large parts of this country where I cannot live, because there are jobs I will never hold, because there are streets I cannot walk down safely, simply because I am a gay man.

Ever the history teacher, I brought it back to that:

I am angry because I grew up in a society where I was taught to expect something different. I remember pledging allegiance every day at school. I remember speaking those words, words that others find so hokey, words that can still choke me up—"I pledge allegiance to the flag of the United States of America and to the Republic for which it stands, one nation, under God, indivisible, with liberty and justice for all." And I believed them with all my heart as a young boy in Lewisville, North Carolina, so proud to live in this country that was so different from any other society. I became angry as I came to understand that those words were not true, and I plan to stay angry until that pledge is fulfilled.

In closing, I returned to Audre Lorde's prophetic words about the agony of hurt and yearning.

When I return to this quote, there is part I left unexplained —the fact that it is "easier to be furious than to be yearning." I yearn to live in a different society from the one we share today. I yearn for the day when it won't matter that I am gay. I yearn for the day when I can walk down the street with my partner and feel safe. I yearn for the day when I will feel like I really belong. But when you yearn, you risk disappointment, and too many disappointments can destroy your ability to believe that things can ever get better.

I know things can get better, but I know they will only get better if we first get angry at the injustices that still exist. We must ignore the voices that say we should be grateful for how far we have come, because they are the same voices that, a few years ago, wanted us to be silent altogether. But most importantly, we must never lose the yearning for freedom that lies behind the anger, for it is this dream that will sustain and nourish us on those dark days when anger is all we can feel. It is our only hope and, as the gay leader Harvey Milk said in a speech shortly before his assassination, "Without hope, we give up. I know you cannot live on hope alone, but without it, life is not worth living." Go forth from this chapel, and give people hope.

The bell rang, and once again hundreds of students lined up to hug me, just as they had done years before. But what I felt this time was not relief but a sense of being drained, of having given all I could to try to make this one small place a better one—with uncertain results. It was time to move on.

Later that week, during the gap between exams and graduation when the school was quiet, I took a lap around the campus. I sat in the chapel and remembered the elation I felt when I did my coming-out talk. I sat in the auditorium and remembered the electric shock that went through the audience the day Robertson identified himself as a gay senior. I stood in the gym and remembered the countless volleyball matches and the innumerable hours on the bus I had spent with dozens and dozens of boys and girls, who affectionately nicknamed me "Sarge" because my style and practices were so intense. I visited my old classroom, the one where the students had graffitied the board with the "We Love You" message the day I came out, and smiled that I had been afraid that they were writing a far different message. I walked back to the school's boathouse on the river and remembered helping Max take Amy on her first canoe ride. I took out my key chain, removed the key to my classroom, and threw it in the river.

CHAPTER 12

Going National

When I got to New York in the fall of 1993, the small community of people who cared about gay students in the city's schools was reeling. A highly divisive battle over a multicultural "rainbow curriculum" and its minuscule incorporation of gay content, as well as over making condoms available in the schools, had led to the ouster of Schools Chancellor Joseph Fernandez. There was a deep sense of depression and hopelessness among those who sought change. Whenever I talked to anyone about the work we had done in Massachusetts, reactions ranged from disbelief to shock. "How the hell did you do that?" was a common reaction. At the same time, I was working on an anthology of writings by gay and lesbian teachers, *One Teacher in Ten*, that would soon be published. Coming into contact with a national network of educators through this book as well as through the increasing number of conferences I was asked to speak at reinforced my understanding that what we had done in Massachusetts was unprecedented. Upon learning of it, other educators would ask, "Could you help us get something like that started here?"

Doing exactly that seemed like a good idea for the next phase in my life. I knew that I had no long-term future at Concord. My relationship with Bob was ending as well, so there was little reason to return to Boston, and the idea of doing so seemed a painful step backward in my life. So I gathered the steering committee of the then all-volunteer GLSTN and suggested we take a shot at going national with the organization. They agreed. When I finished my year at Columbia in May 1994, I set about doing so.

What exactly I was thinking was unclear. Fortunately, I didn't know then what I later learned in business school—that nine out of ten new ventures fail in their first year. Good thing: I was scared enough. I had no idea how to start, but I had read enough to know we needed a board and I started trying to build one from the people I had come across in my travels. Knowing we needed a lawyer, I called Mary Bonauto from GLAD; knowing we needed some financial expertise, I called Donna Crocker, a stockbroker who had stumbled into a speech I gave at Lincoln-Sudbury High School and called to say she'd do whatever she could to help; knowing we needed credibility among educators, I recruited Dick Barbieri, the head of the Independent School Association of Massachusetts, and Van Seasholes, the principal of Newton South, Bob's school. And through an incredible stroke of good luck that is probably the single biggest reason GLSTN made it, I returned a call from Charley Todd, the head of a private school called Watkinson in Hartford, and he agreed to be the first board president.

So we gathered together—two gay men, two lesbians, and two straight men (unwittingly mimicking the Gay, Lesbian, and Straight Teachers Network name we soon adopted)—and had our first board meeting that August. The first item on the agenda was clear to me: money. Over the course of the summer what had once seemed like a good idea became a lot more uncertain when I realized I had no savings, no partner to fall back on, and GLSTN had no money. How was I going to do this? I began to lay out the situation to the board, trying not to sound as utterly panicked as I felt, when Dick Barbieri interrupted.

"Actually, I have been contacted by an anonymous donor who really wants to see GLSTN succeed. He has sent me a check for $25,000 to help us get off the ground."

I felt at that moment something like what I imagined the Israelites felt when manna first fell from the heavens.

With the immediate financial heat off, I began working to build an organization in the fall of 1994. The model seemed clear to me: in Boston we had gathered together a group of volunteers who worked in schools, figured out what we needed to do, and then did it. It seemed that replicating this structure through some kind of local-chapter system was the best way to go, and I began to call back the many people who had contacted me over the years who said they'd like to get this going in their communities. If they said they were interested, I got on a plane and went there. I didn't have to worry about the office when I was gone: the card table in my living room on which I worked every day would be just fine.

I look back with a sense of awe on how people gambled on this unknown organization. The rapid growth of GLSTN showed that we had touched a nerve, that we were meeting a need that had long been ignored, and the bravery of those early volunteers showed me how great the determination to change things was. I never knew what I'd find when I got off a plane, and usually didn't even know what the person I was meeting looked like. In January 1995 I headed to Seattle to meet a guy named Kirk Bell. Kirk had contributed an essay to *One Teacher in Ten* and was the only person I knew in Seattle. When I called him in the fall of 1994, asking if he'd be interested in starting a GLSTN chapter there, his response was an immediate and enthusiastic yes. We still were living off the $25,000 the anonymous donor had given us, trying to save money everywhere we could, and I asked Kirk if I could sleep on his couch while in Seattle. He said, "Of course."

When I got there, he insisted I take his bed, and he slept on the couch instead. This kind of hospitality, this openness, was a hallmark not only of Kirk's personality but also of countless people I would meet through GLSTN, people who opened their hearts and their homes to me. Two nights after I got to Seattle, Kirk drew over a hundred people to his first meeting.

From Seattle I drove down to Oregon. Things were tense in Oregon, which had just been through an ugly election a few months earlier, in the fall of 1994, when an antigay ballot initiative was a major focus. Two gay activists had been killed when their house was set on fire that fall, and a spasm of antigay hate crimes had swept the state throughout the campaign. In one small town, the organizers of the new-chapter meeting told me that they wanted to hold it during the day. I asked if we wouldn't get better attendance at night, when people wouldn't be working, and they replied that they were scared about my safety if I was driving on their lonely rural roads at night. I scoffed, but as I drove into town it felt more like it was 1964, not 1994; that I was in Mississippi, not Oregon; and that my name was not Jennings, but Cheney, Goodman, or Schwerner. I realized then how truly courageous these people were: I got to leave after the meeting—they had to live there.

A few months later I went to St. Louis, where another contributor to *One Teacher in Ten*, Rodney Wilson, offered to organize a meeting and told me I could sleep on his couch, only to also insist I take the bed instead once I got there. Rodney's coming out had been front-page news in St. Louis the year before. As I settled down to sleep the first night, I noticed a baseball bat propped up next to the bed, which I thought was odd. The next morning I asked Rodney if he was a big baseball fan, a question he found curious.

"No. Why do you ask?"

"Because you have a baseball bat by your bed. I thought maybe you played a lot of baseball."

"That's not why the bat is there. After all the news coverage when I came out last year, I started getting a lot of nasty phone calls and even some death threats. I put the bat there in case I needed it."

After the anonymous donor, the next big lucky break came in January 2005 in Los Angeles. My Klingenstein classmate Bob Riddle had agreed to organize our first West Coast conference there and had persuaded David Mixner to speak at it. I was in awe: David Mixner, the confidant of President Clinton, the man who had persuaded Clinton to be the first president to openly embrace gay causes. And then I found out I was to speak directly after David, whose oratorical skills were legendary. (Thanks a lot, Bob.) I must have done okay, because David asked if I could meet with him while I was in Los Angeles. He interrogated me about what I was trying to do and, apparently convinced that I had my act together, turned on his computer, created a list of names and numbers of people in different cities and said, "Call these people and visit them. I'll tell them to take a meeting with you." I was too unsophisticated at that point to know that David had handed me a list of the twenty biggest donors to gay causes in America.

I started calling these people and they started giving me money and, equally importantly, advice, which—as a novice with no experience in management or fundraising—I needed just as badly. I started off seeing them as ATMs: they ended up being my mentors and friends. Some of their tips guide me to this day. Personal-finance guru Andy Tobias, today treasurer of the Democratic National Committee, told me, "Don't feel like you have to know everything. Get a bunch of smart people together, tell them about whatever problems you're facing, and I guarantee that one of them will solve it for you." (He also wanted to know why a nice Jewish boy like me had a name like Kevin, proving he isn't completely all-knowing.) Tim Gill, the entrepreneur who created the software program Quark and then gave away hundred of millions of dollars he made from it to a foundation to help gay people, told me,

"Don't worry about the competition, or the 'opposition,' as they call it in your field. Just focus on your product and make it better and better and better, like I did, and the competition will go away eventually." Ford Motor Company CFO Allan Gilmour, the highest-ranking openly gay person ever at a major American company, listened to me and then said, "Okay, I understand now what you do. Now tell me what you *don't* do," teaching me about the importance of focus. Philanthropist Ron Ansin, who built Cole Haan shoes and had been a cabinet member for Massachusetts governor Michael Dukakis, basically adopted me, becoming the father I'd never had, uttering Yoda-like pronouncements whose wisdom I didn't always get at first but I would later realize were dead-on. Together, these folks took it upon themselves to make sure the little schoolteacher succeeded, and put in the time and money needed to insure I did.

I would also experience one of the unintended positive consequences of fundraising when I met my partner, Jeff Davis, at our first event in New York in December 1994. A nice Catholic boy from Cleveland, Jeff responded wearily to my "Jeff Davis!!" exclamation upon meeting him with, "Where in the South are you from?" With a first-generation Polish American dad who had changed his name from Emile Nowakowski to Clark Davis because he wanted it to sound more "American," Jeff had grown up in the North blissfully unaware he was named for the president of the Confederacy. By the time he met me, though, he was used to rabid white Southerners' enthusiastic response to his name and was known to use it to his advantage on sales calls in the South. We survived our clichéd first meeting, but I remain convinced to this day that his smooth acceptance into my family was aided in no small part by his fortuitous name. But it was his smile, his blue eyes, the touch of gray at his temples, and his big heart that won me over, and soon I was remarried.

One of our first dates was when Jeff came to see me speak to the student body at a school in Washington. From that point on, he was my biggest fan. Where I had passion, Jeff had savvy, having been an executive in corporate America all of his working career. His understanding of how to get things done was an invaluable complement to my passion for what needed to get done. Thanks to his corporate experience, he also moved easily in a world of affluent people and smoothed out some of the rough edges the kid from the trailer park still had. In return for what he taught me, I helped Jeff get in touch with a side of himself that possessed values that corporate America didn't usually put a premium on. He eventually took a year off from his high-flying corporate career to work for PAX: Real Solutions to Gun Violence, a nonprofit dedicated to reducing gun violence, especially among children. When we first met, he was so closeted he would say "Shhh!" if I said "gay" in the back of a cab. Today, he is the highest-ranking openly gay person in the history of financial stalwart Dow Jones. It was more than just the smile and the blue eyes: we turned out to be perfect for each other.

And I needed all the support and help I could get. No one believed it would work. Education groups were still in total denial that there were gay students. Gay groups didn't want to touch anything to do with young people with a ten-foot pole for fear it would give the extreme right ammunition for their canards about "recruitment." And nobody had seen a gay-oriented group put "Straight" in its title and try to build an organization with a genuine cross-orientation membership. Clearly, we were crazy.

But I always thought, when others expressed doubt about the chances of our success—to quote Franklin Roosevelt when asked about the chances of his New Deal solving the problems of the Depression—that "We Can. We Will. We Must." If I was to pick the year when I realized it was going to work, and when I realized exactly how high the stakes were and that we had to *make* it work, it would be the 1996–97 school year. Three names from that year came to encapsulate what GLSTN was all about to me: Gerry Crane, Kelli Peterson, and Leslie Sadasivan.

GLSTN was growing but still tiny then. We'd scraped together enough money to hire two other staff members, John Spear and Deidre Cuffee-Gray, who, like me, were former teachers and workaholics who shared my missionary zeal and would do whatever it took to get the job done. But the growing grassroots activity we were spawning was generating counterattacks, and many of the situations we faced were difficult ones. None was more difficult than that faced by Gerry Crane.

Gerry was an award-winning music teacher in Byron Center, Michigan, just outside Grand Rapids. He was already in the midst of a maelstrom when I met him in early 1996. The summer before, he and his partner, Randy Block, had a commitment ceremony, and somehow news of this got back to some parents in the deeply conservative town where he taught. Although Gerry was not out to his students, these folks still didn't want him around their kids (multiple teaching awards notwithstanding), and they mounted an increasingly vicious campaign to drive him out. The low point was when a quasi-pornographic right-wing hate video, *The Gay Agenda*, was sent to the parents of each student in his classes. Only a very small step up from such nineteenth-century anti-Semitic polemics as *The Protocols of the Elders of Zion* (with its stories of Jews drinking the blood of Christian children during the Passover Seder), *The Gay Agenda* portrayed the entire movement for equal rights for gay people as a plot to enable gay men to molest children and engage in bizarre sexual practices in public. This was about as far from the truth as one could get about mild-mannered Gerry, whose life revolved around conducting his band and choruses and living in domestic bliss with the love of his life. But I was learning that the truth mattered little to our Bible-wielding opponents. Getting their way was all that mattered, and breaking the commandment that "Thou shalt not lie" was a small price to pay for doing what they saw as the Lord's work. God would understand, I suppose, that they just couldn't follow his rules when it came to homosexuals.

Soon the zealots had compelled the Byron Center school board to hold what I guess one would call a meeting (or was it a lynching?) about Gerry in early 1996. In an extraordinary act of courage, Gerry came to the meeting, held in the packed gymnasium of his high school, to face down the witch hunters of Byron Center. Numerous parents and students rallied to his side, attesting to his outstanding record as a teacher (something virtually none of his opponents could talk about, as few actually were parents of any students in the school system). As was the case for me at Concord Academy, the school board soon realized that Gerry's job performance insulated him from the rabid right-wing attack dogs and that he wasn't about to be intimidated, so they had to back off.

Rather than stand by one of their finest teachers, the Byron Center school system chose the coward's way out, which so many school administrators are wont to do. At the end of the school year, they offered Gerry a generous severance package if he would voluntarily give up his job—in other words, a bribe if the faggot would just go away quietly. Gerry was torn by the offer and called me to discuss it in June 1996. On the one hand, having fought so hard, he didn't want the other side to feel like they'd won; he feared they would perceive his accepting the package as a victory for their tactics of terror and intimidation. On the other, he was exhausted, demoralized, and longed to go back to the quiet life of music and domestic happiness he had enjoyed before he was forced into this role of reluctant hero. What was his moral duty? I told him that he had done his moral duty by standing up to the bigots, that he had already won by showing that he would leave on his own terms and on his own timetable, and that now he owed himself and his family a shot at happiness. He didn't have to be a martyr to the cause. He decided to take the package.

The call came from one of our members in western Michigan, Rob, on the day I returned from Christmas vacation in early January 1997. On New Year's Eve, Gerry had a massive heart attack that, according to his doctors, was induced by the incredible stress he had been under for the past year. Gerry was dead. He was thirty-three years old—the same age as I was.

I took the news hard and decided to go to Grand Rapids for the funeral. It was snowing heavily in Chicago that day: my connecting flight to Grand Rapids was cancelled, and so I was put on one to Kalamazoo, an hour south of Grand Rapids, a flight that was also severely delayed. When we finally took off, I realized we were probably going to be so late that I would miss the funeral altogether. Touching down in Kalamazoo in the midst of a growing blizzard, our little regional jet began to skid badly, and I thought what a bizarre coincidence it would be if I were killed going to a funeral. But the pilot got the plane under control, and I bolted out the door of the plane as soon as the doors opened.

Rob was waiting. He told me he had heard that the funeral had been delayed for some reason and that there was still a chance we could make it. We raced through the storm, Rob driving pretty recklessly *(what a bizarre coincidence it would be if I were killed going to a funeral...)*, and we slid into the parking lot of the church in downtown Grand Rapids, the same church where Gerry had his fateful commitment ceremony barely a year and a half before.

Once we got into the church (where some of our members were holding a front-row seat for me), I realized why the funeral was running late. That morning, hundreds of students from Byron Center High School had spontaneously walked out of their classes and made their way to the funeral. Finally the school system commandeered some buses to get the multitude over there, and the seating of the enormous crowd had delayed the start of the service. The seat I took was the last empty one in the sanctuary.

Two images stay with me from the funeral. The first was that of a small and somewhat forlorn-looking floral arrangement directly in front of me. I honestly couldn't help thinking, what cheapskate sent this pathetic little display to a funeral? I leaned forward to read the card. It was from the administration and staff of the Byron Center school system. You bastards, I thought, first you kill him, and now you send cheap flowers to his funeral. Have you no sense of decency, sir? At long last, have you left no sense of decency?

The second was of two teenage girls hugging and sobbing after the ceremony. They clearly must have been two of Gerry's students, and they were overcome by their grief. I thought about these girls, sixteen, maybe seventeen years old, who were learning firsthand the price of bigotry; they would live another sixty years or so, until 2057 maybe, and they would never forget this day, never forget their teacher, never forget the tragic lesson the bigots in their community had taught them by brutalizing this kind, gentle, and gifted man. And then I realized that Gerry wasn't truly dead: he would live on in the hearts of these young people, a memory that would not be extinguished by the hatred that had taken his life. You won, Gerry, I thought. You won.

A few hours away by car, in the Cleveland suburb of Strongsville, Ohio, a woman named Leslie Sadasivan was struggling with her own family tragedy during the same snowy days of early January. I didn't know Leslie yet but would meet her soon. Leslie's son, Robbie Kirkland, had been a happy child in elementary school. But when junior high hit, he changed dramatically. He became moody and withdrawn. School, which he once loved, now became a place he hated to go. A school nurse, Leslie knew how to read these signs, and took her son to a counselor and initiated family therapy as well.

Through counseling, Leslie found out what the problem was. Robbie was gay and was being tormented daily at his public junior high school. Leslie took the news in stride: Robbie was her son, she loved him, and nothing was going to change that. She told him that and promised they'd get him out of that school and into a better place. She'd do whatever it took to make sure her son returned to being the happy boy she remembered so vividly.

A devout Catholic, Leslie enrolled her son at St. Ignatius, Cleveland's most prestigious Catholic school, an all-boys institution with a reputation for outstanding academics. Here, she thought, Robbie would be valued for the academic skills he possessed, and the strict discipline of the Catholic system would minimize opportunities for bullying. But it didn't turn out that way. Robbie continued to be bullied and called names, and he came home from school miserable each day, locking himself in his bedroom on many occasions. Desperate, Leslie approached the school administration, explaining that her son was gay, that the family stood behind him, and that the school needed to do more to address the bigotry that was making her son's life miserable. Despite her pleas, nothing changed.

Christmas break was a welcome respite from school for Robbie, and by all accounts their family had a lovely holiday in 1996. But, as 1996 melted into 1997 and the resumption of school drew near, Robbie must have had a growing sense of dread, a more severe form of my childhood "Sunday funny feeling," about returning to the hallways, the locker rooms, and the playing fields where he got called "faggot" so often. There seemed to be no light at the end of the tunnel: public school hadn't worked out, St. Ignatius wasn't working out, and he had three and a half more years of hell to look forward to. The prospect must have seemed unbearable to a fourteen-year-old. So, the day before school resumed, Robbie went down to his father's home office. He'd figured out how to work the locks on his father's desk and managed to get them open. There, he found the loaded gun that his father, an FBI agent, kept carefully locked away. He took it to his room, placed it to his temple, and killed himself—all so he wouldn't have to go back to school the next day.

I heard this story from folks in our Cleveland chapter shortly after getting back from Gerry's funeral. To channel their grief, Robbie's parents and siblings had decided to speak out against homophobia in schools and had just been the subject of a major front-page feature in the Cleveland daily paper the *Plain Dealer*. They were getting involved with GLSTN and were to speak at our upcoming conference in Cleveland, where I had the chance to meet Leslie for the first time.

Leslie was a delicate, beautiful woman, ten years older than I was but looking like she was the same age, who you could just tell was a school nurse—kindness radiated from her. Her daughter, Danielle, was a student at Miami University in Ohio, where Jeff had gone, and Danielle's boyfriend was at Harvard, where I had gone. We laughed over the coincidence.

If my heart wasn't already breaking for Leslie and Danielle, it broke completely when they showed me pictures of Robbie. He was an angelic boy with a shy smile and an open face that emanated vulnerability. How could anyone ever be mean to this kid? How could Leslie, so small, delicate, and vulnerable herself, possibly have the strength to get up and speak about this precious creature that had been taken from her? All I wanted to do was protect this woman who had already suffered so much.

But I learned that, like the students who had testified for the governor's commission, Leslie didn't need my protection. She needed a venue to tell her truth, to redeem some meaning from the tragedy that had befallen her. It was impossible not to be moved by the beautiful, down-to-earth, Midwestern mom and nurse who had just wanted the best for her son and whose family had been forever ripped apart by the consequences of bigotry. Although terrified of flying, Leslie would board planes repeatedly over the next several years at my request and fly to distant cities to tell her story, changing the hearts and minds of thousands in the process. I fell in love with Leslie Sadasivan.

But there was a second reason why Leslie's story moved me so deeply. Jeff had spent his entire K–12 life in Catholic schools in the Cleveland suburbs. Robbie was dead, and Jeff was alive—simply because Robbie got singled out and Jeff was somehow better at hiding. What if it had been Jeff who had gotten singled out? This thought would haunt my days. And how many more Robbies were there out there, who might have gone on to successful, happy lives like Jeff's, if only their schools had not allowed it to be open season on them every single day? I thought of the waste. I found myself wanting to find every Robbie in the country and tell him it would be okay, to hang on, that school was the worst part and it would be alright when you got out and could make your own path in life. I started thinking that I needed to view every lesbian, gay, bisexual, or transgender child as if they were *my* children and fight for them as ferociously as parents like Leslie had fought for theirs. This responsibility made me want to grab by the throat every timid administrator, every equivocating school board member, all of whom did nothing, and hold their heads under water until they begged for mercy and promised they'd protect my kids. I lost my patience for their excuses because of Robbie.

And then there was Kelli Peterson.

Sometime in the winter of 1996 my colleague John Spear took a call from Camille Lee, a GLSTN member and teacher at East High School in Salt Lake City, Utah. Camille told John that one of her students, Kelli Peterson, wanted to start a Gay-Straight Alliance, and what advice did he have to share with her? John's a smart guy and he immediately got the import of doing this in Utah, the heartland of the antigay Mormon Church. He came over to my office. "You know, Kevin, I think this might turn into something big," he told me.

He had no idea.

All hell broke loose in Utah once the East High Gay-Straight Alliance was announced. The school system immediately tried to ban the group, only to be hoisted on their own, Mormon-made, petard. Utah senator Orrin Hatch had authored legislation in 1984 called the Equal Access Act, which guaranteed the rights of students to form whatever kind of club they wished to form, as long as the school allowed clubs and the students followed the proper process (getting a faculty advisor, etc.). Senator Hatch had done this because he wanted to protect kids who were forming Bible clubs, but he had apparently not looked in the dictionary to understand the meaning of the word "equal." "Equal" access means access for everyone—not just for the Bible Club or the fundamentalist recruitment clubs such as Young Life or the Fellowship of Christian Athletes, one of which virtually every school has today. Our brilliant colleagues at Lambda Legal Defense and the ACLU seized upon this law, arguing correctly that you couldn't ban one club and allow others without violating federal statute.

Having their own law used to block them enraged Utah's politicians the same way a red cape does a bull, and the furor in Utah went into overdrive when school authorities discovered they could not legally ban the Gay-Straight Alliance. The state legislature went into special session to try to find a way to intervene and guard the citadel of Mormonism from the infidel teenage lesbian, Kelli Peterson, who was now on the nightly news. The Salt Lake City school board did the same. It began to grow from front-page news in Utah into a national story. Finally, the zealots hit upon a solution: they would simply ban all clubs so there could be no Gay-Straight Alliance at East High. The stunning disregard for the educational value of student clubs, all of which were to be chucked overboard just to stop a single Gay-Straight Alliance, brought national scorn and derision upon Utah's policymakers. Newscaster Bryant Gumbel literally snorted while reading the story on the next morning's edition of *The Today Show.*

By now, network-news satellite trucks had East High besieged —just in time to witness a massive walkout led by Kelli. Most kids hadn't really cared about the Gay-Straight Alliance, but when they realized that the school board was shutting down their clubs, too, they exploded in anger and rallied behind Kelli. Hundreds streamed out of the school building and marched to the statehouse in downtown Salt Lake City, where hundreds of students from other high schools joined them. The spontaneous rally of teenagers constituted the largest gathering in support of gay rights in Utah's history.

I got news of this in the middle of a speech to a Lesbian Gay

Bisexual Transgender (LGBT) community-center event in Chicago. Robbie's story fresh in my mind, I decided that these kids (and their adult allies like Camille) were not going to fight this fight alone. I announced right then and there that GLSTN was heading to Utah, en masse, to stage our first-ever national conference. I put out a call for every supportive person in our network to join me in Salt Lake City in March 1997.

We had two months to prepare, and we had a total of three staff members to organize the mobilization of hundreds of people to travel to Utah.

John Spear flew to Utah the next day and negotiated a deal with the downtown Holiday Inn to host us. The extraordinarily brave GLSTN members in Utah, led by Doug Wortham, worked feverishly to get ready for the event. People from all over the country started registering. March came, and we all boarded flights to Salt Lake City. The night the conference opened, we held a special reception to honor the students of the East High Gay-Straight Alliance, especially Kelli, for their leadership. When they arrived, they were dressed to the nines. Wow, I thought, this is a little much for the Salt Lake City Downtown Holiday Inn, where I didn't think tuxes were required. It turned out they weren't all dressed up for us. Tonight was their prom, to which they were all defiantly going, mostly as same-sex couples. When they announced this from the podium, pandemonium broke out in the room, with the three-hundred-plus people who had come from across America yelling and cheering their encouragement to these extraordinary young people. This time it really did feel like Mississippi in 1964, but in a good way.

Kelli's story would serve as the narrative thread for a documentary called *Out of the Past*, which producer Eliza Byard (today our deputy executive director), director Jeff Dupre, and I were working on at the time, with the goal of creating something that could be shown in U.S. history classrooms to educate young people on gay history.

A year after our conference, in 1998, *Out of the Past* won the Audience Award for Best Documentary at the Sundance Film Festival. A few months later, in June 1998, it was shown at the White House in the first-ever celebration of Gay Pride Month there. And a year after that, courts struck down the law banning clubs in Salt Lake City schools when it was found that (just as we expected) the administration was letting clubs they liked continue but not ones like the Gay-Straight Alliance. Today, every high school in Salt Lake City has a Gay-Straight Alliance.

Just as the 1996–97 school year closed, we decided to change our name to the Gay, Lesbian, and Straight Education Network (GLSEN), reflecting not only that there were more than teachers involved but also that our struggle was, in the end, one designed to make sure all students got education—that gay students got equal access to an education and that straight students got an education that did not teach them to grow up to be bigots. I was looking forward to a quiet summer after the tumultuous events of the prior months when I got a call from Richard Socarides, the White House liaison to the LGBT community and a senior advisor to President Clinton. Relations between our community and the president had been strained since 1993, when he had gone back on his promise to end the ban on gays in the military and instead instituted a "don't ask, don't tell" policy that codified the ban into law (albeit under a "kinder, gentler" name). The president wanted to repair that relationship and had asked Richard to select twelve leaders from the community who could talk with him about the issues we faced and what he could do about them. Richard asked if I would be one of those twelve.

It was a steaming late July day when I was ushered into a non-Oval room in the White House with eleven other leaders to await the president's arrival. We all had places at a rectangular conference table, nameplates in front of them, but curiously the seat next to me was empty and lacked a nameplate. We were chatting with various White House staff members and suddenly everyone was standing, so I stood too, and a man much taller than I appeared next to me. I looked up and he proffered his hand, saying, "Hi, I'm Bill Clinton," as if he needed to introduce himself. He then sat in the empty seat. He didn't need a nameplate.

The "gang of twelve" had met beforehand to strategize, and we carefully went through our lineup, with different people assigned to address different issues: legal protections for same sex couples, action to fight AIDS, laws to protect gay people from employment discrimination—the list was long because the needs are so great. I waited patiently until it was my turn, when I was supposed to explain the needs of lesbian, gay, bisexual, and transgender youth and the issues they faced in schools. Then I played my trump card. Through a complete fluke, I had spoken to Chelsea Clinton's class at Sidwell Friends three years before and she had introduced herself, asking me to say hi to a friend of hers who was a student at Concord Academy. I started talking about what GLSEN did and dropped Chelsea's teacher's name into the conversation, saying that the best part of my job was going into classrooms like his and talking with students. The president's eyes widened, and he said, "You've spoken to my daughter's class?" I said yes, and he replied, "That's great! I'm going to call Earl Harrison [the head of Sidwell Friends] and tell him how happy I am to hear that!" Having gotten his attention, I sprang into action, running through the figures on gay youth suicide, name-calling in schools, the lack of legal protections, hammering home that every school should do what Sidwell was doing but few did. The president was engaged, I think because we were talking about something that was *real* to him, his daughter's school, and he understood this issue on a gut level, while the other issues were more abstract. Unbeknownst to me at the time, a White House photographer snapped a shot of us intently in midconversation, a photo that hangs in my office to this day.

"Who are you talking to at the Department of Education?" he asked. Turning to an aide, he said, "Make sure this man gets the name and number of the right person over there so we can do something about this."

Two years later, with GLSEN's assistance, the Department of Education issued its first guidelines on schools' obligation to protect LGBT students from harassment.

As the meeting ended, we all stood up and the president turned to me. "I'm going to ask Chelsea if she remembers you coming to her class," he said.

"Well, if she does, Mr. President, tell her I said hi."

If I were more cool, I wouldn't admit that my mind was spinning. But I'm not. On the plane home, I couldn't help but think: I have come a long way from the trailer park, a long way from the hallways where I ate lunch alone every day because I was too scared to go into the cafeteria. It's been a long, long journey, which peaked that day as I was seated next to the president with a chance to get him to take action to protect the Robbies of the world. Nothing could ever top this, I thought.

But I would find out, three years later, that something could.

CHAPTER 13

Going Home

My temperature was 102 when I got off the plane in North Carolina in October 2000. One hundred two degrees: It was the same temperature I'd had to run as a kid before Mom would take me to the emergency room and we would get the only medical care we were guaranteed.

I always get sick in the fall. School reopens; I say yes to every place that asks me to come and help them out; I travel five, six, seven days a week and get so run down that I get sick. Happens every year. Yet every year I do the same thing—because I'm slow to recognize patterns and so stubborn that I tend to ignore them when they tell me to do something that I don't want to do, like slow down.

By October of 2000 I was aware that a dominant pattern in my life was one of improbable journeys: from a trailer park to Harvard; from studying at a modestly funded public high school to teaching at one of the richest and most elite schools in the nation; from being ostracized because I was gay to being seated at the side of the president for the same reason. But heading into Winston-

Salem that October day, I realized I was about to complete the most improbable journey of all: I was to preach a sermon at a church less than a mile from the one I had attended as a child, and my mom was to be in the congregation. This day, truly, had been a long time coming.

Following my graduation from Harvard in 1985, Mom and I had settled into a somewhat unhappy and tense truce of a relationship. Bob and I would spend Thanksgiving with her and Christmas with his family each year. Frankly, the less time we were together, the better I felt. I was angry at her because of the shame she felt about my being gay; she, undoubtedly, was angry at me for my shame around my family's background and my desire to get as far away from her and it as I could. We weren't going to talk about it, but we were mad at each other.

But in all honesty, Mom was not the uppermost thing in my mind during the late eighties. I was caught up in my first real relationship, in starting a career, in figuring out who I was, and Mom wasn't on that list of priorities. Plus, I didn't think she would ever budge from her hostile position, and I wasn't going to back down either (I'd gotten my stubbornness from her). So it was a standoff. Or so I thought.

Unbeknownst to me, Mom found a therapist in the late eighties (how she paid for it, I'll never know) and talked with him about her greatest fear: that she was losing her youngest son. She had been taught her whole life that being gay was wrong, but she could see how her inability to accept me was creating an unbridgeable chasm between us. I don't know how to accept him, she told the therapist. Help me.

The therapist told Mom that she needed to meet some other parents of gay kids, to share her struggle with them and learn from their experience. "Where can I meet them?" she asked. The therapist told her about an organization called PFLAG, Parents and Friends of Lesbians and Gays, about which Mom got excited. But it turned out there wasn't a chapter in Winston-Salem, and she was crestfallen.

"Why don't you start one?" the therapist suggested.

So she did.

I didn't know about it at first. But then students from Wake Forest University, the Baptist college in town—which at that point wouldn't allow a gay student group to form—started coming to her PFLAG meetings for support. They educated Mom about how difficult it was to be a young gay person. Knowing she had a son who was an "expert" on the issue, she began to ask me questions.

"Hey, Kevin, what would you tell a kid about how to tell his mother he was gay?"

"Huh?"

"Well, a young person has asked me for advice on this, and I figured you would know better than I would."

"Someone you work with at the hospital?"

"No, a student from Wake Forest."

This wasn't making any sense to me. Mom was hanging out with Wake Forest undergrads? "How did you meet a student from Wake Forest, Mom?"

"At a meeting."

Now I was exasperated. "What kind of meeting, Mom? Are you in AA now? You don't even really drink."

"It was a PFLAG meeting. He came to our meeting and was asking advice and I thought I'd ask you what to tell him."

As the saying goes, you could have knocked me over with a feather.

"There's a PFLAG chapter in Winston-Salem? Since when?"

"Oh, about a year."

"When did you start going?"

"For about a year now."

I did the math. "So you must have been there almost at the start."

"Well, yes, I was. I was at the first meeting."

"How'd you hear about it?"

"Well . . ." she paused. "Well, I started it."

Long pause. "*You* started a PFLAG chapter?"

"Yeah. I've been seeing this therapist, and he said it would be good for me to meet some other parents of gay kids. I asked him how, and he told me about PFLAG. But the nearest meeting was over in Greensboro, and I don't like to drive that far at night, so he suggested I start one here. So I did."

I was getting too much confusing information all at once, before I had even processed the PFLAG news. "*You're* seeing a therapist? What got you to start doing that?"

Now it was her turn to pause. "Well, I could see how we were drifting apart, and I didn't want that to happen, and I needed some help. He told me I needed to accept that you were gay, that I didn't do anything to cause it, and that is where the idea of talking to other parents came from, so I could learn from what they did."

Who is this woman who knows how to talk about her feelings? This is not my mother! It's a pod person! *My* mother hugged me when I got off the plane my sophomore year of college and I was so confused I whispered, "Why are you touching me?" as her hugging me was not something I could ever remember her doing. Either this is an impostor or this therapist is a friggin' miracle worker.

Once again, I had underestimated my mom. I looked at her with new eyes. Instead of the monster who disapproved of me, for whom nothing I did was ever good enough, I saw her clearly: a lonely woman in her midsixties who had grown up in the hills of Tennessee during the Depression with no running water or electricity, who was forced out of school at age nine, and who had come of age in a world mired in segregation and superstition. She missed her son and just wanted a relationship with him, and she was doing her best to figure out how to get him back.

And I thought: I am a real asshole.

Not that everything was better all at once. Change is a process, not an event, and I had too much hurt and too much history with Mom to let down my guard again all at once. I suppose she did, too. But then I decided to do a chapel talk at Concord about her journey and what I had learned from her (the same topic that had been the theme of my Harvard admissions application essay, something she'd never known). The Concord students were overwhelmed by it and started asking when Mom was coming to visit because they wanted to meet her. So that year I invited her to spend Thanksgiving in Boston with Bob and me rather than us going to Winston-Salem, and after tense negotiations that resulted in a compromise that she could smoke in her bedroom but not the rest of the house because Bob was allergic (she made it clear she wasn't coming if she couldn't smoke in the house; she had her priorities, and nicotine was at the top of the list), Mom came up for Thanksgiving and spent a day at Concord Academy.

I was terrified. I knew she had an accent, that she would have all the wrong clothes on, that she'd never read Proust, that she'd tell embarrassing stories about me, that this would be a disaster. Now they would *really* know I didn't belong. I'd managed to pull off the gay thing, but coming out as white trash was asking them to take a step too far.

The big day arrived, Mom drove out with me to Concord, and everybody loved her. The kids thought she was a rock star and they treated her like one. She was mystified by all the compliments she got as a result of my chapel ("What's so unusual about my life?" she asked me later, the very question revealing how extraordinary she truly was) but the praise clearly pleased her. She was charming, she bonded with the kids and faculty who hung out in the smoking area, she even participated in my classes, adding comments as good as any of the kids (although she hadn't done the reading, but then again, most of the kids probably hadn't either). All day I hovered over her, waiting for her to trip up. She never did. It turned out, I realized, that I was the one who had a problem.

In 1994, when GLSTN decided to go national, I called Mom to tell her about it. But the real reason was that I was doing a segment on the television news program *20/20*, and I thought I'd better warn her about it. It's one thing to be at your little PFLAG meeting talking about the fact your son is gay, but it's another thing to have him on national TV—the next day, everyone at work would be whispering at the water cooler, "Miz Jennings's son is a homosexual!" Mom got very quiet upon hearing the news, which I knew was not a good sign. Remember, Southern women of her generation have a creed: if you haven't got anything nice to say, don't say anything at all.

So I pushed her. "Come on, Mom, what do you think of all this?"

"I understand this is real important to you, Kevin. But do you have to be so *public* about all this?"

"Well, Mom, you made me this way."

The silence was deafening. I kept going.

"It's not what you think, Mom. I'm not saying you made me gay. But remember when I was a kid and we'd go to church and you told me I'd be okay if I just followed the Ten Commandments? Remember how one of those commandments is 'Thou shalt not lie'? Remember how, when I was a kid, if I got in trouble you'd sit me down and say, 'Kevin, whatever it is, the truth shall set you free.' Well, guess what, Mom? You turned out to be right. I have told my truth, and it has set me free."

I was quite pleased with my little speech: I thought she'd gotten it. It was years later before I found out that, caught up in my own drama, I was oblivious to her real concern. Mom had no objection to my new work but, knowing how irrational people can be about their kids, she was terrified that one of the nutcases who regularly accuse gays of "recruiting their kids" would someday decide to knock off the "head recruiter," which would be me. When she told me her fears years later, I laughed and told her she was crazy, that they'd go after Ellen DeGeneres or Barney Frank or someone a lot more important than I. I never told her about the voicemail and e-mail messages in which the exact threats she so feared were regularly communicated to me. (I'm good at hiding. I've had lots of practice.)

In 1996, the North Carolina Gay Pride celebration was to be held in Winston-Salem for the first time and, as perhaps the most famous homosexual from Winston-Salem, I was asked if I would speak at it. This was taking things to a new level: Mom lived there and everybody would now know, if they had somehow missed me on national news. I decided I had to call her and ask how she felt about it. If she was profoundly uncomfortable, I wasn't going to do it.

The phone call was a bizarre experience. It was as if I had been transported back in time, to my childhood, or to my teen years, when I would try to get the car keys without telling her I wanted to use the car to go drinking with my friends—except this time, I was asking, "Can I go outside and play with the other homosexuals?" You're thirty-three, you're an adult, I told myself; you have two Ivy League degrees, you've published two books, you run a national organization. *Then why the hell am I sweating and nervous?*

I began to explain about the march and Mom interrupted. "Oh, Kevin, I know about the march and I figured you were coming," she began. "I have already made my plans to go with you." Now it was my turn to be struck silent. "So, what were you calling about, Kevin?"

Incredulous that she had just passed this event off like it was nothing, I stammered, "Uh, nothing, Mom, that was about it."

"Okay. Well, I'm real tired and, if you don't mind, I'm going to go now because I have got to get up early for work, if that's all you needed to talk about."

"Okay," I said, and hung up. I then stared at the phone with probably the same expression of amazement I suspect a Neanderthal man would have if he encountered such a device.

A few weeks before the march, Mom was diagnosed with emphysema (three packs a day for fifty years will do that to you). She was put on oxygen to help with her increasingly labored breathing and given a portable oxygen tank to take with her when she left the house. Now my concern shifted: should she be coming out to an event in the middle of a June North Carolina day, which means ninety-degree heat and 100 percent humidity? I said maybe it wasn't such a good idea after all. She brushed aside my concerns, saying she wasn't going to stop living just because she had to lug around some dumb oxygen thing.

So there we were at the Pride Festival, where I focused my talk on gay history. Mom loved it (after all, she was the one who had dragged me to the public library and the Civil War battlefields and taught me to love history in the first place) and said she learned a lot. She was delighted to meet so many people who thought so highly of her son, and she would brag about my Harvard degree and the organization I started and my books. I bragged about her for starting the PFLAG chapter in Winston-Salem, and people hugged her for doing it. A good time, indeed, was had by all.

(I didn't yet know that Mom had dropped out of the PFLAG chapter. She told me later that an influx of affluent, professional parents—the kind who always intimidated her, who made her feel shame about her own lack of education and wealth—had begun to make her feel inadequate and out of place, so she just quit going. When I finally learned this, it reminded me that some voices are listened to and valued, and some are not—and that rarely is it the content of what is said that determines which is which, but factors like class and race and gender.)

I started opening up more to Mom and telling her about my life. I called her from the plane on my flight back from my meeting with President Clinton in 1997, and she took it as being as much a triumph for her as it was for me, which was how I told her she ought to view it. She came to the *Out of the Past* premiere in nearby Greensboro in 1998. When a retired teacher named Janet Joyner decided to start a GLSEN chapter in Winston-Salem in 1999, Mom befriended her and went with me to the chapter's first meeting (an event I was not going to miss, come hell or high water).

But 1999 was a bad year for Mom. She had continued to work full time despite her illness. She was never one for charity, refusing my and Jeff's entreaties to help her out financially, but she couldn't live on just a Social Security check, so that meant she had to keep working. But by 1999, at age seventy-four, her energy sapped by emphysema, even my mother, who held the *Guinness Book* world record for stubbornness, had to admit she couldn't do it anymore.

Personally I was delighted that she was quitting her job. I hated that she was still working at age seventy-four. I had always wanted to do something to repay her in some small way for all the sacrifices she had made for me, and had told myself as a kid when I watched her struggle that someday I'd get rich and buy her a big house. Now I had my chance. Jeff and I moved her to a new apartment in a much nicer neighborhood (I never got rich enough running a nonprofit to buy her that house), and I was thrilled to see her settled in her own truly nice place for the first time.

But Mom was the restless type, and I knew she'd need to find something to do, as she wasn't about to sit home all day and watch the soaps. I also knew that if she didn't feel she was helping others in some way, her spirit would die and her body soon thereafter. After all, I knew my mother's favorite story from the Bible.

> And He [Jesus] looked up, and saw the rich men casting their gifts into the treasury. And He also saw a certain poor widow casting in thither two mites. And He said, "Of a truth

> I say unto you that this poor widow hath cast in more than they all: for all these have of their abundance cast in unto the offerings of God; but she of her penury hath cast in all the living that she had."

So I started pestering her to find something to volunteer at, not too taxing, not too onerous. At first she decided she'd volunteer to hold premature babies at the hospital, but then called me, despondent, when she discovered there was a yearlong waiting list of volunteers for that job. Then one day she called me, upbeat, telling me she'd found a place to volunteer. I asked her the name, and she replied, "Holly Haven." Knowing she loved to grow things, I thought maybe it was some kind of plant nursery, so I asked her what they grew there.

"Grow? I don't know what you mean. Holly Haven is an AIDS hospice. It's the first one we've had in Winston-Salem, and I am one of their first volunteers."

Soon our conversations revolved around Holly Haven and the people she met there. They became a kind of extended family to her. I would hear stories about Larry, the executive director; about Lori, a health aide who became her best friend; and numerous patients, most of whose names didn't stick because, well, they weren't there all that long before passing on or recovering enough to move out. The one exception was her friend Ricky, a young gay man who took my mom on as his mother since his own wanted no part of him. Ricky got better for a while and was able to move out, but then he took a turn for the worse. Mom found his body in his apartment when, after several days of his not returning her calls, she got worried and went over there, only to find he had killed himself, overcome by despair over his losing battle with the disease. Mom found his suicide note, which told her that he had left his most prized possession, his Bible, to her.

When I went home a few months later, I went to Holly Haven with Mom, who wanted me to meet everyone. I was surprised at how small it was; her stories made it seem like some major facility, but in fact it was a converted family home with only a handful of bedrooms. Upon meeting each of the guys (they were all guys) and them finding out I was Alice's son, they would light up and say, "We LOVE your momma!" Of course, I think they mainly loved her because, since they weren't allowed to smoke in the house, Mom would wheel them out to the porch where she could smoke with them. Mom was still chain smoking a few packs a day, even with the emphysema and the oxygen: she'd just turn the oxygen off, take the cannula out of her nose, and light up every now and then. (When we came home for Christmas that year, Jeff and I took Mom over to Holly Haven, ostensibly because he'd never been there, but really so that she would stumble across the plaque naming the porch The Alice Jennings Porch in return for a gift we had made to AIDS Care Services of Winston-Salem. It seemed the appropriate part of the hospice to name for her, after all.)

What amazed me the most after my tour was that Mom had neglected to mention a certain something to me about the hospice patients she worked with—something she had been taught as a child was the most important fact about a person. Almost everyone at Holly Haven was black. Why this possibility hadn't crossed my mind, given that AIDS disproportionately strikes people of color, I don't know, but it hadn't. It astonished me that Mom had never brought it up. This, from a woman who had disowned her own son for marrying a black woman, was a rather major omission. Who was this woman, I wondered, and how had she become this incredible person? I thought about Mom's own improbable journey, from an Appalachian, gospel-singing, preacher's wife who took it as given that blacks were inferior and gays were evil, to a woman who spent her days with a group of primarily gay black men. The distance I had traveled seemed slight in comparison. I wondered where she had found the inspiration to make her journey, and decided that maybe she had paid attention in Sunday school too, where someone had taught her to "Love thy neighbor as thyself"; things like race and sexual orientation just don't seem like that big a deal when set side-by-side against such a fundamental commandment. She left me in awe.

So we had both come a long way when I stepped off that plane in October 2000. The founder of the GLSEN chapter in Winston-Salem, Janet Joyner, had gotten her Unitarian church to invite me to be the guest minister on the Sunday closest to National Coming Out Day. Here I was, back in North Carolina, set to preach. It had all come full circle.

The Lord is my shepherd. I shall not want. He maketh me to lie down in green pastures. He leadeth me beside the still waters.

In choosing my theme, I decided to talk about the "Faith of My Father... and Mother," which became the title of the sermon. I talked about how my father's faith was one of fear and suspicion, of self-loathing and self-hatred—a life-negating faith that nearly killed me—but my mother's faith in the power of education had been the one that had sustained me, and had saved and guided my life.

I was both sick and nervous when I got to the pulpit at the Unitarian church—sick because the cold medicine hadn't done much, and nervous because Mom was in the audience to see me give my first sermon, as was my brother Mike and his wife and daughter. So many scary things from my childhood, come home to roost, only a mile from Robinhood Road Baptist Church, the church of my childhood. The Unitarian church was a far cry from Robinhood Road Baptist Church or the Concord Academy chapel, being a modernistic one with wall-to-wall carpeting and chairs instead of hardwood floors and pews. The congregation overflowed the available seats, and their warmth toward me was palpable. As I worked my way through my speech, it was like I was back in the Concord Academy chapel. There are times when you're on a stage and you can tell that everyone in the audience is with you, that they're on your side, that they're pulling for you. This was another one of those times. I wound down by talking about my work with GLSEN, how it followed in the greatest tradition of Christianity, which is one not of judgment but of acceptance, one not of intolerance but of compassion. I closed by speaking about the inspiration I got daily from Mom:

> On those days when my faith begins to flag, I find my mind wandering back to Lewisville, North Carolina, where my mom still lives, and I find my faith again renewed. On those days when my faith in the capacity of people to learn and grow wavers, I look to my mom. Raised in segregation, she has embraced her African American daughter-in-law. Raised with homophobia, she founded a chapter of Parents and Friends of Lesbians and Gays, and regularly attends the meetings of one of the newest GLSEN chapters, in Winston-Salem. Raised to turn her back on those deemed "unclean," she spends three days a week volunteering at Holly Haven, the first hospice for people with AIDS in Winston-Salem—a facility in which each resident is black. When my faith flags, when my soul is weary, when I feel I am too tired to go on with the struggle for justice, I picture my seventy-five-year-old mother holding the hands of a seventy-pound African American man with AIDS as he passes from this life to the next, and I am restored.

Then I added the words of 1 John 4:20–21:

> "If a man says, I love God, and hateth his brother, he is a liar; for he that loveth not his brother who he hath seen, how can he love God whom he hath not seen? And this commandment have we from him, That he who loveth God love his brother also."

When I was done, I asked Mom what she thought. She replied, "You know, you're just like your daddy. You've just got a little bit of a different sermon."

He restoreth my soul; he leadeth me in the paths of righteousness for his name's sake. Yea, though I walk through the valley of the shadow of death, I will fear no evil: for thou art with me; thy rod and thy staff, they comfort me.

The next day, Janet had arranged for me to speak to all the guidance counselors of the Winston-Salem/Forsyth County school system—the very system that I remembered with so little fondness, where my young soul had almost been crushed. At the end of the workshop, a woman who apparently had been one of my classmates said she remembered watching how I was treated when we were in school and that she had promised herself that now that she was a counselor, she would do everything she could to make sure no kid would go through that again.

Thou preparest a table before me in the presence of mine enemies; thou anointest my head with oil; my cup runneth over.

The next morning, a Tuesday, I was up early to catch my 7 AM flight to yet another city. I'm not a morning person, so I was semiconscious as I kissed Mom goodbye at around 5:30. Before I could get out the door, though, she said, "Kevin, sit down. I have something I want to talk to you about."

Even though I was thirty-seven, my inner child immediately went on red alert. These kinds of conversations, beginning with those ominous words, had never gone well when I was a kid, and I braced myself for what Mom had to say, having no clue what it might be.

"What is it, Mom?"

"I have two things to say. First of all, I listened to your sermon, and thought about how awful it was for you growing up and going to school here. I just wanted to tell you I'm sorry. I'm sorry I wasn't there for you when you needed me."

My throat began to close up. "It's okay, Mom. You didn't know. I didn't tell you."

"I know, but that doesn't make it okay. I'm sorry, and I want you to know I'm sorry."

Now I was barely breathing. Mom continued.

"Now, the second thing. I hear about how awful it is for kids like you today, how things haven't changed." She paused. "And I just want you to know how proud I am of you for trying to make it better for them."

What could I say? I had no idea. My heart had stopped by this point, anyway.

"Well, you're going to be late for your flight." She stood up and hugged me, and I held her in my arms, a tiny woman, a small fraction over five feet tall, barely more than a bag of bones, weighing in at slightly over a hundred pounds, sustained by a diet of coffee and cigarettes and chocolate and compassion. "You know how much I love you," she said.

"I love you too, Mom." And I left, off to another city, to do what she called "the Lord's work."

Surely goodness and mercy shall follow me all the days of my life; and I will dwell in the House of the Lord forever,

Amen.

CHAPTER 14

Alpha and Omega

"I am Alpha and Omega, the beginning and the end, the first and the last."
REVELATION 22:14

My story ends where it began—in a North Carolina hospital.

This time it's North Carolina Baptist Hospital in Winston-Salem, about a hundred miles west of Roanoke Rapids. Things have changed in North Carolina since 1966. Baptist Hospital is now affiliated with Wake Forest University and is known for its outstanding care. Helicopters land on the roof, bearing trauma patients to some of the best acute care facilities in the world. Award-winning surgeons do life-saving work in the operating rooms. Fancy diplomas adorn their office walls.

But people still die.

I'm back in Winston-Salem because our roles have been reversed. One fine July Sunday morning I'm spending the weekend in Boston and my brother Mike calls and tells me, "Don't worry, Mom's in the hospital; we don't know what it is yet but if it seems serious, we'll call and you can come down then."

Turns out she'd called 911 the night before and had an ambulance take her to the hospital when a pain in her stomach got to be too much. The hospital called Mike several hours later, but only because Mom slipped up and mentioned her son in town. She'd hidden his existence from the admitting nurse because she didn't want to be a bother. When he got there, she became furious and signed herself out. A few hours later she collapsed again and Mike took her back to the hospital in the wee hours of what would turn out to be a beautiful North Carolina summer day, clear blue skies, sunny, not too hot, not too much humidity: July 21, 2002.

Mike and I exchange nervous phone calls all day, me in Boston, him at Baptist Hospital: "No, we still don't know what's wrong yet; no, I don't think it's that serious; no, I don't think you should come down yet." About six in the evening I go to the gym, and when I come out there's a message on the cell phone: "Kevin, Mom's going into surgery. She's got a blood clot lodged in her intestine, and if they don't get it out, she's going to die in less than twenty-four hours. But it's a dangerous operation—even healthy, young people die from it. It's unlikely she'll survive the procedure, but it's her only chance. You'd better get down here as soon as you can." Mike doesn't have to say the rest: the doctors had told us long ago that, due to her emphysema, Mom could never undergo major surgery; she'd never be able to withstand the anesthetic, her lungs were too weak and most likely would never regain normal functioning. They'd only operate if there were absolutely no other resort.

A happy ending is highly unlikely.

I call Mike back, and he tells me she's in the anesthesia room, "It's too late, you can't talk to her; no, there's nothing you can do." I can't accept this as an answer and tell Mike that—if my mom is going to die in that operating room—he'd better fucking find a way to get a phone in to her. His wife, Donna, comes through. It turns out that she does the anesthesiologist's hair and convinces her to hand Mom a cell phone so we can speak. (Moral of the story: never underestimate the power of a hairdresser in the South.)

This will be our last conversation.

I can't get a coherent sentence out, two Ivy League degrees and an MBA notwithstanding.

Mom is already heavily sedated and talking is difficult for her. She only gets one sentence out but, as always, it's the right one.

"Kevin, I just want you to know one thing: I'm so proud of you."

I jump in a cab and head for the airport, frantically calling U.S. Airways on the way. No, the nice lady says, there aren't any more nonstops tonight, but if you can get to the airport, there's a flight leaving in thirty minutes and you can connect in Pittsburgh and you'll make it into Greensboro at about 10:30. There's weekend traffic in the Callahan Tunnel and it looks like I'll never make it, that it's impossible, that I'll miss my last chance to get to North Carolina that night. A voice is screaming in my head, "Why didn't you get the first flight this morning? Why didn't you get the first flight this morning? Why didn't you get the first flight this morning?"

At Logan, airport security is tighter than a drum (it's less than a year after 9/11, the hijackers left from here, remember?), but I'm in a daze. I walk right past security, the frantic guard stops me, and I look at him in confusion and say, "My mom's dying. I have to get home." A U.S. Airways rep shepherds me through security and I make the flight.

In the air between Boston and Pittsburgh I stare out the window, waiting to land, waiting for the chance to turn my cell phone on, waiting to find the message that my mom has died on the operating table.

I land and I turn the phone on.

She's alive. She's made it through the surgery. She's done the impossible again.

In Pittsburgh we're stuck on the runway for an hour and a half, and by the time I land in Greensboro and get my rental car and get to Baptist Hospital, it's nearly two in the morning. The nurses make an exception and let me into the intensive care unit (ICU) to see Mom. She's still under sedation, they warn me; she's got a lot of tubes in her and a respirator down her throat, which does the breathing for her, and she's terribly swollen and she probably won't know you're here, so brace yourself. I brace myself and walk into the room.

Mom somehow senses I'm there immediately. She opens her eyes, and squeezes my hand.

The next few weeks are a roller coaster. At first they don't think the surgery has succeeded, so they open her up again to see if they got out all of the dead bowel and if the stitches are holding. They find that, unbelievably, all has gone well. The doctors are shocked, and they now tell us that they had given her only a 20 percent chance of surviving the surgery.

But then she starts bleeding internally, and it won't stop. They don't know what to do because if they take her off the blood thinner, she may throw more blood clots like the one that almost killed her, but if they don't take her off it, she'll be prone to bleeding. It doesn't look good; then, miraculously, the bleeding stops. Now they're trying to get her off the respirator—and you understand, Mr. Jennings, that your mother will probably never get off the respirator; she'll probably have to live the rest of her life in a home tied to a machine. But we'll try and, well, she's doing better than we expected, so let's cut back on the respirator pressure, and, well, she *is* doing remarkably well, so let's try turning the thing off for a few hours to see if she can breathe on her own and, well, I'll be damned, she did fine. It looks like she may indeed get off the respirator, so let's transfer her to intermediate care as it looks like we don't need to keep her in intensive care anymore. Have you made plans for where she's going to go when she's released, Mr. Jennings?

It's now been almost four weeks in the ICU, four weeks in which my mom's been on a respirator, unable to speak, but sure as hell still able to communicate. Disgusted with the slow pace of her recovery, she mouths to my sister-in-law Donna one night that she should "bring the car around!" because she's planning to sneak out and go home and is stopped only when she sets off the alarm on her bed as she tries to climb out of it. After I demand that she stop pulling out her tubes one afternoon, she gestures, as I am leaving, for me to come closer. I lean in, expecting a kiss, which brings me into close enough range for her to slap me. The nurses love her and the doctors call her feisty and say that's why she's still alive. Look, Mr. Jennings, you and your friend Jeff have been here every day, for each of the four visiting periods, morning, afternoon, evening, and night, for four weeks. You should go home and rest some, as your mom's really going to need you when she gets out of the ICU and isn't getting the kind of intensive care she's getting here. She'll be out of here, into intermediate care, any day now, once a bed opens up.

I don't feel right about leaving. Mom never left my side in Roanoke Rapids and it doesn't feel right for me to leave hers. I've been all over the doctors throughout Mom's stay, demanding information, questioning every decision they make until I am satisfied it's the right one, confirming every stereotype that Tar Heels have of Yankees from New York with their pushy-pushy ways. At first they're resistant, but then one day a surgeon takes note of my Harvard class ring and all of the sudden audiences are granted to me whenever requested. I am treated with a deference and respect that I note other families in the ICU waiting room, families with less means, families with little education, white-trash families—families like the one my mother grew up in, families like mine before I got my fancy Ivy League education, which changed the balance of power—are rarely given. I find myself giving them tips on how to get what they want out of the doctors, and suddenly we're like a family, all united against a system that holds our loved ones' futures in its hands but doles out access and information about them only when cornered. I worry about who will monitor the doctors if I go away, who will keep them honest, but my brother says, "Don't worry, go home, Donna and I are here."

"Don't worry," my nephews and nieces tell me, "We'll be there every day." "Don't worry, Mr. Jennings," the doctors tell me, "She's on her way to intermediate care as soon as a bed opens up." And against my better judgment, I book a flight back to New York to catch up on work for a few days.

The morning of the flight, Thursday, August 15, 2002, it still doesn't feel right to leave, and so Jeff and I stop by the hospital on the way to the airport, thinking that, if she doesn't look good, we'll just stay. We're on the first flight in the morning, so we get to the hospital about 5:30 AM; the nurses know us by now, and they let us in outside of visiting hours. Mom seems okay and nods her head that she understands that we're going back to New York, that it will be only a few days, and that when we come back she'll be in intermediate care and we'll make plans for her to go home. "Don't worry," the nurses say, "We'll take good care of her." We climb into our rental car, drive to the airport, board the flight, and are back in New York for the start of the workday.

My family's been sworn to update me after every visiting period, and in the afternoon, my brother tells me Mom's running a pretty high fever. Alarm bells start going off in my head and I say maybe I should fly back. But he tells me, "Calm down, I talked with the doctor and they're giving her medication. She'll be okay." The fever goes down again and the next night my nephew Michael calls my cell phone during dinner after the last visiting hour. He tells me how great Grandma was, how the nurses had brought a TV to her bedside so she could watch an Elvis special because it was the King's birthday. "You know how Grandma loves Elvis. She seemed in really good spirits. I think everything's gonna be okay, Uncle Kevin," he says. When I say good night to him, I am so happy, so relieved, that I go back to the table and have a second martini to celebrate. I go to bed and sleep like a baby, but of course I leave my cell phone on because, hey, you never know.

At 6:30 AM my cell phone rings twice and goes to voicemail before I get to it.

I am frantic and I note that the missed call is from my brother Mike. I punch in his cell phone number and he gets on the phone and says, "It's over."

"It's over? What do you mean, 'it's over'?"

"Mom died about an hour ago."

I can't believe it and I can't believe I wasn't there and I can't believe I didn't say goodbye. I can't believe anything.

I'll learn later from the autopsy that, on the Thursday I left, the doctors found that Mom had developed a septic infection that had spread throughout her entire body and, as my own doctor told me later, she didn't really have a chance from that moment forward. Even a healthy young person wouldn't survive such an infection, much less a seventy-six-year-old woman with chronic pulmonary disease who's been lying in an ICU for four weeks and had four surgical procedures during that time.

But I don't know this yet, which may be a blessing, because for a few weeks I am spared the guilt of thinking that, had I stayed, I might have somehow compelled, through force of will, the doctors to deliver the right treatment, I might have found the magic bullet to stop the infection, I might have saved Mom the way she had saved me thirty-six years before when I was helpless, lying in an oxygen tent in the Roanoke Rapids General Hospital, given up for dead. Sure, my rational mind tells me that, this time, there was no way we could have defied medical science and beaten the odds—but if I'd listened to my rational mind all along, I'd be living in a trailer park in the backwoods of North Carolina today instead of in New York City.

As always, the nice lady at U.S. Airways gets me on the next flight, flight number 6857 to Washington, changing to flight number 3118 to Greensboro, and I find I've developed a bizarre attachment to the airline I used to laughingly call "U.S. Scare" and swear I'll fly them for the rest of my life out of gratitude for how they've shuttled me back and forth during the last few weeks. The regional jet we take out of D.C. is small, so small Jeff can't stand all the way up in it. About a half hour outside of Greensboro, the pilot warns us that severe thunderstorms are striking North Carolina on this typical, hot, humid, summer afternoon, Saturday, August 17, 2002, the last day of my mother's life; the storms will rock the plane and we'd better buckle our seatbelts and brace ourselves for a rough descent and landing. At just that moment, a rainbow appears outside my window. Suddenly it's a double rainbow, and it seems to be following the plane. I'm crying, Jeff's crying; we know it's Mom's spirit guiding us in. The flight attendant passes us with a quizzical look and wonders if we're psycho, but the double rainbow follows us all the way to Greensboro, and our descent and landing is as smooth as silk. We get off the plane and my brother and sister-in-law and niece and nephew can't quit talking about the thunderstorm; it's the worst they've had in years. Even I-40 was closed for a while due to flash floods—who'd ever heard of that happening? Boy, it must have been one hell of a flight. No, we tell them, it was just about the smoothest one we'd ever had.

I go to the hospital, and the nurses let me in one last time because I need to see the ICU, to see that Mom's not there. When I see her empty bed and the nurse confirms that, yes, that's the bed your Mom lay in for the past four weeks, it hits me, and I cry in a way I haven't ever cried before. That night I get drunk with my family, something else I've never done before, and the next morning I take a dull hangover to the funeral home.

Mom had left clear instructions about her funeral. She was to be cremated, because coffins and burials were a big waste of money, and there were to be no flowers, because they're just a big waste of money, too. She won't even be around to see them, so what's the point?—you know that kind of money should be used to help other people. So we create a fund in her memory at the Appalachian Community Fund, a fund to help low-income women in the place where she grew up have a better shot at the American Dream than she ever got (to which my friends and people who have heard me speak about her start sending checks and checks and more checks—eventually $30,000 in checks—all because her story had so touched them). We make the arrangements for her cremation and for a memorial service to be held a couple of days later. The funeral director fills out the paperwork and says, "All we have to do now is have someone identify the body so we can proceed with the cremation."

Everyone freezes.

After a few awkward minutes it's decided I should do it, especially as I hadn't yet seen her body. I go into the room where she's laid out on a gurney, a gurney that looks like it's meant for a small child, and for the first time I realize how incredibly physically small my mom was—five feet, one inch tall, 103 pounds when she was admitted to the hospital, probably less after four weeks in intensive care. And I realize that she never seemed small when she was alive because her sprit was so strong that it dwarfed her body and gave her a presence that filled every room she entered. I also realize for the first time that she looks just like her mom, and that in many ways her life turned out just like her own mother's had, with her horizons curtailed by the fact that she was born poor and a woman and in Appalachia. There's so much I want to say, but there's only one word left to say because this is the last time I'll ever see her body. That word is goodbye.

The next few days we sort through Mom's belongings in search of some remembrances and pack up the rest to go to charity or to her grandchildren, who could really use this toaster and that coffee maker and those nonstick pots and pans (which I had bought her for Mother's Day just three months before and which she had used but once, to make my beloved chicken and dumplings); they're just starting out in life and they can't afford those kinds of things and having them will be a blessing. Little fights break out over material possessions and I am amazed at how some people can find a way to sink to the lowest common denominator at a time like this, but I guess everybody's family has those kinds of people, after all. It's all just so sad to me, how in the end they're just things, and Mom deserved much nicer things, a beautiful life filled with beautiful things, and now we're grasping at these cheap little things to try to hang on to her, to hang on to something that will keep her in our lives in some way, when this is a challenge beyond the reach of any material object.

I sort through and pick a few items that matter to me. I take a jar of green beans she had canned that spring, and smile over how she was still canning beans in this day and age when you could buy any vegetable you wanted fresh at the supermarket any time of the year. She canned them, I guess, because she learned to do that in the hills of Tennessee in the 1920s from her mom; she did it each spring, the way the groundhog still crawls out of his hole each year and tells us if there are going to be six more weeks of winter or not, even though meteorological forecasts do a much better job than rodents nowadays. I take her souvenir spoon collection, a collection made up mainly of little spoons I had bought her, spoons with handles reading Paris and Tokyo and Cape Town and a host of other places that Mom had always dreamed of visiting but never had the means to until she was too sick with emphysema to fly and thus had to live vicariously through me and the spoons I would bring her. I find a letter, my most-prized remembrance of her, a reference letter from her boss during my senior year of high school, when she worked a pushcart for minimum wage on the Pearl Harbor naval base five days a week, eight hours a day, standing all day in the blazing Hawaiian sunshine, selling hotdogs to sailors so that I could quit my part-time job at Taco Bell. She worked in the shadeless heat so I could spend my senior year studying and getting good grades and getting high and getting ready to leave her and the kind of life she'd had far behind. So I could go off to Harvard and develop airs and break her heart for years until I realized how wise she had been all along, how much smarter than I she was in so many ways, and how much more *she* deserved the life I had been given. The letter read, "Alice Jennings is very reliable and very conscientious.... She has improved her sales. . . . She has worked hard in her job, and has improved the overall operation of the Hot Dog Stand. She is enthusiastic and handles the customers real well. She gets along well with everyone."

At the end, the reference request asked, "What kind of position do you see this employee holding in the future?"

Her boss had written, "Leader-type position."

Epilogue

"O Lord, I am in derision daily, every one mocketh me.... All my relations watch for my halting, saying, Peradventure... we shall prevail against him; we shall take our revenge on him. But the Lord is with me as a mighty terrible one; therefore my persecutors shall stumble, and they shall not prevail; they shall be greatly ashamed."

JEREMIAH 20:7,10–11

Three days after Mom died, Tuesday, August 20, 2002, I organized her memorial service and delivered the eulogy. In it I spoke of her journey, from the Appalachian shack where she grew up to her final days as a volunteer at Holly Haven. A few days later, I sent the eulogy out to a list of e-mail addresses of my first cousins on the Johnson side that my cousin Margie had put together. My cousin Nathan, whose father, Fred, had tried unsuccessfully to recruit my dad into the Klan five decades earlier and had tried to block school integration in the early seventies, sent me a reply, quoted here with its errors intact. Although it opened with "Kevin, let me express my deepest sorrow at the lost of Aunt Alice," Nathan made it clear that "we donot approve or will ever except your livestyle." Not only was I "a disgrace to the family," but "worst of all you promote your sickness around this great country corrupting the minds of our young.... The gay community will be the downfall of all America." His well wishes consisted of asking me to "please consider what evil path you have taken before it's to late" but, if I didn't, "hopefully we will one day get a government in office to rid us of people like yourself."

Shocking as it was to be the target of such visceral hatred, I was hardly surprised. Nothing Nathan had to say was new to me; I am used to such rhetoric. As it says in Psalms 129:2, "Many a time have they afflicted me from my youth; yet they have not prevailed against me." I grew up hearing it, believing it, hating myself, hating those like me—and the struggle of my life has been to unlearn it, to see it as the lie that it is. But I *was* amazed at the timing (would Miss Manners call this a condolence note?), at the author (Nathan had been the hardest-drinking, most dissolute of my cousins, so much so that my brother Mike snorted when I sent him the e-mail and said, "Nathan wrote this? You *gotta* be kidding me"), and at the moral certitude of the e-mail—its conviction that I was evil and that people sharing its point of view were good. I have always found notions of good and evil tricky and rarely like to make pronouncements on them ("Judge not, lest ye be judged"), but in this case, the answer was clear.

I'm not the evil one here. And neither is anyone associated with GLSEN.

So let's talk about moral values. It says in 1 John 4:20, "If a man says he loves God, and hates his brother, he is a liar." Four out of five LGBT students are physically, sexually, or verbally harassed *every single day* at their schools. They are over twice as likely as their straight peers to be threatened or injured with a weapon. Consequently, they are six times more likely to attempt suicide than their straight peers. We're trying to protect them from that. To do so is the only moral choice.

To do anything else is immoral. As it says in Matthew 18:6, "Whosoever shall offend one of these little ones . . . it were better for him that a millstone were hung about his neck, and that he be drowned in the depths of the sea." I'm becoming something of an avenging angel in my middle age—more Old Testament prophet than New, I'm afraid. I'm not about to cede the moral high ground to people who claim they're "protecting children" while actively working to deny them protections if they are gay. I am not about to allow people to say they are for "family values" when they teach values that turn parents against their own children if they are gay. I am not about to let people claim they are American patriots when they teach children to violate their pledge of allegiance to "liberty and justice for all" if a fellow citizen happens to be gay. I am not about to let people call themselves Christian who then ignore the commandment of the Lord that we love one another. And I'm not going to let them hide behind that "love the sinner, hate the sin" malarkey, which reminds me way too much of how my dad would say, before spanking us, "This is going to hurt me a lot more than it's going to hurt you." I didn't fall for it at age five, and I'm not falling for it now. As Mom would have said, "No siree, Bob." My capacity for forgiveness has been exhausted: I can't turn the other cheek anymore. Instead, I'm trying to figure out how I can carry millstones around with me. If I do, I know where to hang them.

Matthew, chapter 25, offers perhaps the clearest Christian moral yardstick:

> Then shall the King say unto them on his right hand, Come ye, blessed of my Father; inherit the kingdom prepared for you from the foundation of the world. For I hungered and ye gave me meat; I was thirsty, and ye gave me drink; I was a stranger, and ye took me in. Naked, and ye clothed me; I was sick, and ye visited me; I was in prison and ye came unto me.... Inasmuch as ye have done it unto one of these the least of my brethren, ye have done it unto me.... Inasmuch as ye did it not to one of the least of these, ye did it not to me. And these shall go away into everlasting punishment; but the righteous into life eternal.

This, in the end, is the essence of the difference between good and evil, the test of a just society and of a just people: how do we treat those who are the least among us? Do we walk by their side offering them comfort? Jesus set an example by walking with the diseased, the poor, the "strangers" of his time, yet so many of those who claim to follow him today urge us to turn our faces from the Robbie Kirklands of the world, or to offer them a "comfort" like "ex-gay ministry" that will "cure" them, which only deepens their sense of worthlessness and hopelessness. To create by one's action or inaction a culture, an institution, a school, or a community that makes some young people feel so much the very least of their brethren that they choose to take their own lives—well, I have a name for the people who do this: child abusers. They're the immoral ones, Nathan, not me, and for their sake, I hope there exists a merciful God, because they're going to need one.

How ironic that, in my middle age, I have returned to the book that shaped the lives of my father and mother, the book whose misreading almost destroyed me as a child, and have found in it the inspiration I need to continue my work. I guess so doing honors them. "Honor thy father and thy mother that thy days may be long upon the land" (Exodus 20:12).

Maybe I *am* just like my daddy, preaching a somewhat different sermon, as Mom told me. But the reminders I see daily are those of my mother. Next to my home computer, I keep her friend Ricky's Bible, left to her after his suicide, to remind me of the waste and sadness that result from bigotry that goes unchecked. On my desk at work, I keep the little plaque she got from AIDS Care Services of Winston-Salem for her volunteer work at Holly Haven, to remind me that every person, no matter what their resources, can grow and change and can make a difference. Next to that, I keep her Bible, the one my siblings gave her before I was born, whose colorful pictures distracted me during many an interminable prayer meeting or crusade during my childhood. I look at it whenever I get discouraged, knowing that the woman who carried it made a far longer and more difficult journey than I have and that, if she could do it, I can do it. And around my neck I wear a necklace given to me by a colleague who went to an antique store and bought a mite like the widow's mite, the coin that would have been put in the treasury in the story my mother so loved.

Thanks, Mom, for teaching me the difference between right and wrong. I honor you by passing the lessons you taught me on to the next generation. And I know that those who oppressed and opposed you once and who try to oppress and oppose me still will one day be greatly ashamed. I know this because I'm your boy, and because I'm a preacher's son.

And because the Bible tells me so.

Acknowledgments

I would like to thank Joanne Wyckoff, who brought me to Beacon Press, for her important role in getting this project going. Joanne's role was ably assumed after her departure by Helene Atwan, whose commitment to and support of this project never wavered. Helene convinced Michael Denneny to assist by editing the final version of the book, and I am indebted to him for his insight and guidance. Tom Hallock, Pam MacColl, and Lisa Sacks at Beacon also provided invaluable contributions and support during the process. Two of my colleagues at GLSEN, Tom Falvey and Josh Lamont, did close readings of the text: I am deeply grateful for their very helpful critiques.

Writing a book like this makes me realize how many wonderful people I have encountered at different junctures in my life, how I wouldn't be where I am today without the many helping hands that pulled me along. The idea of listing them all is daunting and to do so would be impossible. I do, however, need to make a few thank-yous to:

My dedicated and gifted colleagues at GLSEN, especially Tim

Pappalardo, who did an incomparable job as my assistant 2003–2005, and my partner in virtue, deputy executive director Eliza Byard;

Christie Vianson and Jim Johnson, during whose tenures as GLSEN board president this book was written, and whose friendship, wisdom, and support have sustained me in more ways than one;

Graciela Kaplan, who has gamely filled the shoes of my mother since she died in 2002; and

Ron Ansin, my mentor and guide.

In August 2005 I suffered a massive heart attack just after coming off the ice following yet another victory for the New York Gay Hockey Association, in which I played my usual completely inconsequential role. I want to thank two of my teammates, Eric Moon and Neil Nerich, whose swift actions the doctors credited with saving my life. My friends Dr. Greg Kerr and R.N. Jeff Webb have spent countless hours helping me navigate the aftermath of this event. Greg led me to the incomparable Dr. Erica Jones, who has overseen my care since the heart attack and whose unstinting availability, compassion, and expertise have made all the difference. Innumerable people have come out of the woodwork since my heart attack, and I am touched by and grateful for all the love and support I have received, but I must single out my friend Nerijus Bagdonas, who has been at my bedside every single day of every single hospitalization, and my brother Mike, who has used his own heart attack experience to help me deal with mine.

The reason I am alive and wish to go on living is my partner, Jeff Davis. There are times when he holds my hand and looks at me with those big blue eyes that I think my heart is going to burst. I must have been a very good person in one of my past lives to have landed him as my partner and to have had as our "children" our golden retrievers Luke (1989–2000) and Amber (2000–present).

In many ways this book is a tribute to my mother, in whose memory I have established the Alice Jennings Fund at the Appalachian Community Fund, which provides support to organizations serving low-income and battered women in my family's homeland so that the next generation of women will have the opportunities my mother was denied. I will donate a portion of the proceeds of this book to ACF, and I urge readers to support their work.